THE RAPE OF GREECE

SURREY COUNTY COUNCIL
WITHDRAWN FROM STOCK
AND OFFERED FOR SALE
WITH ALL FAULTS BY
SURREY COUNTY LIBRARY

Also by the author

The Boss (with Joe Joyce)
Blind Justice (with Joe Joyce)

The RAPE of GREECE

The King, the Colonels and the Resistance

Peter Murtagh

SURREY
WDR
949
.5
94
COUNTY LIBRARY

SIMON & SCHUSTER

LONDON·SYDNEY·NEW YORK·TOKYO·SINGAPORE·TORONTO

First published in Great Britain by Simon & Schuster Ltd, 1994
A Paramount Communications Company

Copyright © Peter Murtagh, 1994

This book is copyright under the Berne Convention
No reproduction without permission
All rights reserved

The right of Peter Murtagh
to be identified as author of this work
has been asserted in accordance with sections
77 and 78 of the Copyright Designs and Patents
Act 1988

Simon & Schuster Ltd
West Garden Place
Kendal Street
London W2 2AQ

Simon & Schuster of Australia Pty Ltd
Sydney

A CIP catalogue record for this book
is available from the British Library.

ISBN 0–671–71038–9

Typeset in Garamond 11.5/13.5 by
Hewer Text Composition Services, Edinburgh
Printed in Great Britain by
Butler & Tanner Ltd, Frome and London

Contents

Preface

Any student of contemporary Greek affairs will find himself dragged back into history. Nothing happens in Greece today that does not have a resonance in the past. That is why virtually the entire nation has appeared willing to risk all to prevent the coming into being of Macedonia, the neighbouring former Yugoslav republic of the same name – a name to which Greeks believe they have exclusive rights stretching back to Alexander the Great and beyond. For similar reasons, Greece has taken the side of Serbia when self-interest – as an aid-hungry member of the European Community and of NATO – would appear to suggest otherwise. But Greeks and Serbs share an outlook and heritage, religious and historical, that means more to each and does much to explain recent policies.

The past and what happened there explains why Andreas Papandreou, who staged a remarkable political comeback last year, and Constantine Mitsotakis are in opposing political parties and loath each other with a depth equalled only by the obscurity – at least to the outside world – of what divided them in the first place. The past – the immediate post Second World War years – and what happened to Greece then laid the foundations for the horrors of the colonels' 1967–1974 dictatorship. Anyone wishing to examine those years must delve into the ones that preceded them.

This book is a work of journalism, not academic scholarship. It is an attempt to tell the story of Greece after the war and to tell it largely through the recollections of a number of key players. It is a story of how a small, southern European, slav-bordering country was turned into a pawn of the United States in its Cold War jousting with the Soviet Union. The country thus bred comprised a lethal brew of regal degeneracy and political corruption. Crucial issues in the life of Greece that ought to have been resolved at the end of the war were not. They remained and festered, distorting normal political development and breeding hatreds and feuds that were passed from father to son into the present day.

The issues included the fate of those Greeks who had collaborated with the occupying Nazi forces, the brushing aside of a genuinely national resistance force in favour of groups and individuals more suited to British and American post-war needs. There was the virtual re-imposition of a widely discredited monarchy and the crushing – first in a civil war and later through state-orchestrated oppression – of dissent and opinion not supportive of the pro-Western establishment. It was in Greece that US napalm was used against civilian and guerrilla forces long before anyone in the Pentagon heard of Vietnam, and it was in pursuit of Western interests in Greece that the Truman doctrine of American intervention to stop the spread of communism was invented.

The internal strains eventually brought into being the dictatorship of the colonels. The fact that their regime lasted just a shade over seven years, despite covert and overt US support and access to one of Europe's better equipped armies and state security networks, is testimony to the lack of popular support it enjoyed. A small number of people – usually brave, sometimes foolhardy but always well intentioned – fought the regime. In telling part of the history of resistance to the colonels, this book deals mainly with one such group, Democratic Defence. There are others and their role is no less diminished for lack of comprehensive examination here.

There are many people to whom I owe a debt of gratitude but many would not thank me for mentioning them. All interviews were conducted on the basis that sources would not be identified by direct attribution, if they so requested. Several former US diplomats and Central Intelligence Agency employees who served in Greece in the Sixties and Seventies gave their account of what happened. I thank them for giving me their time, though they may not thank me for reaching conclusions I know they do not share. The same may be said for official sources in Britain.

I could not have written this book had I not had the co-operation of many of the former members of Democratic Defence. The story of their heroism in devotion to the principles of individual freedom, democracy and justice fills these pages. For the most part, they remained silent after the restoration of democracy and it is to them that I dedicate this book. I would like to thank in particular one of their number, an Englishman named Martin Packard, who refused no request for help and introduced me to many of his former resistance colleagues. I would like also to thank his wife, Kiki Packard. Four other Democratic Defence activists deserve special thanks, too: Vassilis Filias, George Kouvelakis, Stellios Nestor and Nicos Leventakis. All freely gave me their time and their memories. Colleagues and friends at the *Guardian* who helped me include Peter Preston, who drew my attention to Martin Packard and his extraordinary story and indulged my determination to write this book; Joe Joyce, David Pallister, Victoria Brittain, Michael Simmons, Martin Woollacott, and Paul Webster. I am indebted also to Bob Fink in Washington who advised and encouraged me, searched obscure records for crucial names and never failed to respond to a request for help; to Mark Hosenball also in Washington; to Paul Eddy and Sara Walden for encouragement and friendship that endures long absences; to the Library of Congress wherein are stored many de-classified documents; to Washington's National Security Archives, and to the British Library in London.

I am indebted finally to my wife, Moira, who has indulged me far too long.

Peter Murtagh
London, October 1993

Introduction

The Best Since Pericles

'You are nothing. Be grateful we've only tortured you a little. In Russia they'd kill you.'

Inspector Basil Lambrou

The army car hurtled through the streets of Salonika at great speed, bouncing from bump to bump as it careered along the mud surface roads, breaking the night silence as it went. The headlights rocked up and down in the darkness, one moment lighting the way ahead, the next shearing up and down the facades of the buildings on either side. There were few people about. Most preferred to stay indoors, fearing that to venture out might be construed as opposition.

Thumping about inside the car boot, arms handcuffed behind his back, was Stellios Nestor, a 32-year-old barrister and former Assistant Professor of International Law. The Secret Police had placed a hood over his head but he was still able to see when the yellow street lighting of the town centre gave way to the white lights of the suburbs. Each time the car lurched to the left or right, Nestor counted the turns. He was filled with dread as it dawned on him that he was heading in the direction of the military base near the airport, a base that was used by the Greek intelligence agency, KYP.

Nestor's arrest in the early hours of 24 May 1968 was as routine as his subsequent treatment. In his law office, there had been a young girl whose boyfriend worked with the Patriotic Front, a communist dominated resistance organisation and the first of several to spring up in the days immediately following the military coup one year earlier. The girl's connection had proved useful to the organisation to which Nestor belonged,

Democratic Defence. DA, as it was known from its Greek initials, championed the cause of liberal democracy and took its inspiration mainly from the social democratic politicians of Scandinavia, Germany and England, as well as from some of Greece's younger generation left wing theoreticians.

Nestor was a typical member of the organisation. He was one of Salonika's social and intellectual elite and had been educated partly in the United States. He was secretary of the city's European Movement, read serious books avidly and enjoyed discussing politics. The question at the centre of political debate was always the same: How could they, the best and the brightest of their generation, change Greece and, most important of all, what sort of a country did they want to see emerge? The powerhouse of political debate was, of course, Athens, to where many of Nestor's friends had drifted, either from provincial cities like Salonika or from spells at academic institutions in northern Europe and America.

But Nestor remained in Salonika, a respected and rising member of the legal establishment. When the army colonels staged their coup in April 1967, he had been entirely opposed to their action. The day it happened, the first he knew was when a phone call from a friend advised him that he might be better staying at home that day. Nestor escaped the immediate wave of arrests and in the succeeding months, watched events unfold with a deep sense of gloom.

Gradually, as the military dictatorship took hold, people like him began to wonder what they could do. Through his friends in Athens, he became a willing activist in DA, to the extent that within a year of the coup his legal work was all but set aside in favour of the greater challenge. With legal colleagues and others (one a businessman, another a film critic and organiser of Salonika's International Fair), Nestor created a nucleus of DA activists in the city, determined to do all they could to overthrow the dictatorship. Their activities mainly involved producing and secretly distributing resistance propaganda – posters, leaflets and car stickers – and writing to prominent people in Greece and abroad, urging them to oppose the regime, or at least have nothing to do with it.

But this well meaning band of middle-class intellectuals was chronically undersupplied with the basic tools of the trade – a printing machine and paper. So they were grateful when Salonika's Patriotic Front activists allowed them to share facilities. Luck ran out when Nestor's link to the front, the boyfriend of the girl in his office, was arrested. Under torture, the young man disclosed her name and the fact that she had DA connections. An entirely predictable chain of events ensued, in which Nestor's arrest was but one of many.

The KYP officers who had dragged him from his home at 1 a.m. eventually arrived at the army barracks and lifted him out of the car boot. He was brought at once to an interrogation room where a young captain and four associates ordered him to speak. Their demands were straightfoward: they wanted to know everything about Democratic Defence, names, dates, places, objectives. Nestor refused to say anything.

The men then set about their task with a familiarity and routine which suggested they were well used to it. Two of them told Nestor to take off his shoes while the others twisted the shoulder strap of a rifle around his ankles. One man held the barrel of the rifle, another the butt, and Nestor was hoisted aloft, dangling upside down with his head inches above the concrete floor. One of the men produced a leather whip and began lashing his bare feet. The crack of leather on flesh was punctuated by the captain's insistent demands for information.

The initial beating lasted only a few minutes after which the men lowered Nestor right side up and ordered him to jump on the floor. Buckets of cold water were thrown over him to make sure he remained conscious. After this, the foot-beating resumed and was repeated time after time, until gradually Nestor began to lose consciousness. Each time he fainted, the men threw more water, woke him up and started the process over. When Nestor's legs became so swollen and his wounds were bleeding so much that he could no longer stand (the bones in one foot were by now shattered), two of the men held him up against a wall while the others punched him in the chest and stomach and plucked hairs from his moustache.

Nestor lost all sense of time. The session almost certainly

lasted several hours and stopped only when he screamed about a pain in his chest and the torturers feared they might kill him if they continued.

He was thrown wet and bleeding into a cell where he remained in solitary confinement for 47 days, relieved only by periods of interrogation which included threats that if he did not talk, his wife would also be submitted to *falanga*, as the foot-beating was called. During his period in solitary, his pleas for a doctor were ignored. After the 47 days, he was removed to a basement cell in a Salonika prison camp where he was held for three and a half months. Twenty-one hours a day were spent lying or sitting on the floor with other prisoners. For one and a half hours each morning and afternoon, they were allowed to walk around a small yard, its walls so high they blocked out direct sunlight permanently. Six months later, a military court jailed Nestor for sixteen and a half years.

Another man arrested on the same day as Nestor was George Sipitanos, Nestor's business associate in Democratic Defence. Like Nestor, he was taken from his home in the early hours of the morning by members of the Secret Police and transferred shortly after to an army barracks. An army major began lashing his bare legs and feet with a strip of rubber. From time to time during the beating, a captain would leap from a chair to prod his chest with a rifle butt.

'You will die, dirt,' screamed the captain as Sipitanos refused to divulge the 'illegal activities' of his friends in Democratic Defence. The captain was fond of loading his gun, cocking it and placing it against his temple. 'Speak or I'll shoot. Answer the major or I'll blow your brains in the air.'

Sipitanos was later transferred to KYP's headquarters in Salonika where he was held in a darkened room, measuring about five and a half feet by nine feet, for 40 days. The military court gave him seven and a half years.

Nestor and Sipitanos were treated lightly compared to others routinely arrested by the Secret Police and KYP agents. Take the case of Pericles Korovessis, a 28-year-old actor whose father had royalist political connections though Pericles himself had left-wing leanings. At 3 a.m. on 8 October 1967, plainclothes police burst into his home in Athens and dragged him away from his wife after a search of their apartment. The men seized the usual paraphernalia which, in the eyes of the dictatorship, amounted to incriminating evidence.

'Every thick book is a communist book,' declared the officer in charge of the raid as his men grabbed the works of the ancient philosophers Aristotle and Sophocles, the playwright Aeschylus, a number of folk-song tapes, a teach-yourself-English tape produced by the BBC and a typewriter. An unmarked black sedan whisked Korovessis to the Athens headquarters of the Secret Police, a notorious building in Bouboulinas Street, where his nightmare was only beginning.

'It's a horrible mistake,' Korovessis insisted as they led him to a fourth floor interrogation room. Left alone for a moment, the first person to enter the room brought with him an air of carnival madness. The man danced around the floor, shouting wildly and accusing Korovessis of having killed his father in some resistance operation. The accusation was untrue and when the man lifted a chair and was about to beat Korovessis, the other men returned and grabbed it from him. But they were no guardian angels. When Korovessis continued to plead his innocence in the face of determined interrogation, the officer in charge, Odysseus Spanos, punched him in the face, smashing a tooth and causing blood to spurt out.

'If you dirty my shirt, you'll pay for it,' said Spanos.

Spanos and the other officers then led Korovessis up to a small room on top of the building's roof terrace – their favourite place for beating people, a sort of penthouse of torture. In the middle of the room there was a long wooden bench, smooth from over use. Korovessis was tied down and beaten on the feet with a pickaxe handle. Unlike their counterparts in Salonika, the Athens Secret Police often preferred to leave their victims' shoes on, apparently to minimise the number of scars. However, this method also meant that as the feet swelled up, the shoes burst open, puffed up flesh and blood oozing out through the splits.

'Do you like this?' asked the man wielding the stick as Korovessis screamed in agony. 'This is just a sample.'

Spanos went over to a toilet hole, poked it with a stick and began lifting out a urine soaked rag. 'Sir, that's my job,' said one of the men rushing forward to assist. 'That's too dirty for you.' The underling took the rag and stuffed it into Korovessis' mouth to muffle his cries. The beating continued until dawn with Korovessis occasionally vomitting, the rag bursting out of his mouth under the pressure. Before being taken down to cell number 17 in the basement, the men made him lick up his sick.

The following day, the interrogation resumed, this time in the presence of Inspector Basil Lambrou, the head of the Athens Secret Police. Lambrou was a dapper man, a relative sophisticate among the thugs under his command, though some of his victims detected a tell-tale facial twitch whenever he got excited.

'We are all democrats here,' he was fond of telling his victims. 'Everybody who comes here talks. You're not spoiling our record.' He assured all protesters that no one would believe their tales of torture and ill-treatment. 'We are the government, you are nothing. The government isn't alone. Behind the government are the Americans,' he would say. He was given to expounding his theory of contemporary global politics. 'The whole world is in two parts,' he informed Korovessis, 'the Russians and the Americans. We are the Americans. Be grateful we've only tortured you a little. In Russia, they'd kill you.'

Lambrou had a sort of Jekyll and Hyde personality that could produce, out of the blue, gestures of apparent humanity. One instance was the time when the seven-months-pregnant wife of a man taken into Bouboulinas Street ventured inside to ask of his whereabouts. As the husband was being subjected to electric torture in one part of the building, Inspector Lambrou happened upon the pregnant woman in the foyer. 'My dear, my darling,' he cried when he saw her. 'A baby on the way! I am so happy for you. May I be the godfather?' The husband was set free immediately.

No such gestures were available to Korovessis, however. When he told the inspector that he had no information of use to him, an officer was ordered to bring him back up to the terrace torture room. 'I'll give you to Gravaritis,' said the officer. 'He'll kill you. He enjoys it.' Gravaritis stroked the young actor's shoulder. 'Why fight the boss? Tell the whole story. It'll be good for you.' With that, Korovessis' head was smashed against a wall. Then he was stripped naked and bound once more onto the wooden bench for *falanga*. But this time, the beating was not confined to his feet. They pummelled his ankles, knees and pelvis with a metal bar which was later shoved up his anus. After that, Korovessis was dragged to the edge of the terrace and pushed over. But the drop was not onto the street over 100 feet below. Korovessis fell just a few feet onto the roof of an adjoining building.

Back inside the torture room, his efforts to feign unconsciousness appeared to have them fooled until the bar was thrust against his testicles, provoking a cry of pain as he writhed in agony on the floor. 'Oh, you're all right,' said Gravaritas, casually combing his hair in the reflection of a window. 'We've become tired of this kind of man,' he declared as Inspector Lambrou strolled in. One of the men with Lambrou produced some red peppers, the sort usually found gracing meals served to tourists in the tavernas of the Plaka. As Korovessis lay there, the peppers were stuffed into his mouth and up his nose. Liquid detergent was poured over his mouth and a cigarette shoved between his lips.

'You see what happens to people who don't like democracy,' said Inspector Lambrou.

Korovessis was taken to military hospital number 401 where he might have expected to receive medical attention for his wounds. Instead, during his two-week stay, a doctor came most mornings and twisted his genitals as a prelude to even more vicious torture. Two years later, giving evidence to a European Commission of Human Rights investigation of torture in Greece, Korovessis recalled what was done to him in the hospital.

'They took me to the surgery. There they put me on a leather bench. They put behind my head a small napkin and a pillow. There was a machine like a tape recorder with buttons ... somebody would [monitor] my heart and he would let current go from behind my ears. It was extremely terrible, the most terrible torture of all because with the other tortures you could see, while with this one you didn't know to what extent it could go and it was mainly the sensation that your tongue had become leaden.

'The most terrible of all these things was that the more they tortured you with electro-shock, the more you were in a state of awareness. You were sort of raised up, you had more endurance. With the *falanga*, the more you were beaten, the quicker you fainted. On the last day I think they did electro-shock all over my body. They touched me everywhere.'

Once during this torture, Inspector Lambrou entered the room. 'Your soul is tortured because you have many sins. Write them down and save your soul,' he said. Korovessis never did because like so many others who were tortured all over Greece, he had nothing to tell. He was eventually removed to prison from where he was released in March 1968 as a result of a government amnesty. Like so many who shared similar experiences, Korovessis was neither tried nor convicted of any crime.

The experiences of Stellios Nestor and Pericles Korovessis were duplicated in varying degrees by thousands of Greeks throughout the country in the early years of the dictatorship. Many of those arrested were actively opposed to the regime – many more were not. They happened merely to be linked, often obscurely, to someone who had already been arrested. Sometimes a person was arrested because he or she lived in the same apartment block as someone else brought in for questioning. A person might be detained because he was seen at some time sharing a few moments in a cafe with a suspect. Or they might be arrested because, under pressure of torture, someone named them in the hope of sending their tormentors off on a wild goose chase.

Whatever the reasons for detaining people, the junta arrested at random. In the first five hours after the coup, more than 10,000 people were rounded up and taken to what the regime called 'reception centres' where they were subjected to initial beatings – like the 65-year-old leader of a small left-dominated political party who was pistol whipped unconscious in the middle of the Athens football stadium. The man who did this was a young lieutenant, a man who was young enough to be the politician's grandson. Most arrested in the initial round-up were removed to police and army cells where many were tortured, held in prison camps and eventually convicted by military kangaroo courts and sentenced to long periods in jail. Apart from *falanga*, electric shock and beatings, common methods of torture included sexually molesting women (in some cases to such a degree that vaginal flesh was ripped apart by hand), inserting a rubber tube into a person's anus and driving water inside them under pressure, pulling out pubic hair and removing finger and toe nails.

The junta explained its coup and programme of mass arrests as necessary to forestall a communist take-over of Greece. The claim was investigated by international bodies such as Amnesty International and the Council of Europe, which found as a matter of fact that no such threat existed to justify either the coup itself or the subsequent massive abuse of human rights by the regime.

For their part, leading members of the junta believed they had a mission to save Greece and to re-establish the country as a dominant force in the region, worthy of the inheritance of classical and Byzantine Greece. Those who criticised them were, *ipso facto*, communists or fellow travellers. The colonels' lust for self-aggrandizement was coupled with a fear of things modern. In the demonology of the regime, many of the youthful trappings of twentieth-century life were placed on a level pegging with the more predictable enemies of the junta. In the first few hours of their rule, for instance, when the constitution was suspended and civil rights abolished, it was also announced that long hair and miniskirts were banned.

The army officers responsible for all this were sycophantic towards the United States. If official US policy towards the regime was characterised by mild public embarrassment but a willingness to work with it, unofficial American attitudes were supportive. In a grotesque reference to the father figure of classical Greek democracy, a US general remarked at the height of the junta's torturing that Washington's loyal allies in Athens were 'the best damn government since Pericles'.

PART ONE

Chapter One

Ugly Worms from a Dirty Past

'Whoever is interested in human rights in Greece is a
communist.'

Brigadier-General Stylianos Pattakos

When the Greek army – colonels and middle-rank officers for
the most part – seized power in the early hours of 21 April
1967, they took hold of a country that was deeply divided.
It was split between the political rivalries of the Left and
Right, was economically backward, and intractably at odds
with Turkey, its powerful neighbour and co-member of the
North Atlantic Treaty Organisation. Many Greeks were deeply
suspicious of the world beyond their shores and although the
political establishment aspired for Greece to be accepted as
an equal player on the international stage, looking longingly
to membership of the European Economic Community, the
country as a whole exhibited symptoms of post-colonial schizo-
phrenia. On the one hand, politicians were given to robust
declarations of Greece's sovereignty and independence, while
on the other, they dismissed as nonsense any suggestion that
the country could survive without the protection of a powerful
patron, first Britain, then the United States. Political activists
displayed inconsistent attitudes towards their patron – they
would denounce any suggestion of foreign intervention in
domestic affairs but, in disputes with rivals, would canvass
American diplomats to take sides. In this, the Americans were
not found wanting.

This swirling mass of internal political tensions, contradic-
tions and persistent outside interference led inexorably to
the 1967 coup and the seven years of neo-fascist horror that

followed. If the Americans did not actually orchestrate the take-over, they relentlessly massaged the right-wing political establishment, the royal family and the army to the point where those who acted to destroy democracy had every reason to believe they had Washington's full support.

The men behind the regime to which this situation gave rise believed that Greeks who advocated democracy were communists – 'monsters from hell . . . demons and treacherous devils' as one member of the junta put it. To those who stood in the way of the dictatorship, one of its leading strongmen, Brigadier-General Stylianos Pattakos, had a simple message.

'Break the ribs of these dishonest beings,' he urged. 'Step on these ugly worms and smash these parasites from the sickened public life of the dirty past!' To a visiting member of the British parliament, he divested himself of the opinion that 'whoever is interested in human rights and human dignity in Greece is a communist . . . All those who are against the government are communists.'

For seven years, Pattakos and his associates ruled Greece by the simple mechanism of terrorising its eight million people. They denied democracy, brutalised and tortured dissenters and disrupted political development to such a degree that the country has not fully recovered almost twenty years after the collapse of their regime. Throughout the entire sorry episode, the United States raised hardly a murmur of protest and indeed behind the scenes urged those who did to desist. Opposition was left to the liberal governments in Scandinavia, West European social democrats, exiles abroad when the coup happened and others who joined them as soon as they could get out. Their efforts were augmented by some intensely brave people who remained in Greece and fought the regime as best they could and a rag-bag assortment of well-meaning intellectuals, academics and adventurers.

Opposition to the dictatorship became a great *cause célèbre* of the 1960s, ranking equal for a time with opposition to the apartheid regime in South Africa. Like opposition to apartheid, the campaign against the junta also involved efforts to boycott Greek produce and Greece as a holiday destination.

The varying campaigns against the junta had their effect but, in the end, the dictatorship did not collapse because it was overthrown. It simply imploded due to a near total lack of internal support. The catalyst was a foreign adventure: the junta sponsored a coup in Cyprus, seeking to replace the legitimate government there with a puppet regime. That in turn provoked an invasion and division of the island by Turkey and the consequent collapse of the regime in Athens.

Today, the events which convulsed Greece in the late 1960s seem somehow not to belong to the history of modern Europe, nor to a country that prides itself on an unrivalled heritage in politics, philosophy, literature and the arts. Now a democratically elected government in Athens is a member of the European Community. A Greek commissioner holds a Brussels portfolio and elected politicians represent their country in the European Parliament. Greece remains a member of NATO and plays host to thousands of US troops and airmen. Millions of tourists descend annually on its famous islands, delighting in the natural beauty of the place and the easy-going nature of a friendly people for whom the concept of relaxation appears to have been invented.

Yet this nation produced Europe's most vicious military dictatorship to seize power since the end of World War II. A supposedly modern, independent European country, Greece in 1967 was in reality a client state of the US, used and abused for Washington's strategic self-interest. It was a victim of the Cold War just as surely as were the East European nations trapped inside the Soviet Bloc. But whereas Soviet domination of Eastern Europe was achieved by conquest, subversion of popular will and massive repression backed up at times by Red Army tanks, the long-term US domination of Greece was for the most part a more subtle affair, even though it peaked in the horror of the colonels' regime.

After the Greek civil war, in which the Americans played a decisive, bloody role, the US had its way by massaging Greek politics to ensure governments comply with Washington's needs. In an economy that was backward with a huge gap between rich and poor, the vast bulk of US aid went to the military. American spies infiltrated the royal family, the army and internal security apparatus, and virtually ran the right-wing political establishment.

The Americans, however, were merely following a lead set by European imperial powers over 100 years before and from which Greece seemed unable to escape. When the country became independent from the Ottoman Empire in 1832, three other imperial powers – Britain, France and Russia – vied for influence. The measure of their success may be gauged by the fact that through much of the nineteenth century Greece's main political parties were known not by names reflecting the different policies they espoused but ones indicating to which outside power they were attached. Hence there was the English Party, the French Party and the Russian Party. The British imposed a Bavarian prince, Otto, who was dispatched to Athens on board a Royal Navy frigate to rule as king for almost 30 years.

At birth, independent Greece comprised the Peloponnese, Attica and land north to the border with Thessaly, the island of Euboea and the Cyclades islands of the western Aegean. Throughout the nineteenth century, the country expanded further to include, first, Corfu and the other Ionian islands and then Thessaly. Expansion continued apace in the early twentieth century to include in turn Macedonia and Crete, a large chunk of western Turkey (ancient Asia Minor) and Thrace, right up to the Bosphorus and the ancient capital of Constantinople. War with Turkey in 1920 resulted in the loss of Asia Minor (and the consequent migration to mainland Greece of about one million refugees) and eastern Thrace, Constantinople along with it.

The return of this sacred land became an all-consuming quest for those jingoistic Greeks – not least the junta of colonels – who harboured fanciful notions of a Greater Greece. This was the Great Idea that Greece could expand to 'liberate' Greeks trapped inside the remnants of the Ottoman Empire and restore to itself the regional position it held in Classical and Byzantine times.

The consolodation of Greece into a modern nation state had been messy and inconclusive, just as it was in many parts of Central and Eastern Europe and the Balkans. From the mid-twentieth century onwards, Greeks were subjected to massive foreign interference in their affairs. In the 1930s, the country produced the dictatorship of General Yannis Metaxas, who ran a totalitarian regime built upon his own version of fascism. Invasion by Mussolini caused his downfall and Greece's entry into World War II on the side of the Allies. Few countries generated more valiant resistance to German occupation, but immediately after liberation Greek partisans were betrayed by the British, leading ultimately to a civil war in which tens, possibly hundreds, of thousands of Greeks lost their lives. A far greater number were forced to flee to neighbouring Eastern Bloc countries where they languished for decades, banned by successive Athens governments from returning home.

At the end of World War II, Greece's relationship with Britain was such that the British prime minister, Winston Churchill, could hand-pick his Greek counterpart, George Papandreou, only to dismiss him later as 'this old fool' whom he recommended be 'locked up until he comes to his senses' – until he agreed, that was, to what London wanted. Churchill was unapologetic about the British army's destruction of the Greek resistance upon whom Britain's own forces had so depended in Greece's war against Hitler. He dismissed the resistance as a communist front, despite evidence, much of it supported by documentary accounts from his own officers serving with the partisans, that it was in truth a broadly-based and massively popular army.

When the resistance liberated Athens and paved the way for a British entry to the city, partisans soon found that they were now the enemy. Under British supervision, Nazi collaborators were inducted into a new Greek army, already heavily dominated by royalists due to earlier purges ordered by Churchill. When relations with the resistance broke down, their leader, Major-General Stephanos Sarafis, pleaded with the British to end unconstitutional impositions about the nature of the emerging post-war Greek government and allow the people of Greece to decide for themselves.

Sarafis' bitter recriminations were contained in a letter to the British commander of Athens, Lieutenant-General Ronald Scobie, written even as his own men were being killed by

British bullets. Sarafis regretted that the British government
and its army in Athens appeared determined to 'impose on
a people who had fought fascism and invaders for eight years
a government which did not enjoy their confidence, but was
appointed by a king whose own position was far from secure'.

Sarafis charged that Churchill drove his forces 'to attack the
Greek people and its army, which had rendered you such great
service, and to proceed to the conquest and occupation of
Greece, thereby replacing the Germans and treating Greece
as they did, while ignoring all its services and sacrifices up to
the present day . . . As free men, in solidarity with the fighters
in Athens, we shall continue to struggle wherever there is a need
until such time as, realising your historical responsibilities, you
reverse your decisions and cease your attacks so that it may
become possible to form a truly national government which
will guarantee the free expression of the people's beliefs . . .' But
for all Sarafis' tough talking, the resistance forces were totally
unable to defeat the might of a British army.

As Britain moved into its post-Imperial decline and the Cold
War loomed, the Americans took over and turned Greece into
a client state. As the Russians resorted to brute force and
terror to create regimes in the Soviet image throughout eastern
Europe, so too during the 1950s did the Americans manipulate
domestic Greek politics, subvert elections, and hire and fire
prime ministers to ensure governments in Athens that suited
Washington's needs, not those of a free-choosing Greek people.
Institutions of state security were created and run by Americans,
some of them Greek–Americans, until native Greeks in whom
Washington had confidence were put in their place. No Greek
government could alter the size of the Greek army without first
obtaining permission from the Americans.

The degree of American determination was evident in a 1948
report to President Harry Truman by his National Security
Council which noted in its introduction: 'One of the greatest
dangers to world peace may be the failure of the Soviet Union to
understand the extent to which the United States is prepared to
go in order to maintain the security of the eastern Mediterranean
and the Middle East.'

That security hinged on Greece remaining a friend to Washington. It was the view of US policy makers and analysts that if Greece fell to communism, so too would Italy. Access to the Middle East would then be impaired seriously and Europe's southern flank would be exposed to threat by the Soviet Union. To ensure this did not happen, America embraced the Greek Right, and with it an avowedly pro-fascist, collaborationist element that had sided with the Nazis and after the war joined forces with the Right, all with Washington's knowledge. Washington applied to Greece its black and white view of the world in which there were only pro-communists and anti-communists, and it was the anti-communists who were America's friends. In the end, it was these friends of Washington, some of them actually employed by the Central Intelligence Agency, who in 1967 seized Greek democracy by the throat and throttled it to death.

To support the Greek state created out of the ashes of World War II and the civil war, the United States funded an enormous military complex. Almost the entire Greek officer corps of over 10,000 men received US army training during the 1950s. US military bases were established all over the country and Greece became the hub of CIA activity for the entire eastern Mediterranean, as well as the Middle and Near East as far as Iran. During the 1950s, over 75 per cent of all US aid to Greece went to the military and, between 1957 and 1960, such aid was five times greater than aid devoted to health, education and civilian infrastructure.

US military officials vastly outnumbered US civilians. The pattern continued right up to 1970 when there were some 3,000 US military and Defence Department employees stationed in Greece compared to just 210 US government employees who were not attached to America's military interests. The extent of US military spending forced Greek governments to keep to a pace which the economy could well have done without. By 1971, the junta was spending over one quarter of its gross national product on 'defence'.

At the same time, the country's economic profile had changed little since the 1950s. At that time, just six per cent of the people consumed 22 per cent of GNP. The gulf between the rich and poor was huge: the average income of people in poor rural areas was just 16 per cent of their countrymen in the more affluent parts of Athens. In 1970, income tax accounted for between 16 and 17 per cent of government revenue. The remaining 83 per cent came from indirect taxation, levying rich and poor equally. Laws which favoured the rich allowed one wealthy shipping magnate to boast profits of $433 million in the early 1960s while at the same time paying virtually no income tax.

In 1964, three years before the coup, 48 per cent of Greek industry was controlled by foreign capital, 75 per cent of it American. Ninety-seven per cent of commercial banking was controlled by just two banks, 70 per cent of industrial credits were extended to just 30 enterprises, and 50 per cent of the people lived off the land at a time when agriculture accounted for only 30 per cent of GNP.

Much of the tragedy of America's post-war involvement in Greece lay in the fact that it was so overwhelming, so all-embracing. Unlike other countries in western Europe – West Germany being perhaps the most notable example – the extent of US influence in Greece did not allow for the emergence of internal stability. The post-war order imposed on Greece was never accepted by a sufficient number of its citizens for those who continued to dissent to grow irrelevant as the years passed. Instead of helping to nurture democracy and fair competition between diverse political trends, US involvement had a smothering effect. Democracy such as it existed was immature.

When the coup came in 1967, Greeks were unable to look even to their king for adequate support. From the time the monarchy was imposed by the British in 1832, it was a controversial institution. Kings were overthrown on a number of occasions and when George II (who acquiesced in the Metaxas dictatorship) was re-imposed by Churchill at the end of World War II, it was done in circumstances that guaranteed his continued rejection by a substantial segment of society.

Throughout the 1950s, the royal family acted as if Greece owed it a living. More often than not, the palace seemed to regard itself as being at war with the country's elected representatives. It retained a near-total hold on the army, whom King Paul regarded as personally his, royal corruption was rife (and pandered to by the CIA), and the relationship with the Americans was regarded by the palace as the ultimate guarantee of the monarchy's continued existence. In Spain, when remnants of the regime of General Franco tried to seize power in 1981, five a half years after the dictator's death, King Juan Carlos crushed the embryonic coup with little more than the inspiration of a robust clarion call in defence of democracy. In Greece in 1967, his brother-in-law Constantine was so lacking in mettle that he swore into power the usurpers of democracy, an episode recorded by photographers for all his people to see.

The king's conduct was hardly surprising. He had been brought up by a domineering mother with an unbridled contempt for democracy, a woman who had, in the words of one former courtier, 'a fourteenth-century mind'. Constantine inherited the throne as a young and inexperienced man. His palace was staffed by advisers many of whom believed that his role was not that of a figurehead, a focal point of unity for all his people: they believed rather that the king should run the country himself, through appointees responsible ultimately to him alone.

Faced with a popularly elected prime minister who did not do the royal bidding, Constantine sacked him. Faced with the probability that the same man would win overwhelming support at a general election, Constantine explored with the Americans the idea of a coup. When the wrong group of army officers then staged their successful coup, Constantine made a pathetic and poorly organised effort to oust them. And when that failed, he fled to exile – an irrelevancy doomed forever to seek a role for himself where one no longer existed.

Chapter Two

Miseries and Triumphs

'Athens is the saddest city in Europe. For some, it's a
city of rejoicing and revenge. For others, a dark well of
fear and despair. Day and night the manhunts continue in
Athens.'

Leland Stowe, reporting from Greece
for ABC News, 20 January 1945

Britain's post-war betrayal of Greece began behind the scenes,
unknown to those whom it most affected. There was an initial,
bloody encounter in Athens and then a pause followed by a
vicious, prolonged clash that left a scar which persists to this
day. The betrayal started in the early years of World War II,
when Greece was under German occupation, and the intentions
of those responsible were clear by August 1943. By that stage in
the conflict, Winston Churchill had already decided upon the
post-war shape of Greece, come what may.

Churchill had a romantic view of the country. Like many
Englishmen, he looked to classical Athens for the origins
of a civilisation he believed found its continuity in British
parliamentary democracy. So far as modern Greece was concerned, Churchill's trenchant view was that it must have a king
when the war was over. This reflected his passionate faith in
monarchy as an institution and his belief that Greece could
be held together only by a royal family. As for Britain's
own strategic interests, Churchill shared the Allied view that
a Western inclined government in Athens would help contain
any post-war Soviet advance through the Balkans.

Churchill's designs turned to tragedy for two main reasons.
First there was the antipathy towards the monarchy felt by those
Greeks who fought and beat the Nazis and who did not want

to see the return of a king who had acquiesced with the fascist dictator Metaxas. Second, when the United States took over Britain's role in Greece, its Cold War policies determined its support for the Greek Right. It was the view of the Greek Right that almost anyone to its left was either a communist or was so willing to compromise with communists that a full-blown Soviet take-over of Greece would be inevitable.

The reality of Churchill's wartime policy towards Greece was laid bare on 3 December 1944. Six weeks earlier, the Germans had retreated, hurried on by the country's main resistance army. A few moments after 11 o'clock in the morning, a group of Athenian protesters between 200 and 600-strong walked into Syntagma Square, the city's main square in front of parliament. Among them were women and children in festive mood according to contemporary reports. They were part of a much larger group of 60,000 delayed by police road blocks. The demonstrators supported ELAS, the National Liberation Army, and its political wing EAM, the National Liberation Front. Together they controlled some four-fifths of the country and numbered up to two million members. The protesters were angry about British interference in the new post-liberation government of national unity and, specifically, British orders to the resistance to disarm. By contrast, the British were not only allowing German collaborators and recently returned pro-monarchist forces to hold onto their guns, but were inducting them into a new national Greek army.

As the small group of protesters ambled into the square, they were met by a line of armed men, a motley collection of police and freelance gunmen, some of them collaborators. British troops were also present and police with machine guns were positioned on the roof tops. A man in uniform stepped out from behind a wall and began giving orders.

'Shoot the bastards,' he shouted without warning. The protesters scattered in all directions but the firing went on for an hour. When it stopped, 25 unarmed protesters, including a six-year-old boy, lay dead and 148 others wounded. During the shooting, a lone British officer attempted to kick the guns high into the air so the bullets would fly over the heads of the protesters but by then it was too late.

Not long after the killings, the main group of protesters arrived. In a display of extraordinary restraint, they held an emotional and entirely peaceful rally. Many carried American and Greek flags. Some flew the red flag of socialism but few the Union Jack of Great Britain. They set up a chant: 'Roosevelt, Roosevelt.' Banners dipped in the blood of the slain demanded that the British government and General Ronald Scobie, Churchill's military commander in Athens, stay out of Greek affairs.

In London, Churchill faced an angry House of Commons but was unrepentant. He agreed it was a 'shocking thing' that the police fired on unarmed protesters. But he added: 'We should also reprobate the massing and leading of large numbers of unarmed children to a demonstration, the scene of which had been banned by the government, in a city full of armed men and liable at any moment to an explosion.' And then he dismissed the matter with a quip: 'So much for that.' Churchill's ambassador in Athens, Sir Reginald Leeper, took the only course open to him when questioned about the incident by an American reporter. He lied. 'The police did not shoot first,' he asserted. 'Grenades were thrown first by [resistance partisans]. The communists put their women and children in the front row, as they always do, to hide their armed men. They had their guns behind and were shooting.'

Greeks found the incident less easy to dismiss than Churchill. In the immediate aftermath of liberation, it became clear that Churchill was throwing the full weight of the British army behind one side of a political schism that had dominated Greek politics for most of the century: monarchy versus republic. The division found its sharpest focus in the pre-war years under the regime of General Metaxas, leader of the misleadingly titled Party of Free Opinion.

Metaxas was declared dictator in August 1936 when Greece's King George II signed a decree dissolving parliament. The alliance between the monarchy and the fascist general was born of palace fears that the Greek Communist Party was about to organise a general strike. Whatever the merits of the case for emergency measures, the colour of the new regime quickly became clear. Metaxas took his cue from Mussolini and Hitler by organising a youth movement, repressing free speech and pandering to the military. The fascist salute, the rigid outstretched right arm, was introduced. Industries whose output was geared to serve the needs of the military were protected by special tariffs. A network of secret police saw to it that taverna talk steered well clear of current events. Neighbours – recruited as informers by inducement or threats – spied on each other. Individuals who questioned the regime or showed any sign of outright opposition were sent into exile in the Aegean islands, or worse.

When Mussolini invaded in October 1940, the Greeks united against him in a way they had been unable to against Metaxas. The Greek forces, a combination of the national army and the pre-invasion resistance to Metaxas (swelled by the thousands of political prisoners the regime felt obliged to release) pushed the Italians back to the Albanian border and almost into the Adriatic.

By the time Hitler came to Mussolini's rescue, Metaxas was dead by natural causes and the ability of his successors to resist the more powerful and better organised German army much diminished. By April 1941, Greece was conquered and a quisling government installed soon after. King George fled with a handful of officials who set up a government in exile.

The first resistance organisation against the German occupiers was formed late the same year. EDES, the Greek National Democratic League, was born in Athens when it became apparent to the elders of the Liberal Party that they were in no position to mount an effective challenge to the Germans by any other means. Those who set up EDES were mainly professional, middle-class people who were conservative, though not necessarily monarchist, in their political outlook. Their nominal leader was General Nikolaos Plastiras, a republican living in exile in France following failed coups against the monarchy. The actual leader was Napoleon Zervas, also a republican and a man of undoubted military ability from western Greece who was nonetheless distinguished mainly by his appearence. Known to his followers as Papa Zervas, he wore an enormous black beard that rested on the top of his chest, completely obscuring his neck.

It was not until June 1942 that Zervas established a base in western Greece and only then under duress from the British. London was exasperated that funds to Zervas had produced few apparent results and so threatened to denounce him to the Germans. Zervas caved in and, with officers and equipment from Britain's Special Operations Executive, began harrying the Germans.

Although the League grew to be a force of some 5,000 partisans within eighteen months, it did not become the major element of the resistance because it lacked an effective and aggressive political organisation recruiting into it. Partisans spent as much time during the war fighting with the Germans as against them. In the blunt assessment of one historian, the League 'never achieved any wide popular base but remained little more than a cabal of ambitious politicians or would-be politicians in Athens'.

The same could not be said of the National Liberation Front and its army. The Front was founded in September 1941 inspired largely by the Communist Party and its political allies. But it was a broad based organisation of the Left – embracing communists, socialists, Popular Democrats, a rural party, the Republican Party and younger members of the Liberal Party. The Front relied initially on the superior organisational abilities of the communists, long used to operating underground.

Through the harsh winter of 1941/42 during which 300,000 Greeks died, many of them from starvation, the Front established a village-by-village cell structure in central Greece. Women were much attracted to the organisation due to the fact that they were accorded equal political treatment, a major break with the past.

By April 1942, the Front was ready to establish its military wing, ELAS. The army recruited heavily among workers, peasants and intellectuals who were first screened by local Front leaders. Those accepted were subjected to strict military discipline. Deserters were shot. Each ELAS unit was led by three people: a military commander, a Kapitan (frequently a communist) who was in charge of education and propagating the role and aims of the organisation, and a Front representative whose main function was to liaise with the local population. All major decisions had to be agreed unanimously, thus ensuring ultimate civilian control of the army.

The organisation eventually published its post-liberation plans for the country: Greece was to be a republic and a democracy founded on the principles of free elections, a free press, freedom of assembly and free speech.

The Front and its army quickly became a mass popular movement, by far the largest and most effective resistance organisation with which the German occupiers had to contend. In a country of some seven million people at that time, the two wings of the organisation together enrolled between 1.5 million and two million members, of whom about 50,000 were actively involved in ELAS, later supplemented by a 10,000 to 15,000-strong reserve in Athens and Piraeus.

ELAS, like the National Democratic League, was supplied weapons by the British and a small team of British advisers was dropped into Greece in 1942 to help direct operations and co-ordinate the two groups. ELAS, however, was less dependent on donations of British arms because it had captured about 10,000 Italian rifles. As the League grew steadily more conservative and anti-republican, it eventually became the sole recipient of British military aid. Despite tensions between the two organisations (often breaking out into conflicts over territory), they co-operated occasionally to fight effectively against the Germans and, under British direction, helped disrupt the wider Axis war effort, notably by disrupting the German supply route to Rommel in north Africa.

The Germans took harsh revenge for the activities of the partisans. At the height of German power, they had a policy of executing 50 Greeks for every one of their own people killed. By the time of liberation, around 550,000 Greeks – about eight per cent of the population – had lost their lives, among them over 58,000 Salonika Jews, rounded up and murdered.

In fighting the Germans, the resistance had to contend not just with a quisling government but two quite distinct groups of collaborators as well. The most serious were the so-called Security Battalions, composed of pro-fascist Greeks. The battalions were set up in late 1943 under German direction and with German arms and uniforms. Members roamed the countryside, killing partisans and anyone thought to be helping them. The battalions numbered among their members several individuals who were to play prominent roles in the immediate post-war years and for a long time after. The best known of these was a young soldier named George Papadopoulos.

Another man who collaborated with the Nazis and later played a role of almost equal importance in Greek affairs was a Cypriot soldier called George Grivas. Grivas harboured extreme right-wing, quasi-fascist views. He formed an organisation called the X Bands which dealt initially with British agents dropped into Greece to help the resistance. But as the war progressed and ELAS grew in strength with defeat for the Germans an inevitability, Grivas changed sides and began working for the Germans and the quisling government. He ended the war doing his best to murder members of ELAS but his X Bands never received popular support, numbering at their height no more than about 600 men.

While the war against the Germans continued inside Greece, the royal family moved in exile between Egypt, South Africa and London. The government in exile, presided over by a banker appointed prime minister by King George II, settled finally in Cairo where it remained firmly under British control. With the government, and equally under British control, were Greek soldiers and naval officers who had chosen to go into exile after the German conquest. While they fought bravely alongside their colleagues in the British army, many of the soldiers had strong views as to the sort of Greece that should emerge after liberation – views that placed them at odds with Churchill.

In March 1943 they staged a mutiny demanding the resignation of the Greek prime minister and a post-war referendum on the question of the monarchy. The mutiny was put down quickly by the British. Churchill acknowledged in his memoirs that, in crushing the revolt, he had to accept 'very direct personal responsibility'.

Churchill supported a restoration of the monarchy despite intelligence reports from his own resistance liaison officers which pointed strongly to a widespread dislike of the king. His zest for monarchy led him to sack British officers who submitted reports that ran against the grain of his own view. In one such report at the height of the war, a British liaison officer noted: 'One of the chief dead things in Greece today is the monarchy. We crossed parts of Greece which were strongholds of royalism in the past. Now people appear ashamed if you ask whether they would vote for the return of the king . . . What amazed all of us is the amount of control [that ELAS] exercises in every part of Greece . . . [ELAS] has established self-government in most of the country and [is] very popular.'

Churchill's hopes of a smooth restoration of the monarchy after the war received a new blow in April 1944 when the Greek army in Egypt again demanded a referendum over King George's future role. The mutiny was put down with even greater severity than before: some 10,000 Greek soldiers – about half the entire Greek armed forces – were interned in British-run concentration camps. Eighteen months after the mutiny ended, the British were still keeping jailed some 1,500 Greek soldiers in a remote concentration camp in Eritrea.

Churchill underlined his contempt for the motives of the rebellious Greek troops when he described them as 'contaminated by revolutionary and communist elements' led by 'ambitious emigre nonentities'. He decided to lance the boil by purging most, though not all, officers and men who had republican sympathies. He told his foreign minister, Anthony Eden, that the Greek troops needed 'a good smack over the head'.

A new Greek army unit was established, which came to be known variously as the Greek Mountain Brigade, the Hellenic Raiding Force, or LOK, its Greek acronym. Excluded from the unit were almost all men with views ranging from moderative conservative to left-wing. Under British military supervision and at Churchill's express orders, the unit was filled with royalists and anti-republicans.

With the purge complete, Churchill sought a measure of
political compromise by installing George Papandreou as the
new prime minister in exile. Papandreou was a liberal destined
to dominate centre-left Greek politics for over twenty years,
mostly in opposition. After his appointment, he attempted his
own compromise by convincing six senior members of the Front
to participate in a government of national unity to take over
once the Germans had been expelled from Greece. This new
government in exile agreed that after liberation, free elections
would be held, the Greek army would be re-constituted and
re-organised, and collaborators put on trial. The divisive issue
of the monarchy was set aside, to be resolved after liberation.

Through the middle of 1944, the German army was forced to
withdraw from Greece under pressure from ELAS and looming
defeat in central Europe. But at the time, the world was denied
knowledge of the role being played by the resistance. In August,
Churchill ordered the British Broadcasting Corporation to
eliminate 'any credit of any kind' to the Front and its army
when broadcasting reports on the fighting in Greece. On 12
October, Athens and Piraeus were liberated by resistance troops,
and two days later the British army, along with the Greek army
in exile, marched into the city, welcomed by huge crowds and
banners saying, 'We greet the brave British army'.

A few days after liberation, one of Britain's resistance liaison
officers, Brigadier Karl Vere Barker-Benfield, a former British
Army inspector of intelligence training and chief of army
intelligence, extolled the resistence. 'We would never have been
able to set foot on Greece had it not been for the magnificent
efforts of the resistance,' he said. Two days later, he shared the
fate of other colleagues who had dared put a different gloss on
events to that favoured by Churchill. He was removed on the
orders of Ambassador Leeper.

Within six weeks of liberation, Churchill's policy led inexorably to a bloody battle for Athens in which some 4,000 civilians
died as ELAS and the British turned their guns on each other. In
London, members of parliament turned their wrath on Churchill
who faced an unprecedented wartime motion of censure. He
remained unrepentant and instructed Papandreou, who offered

to resign, that on no account was he to leave office. Churchill told Leeper that if Papandreou, to whom he now referred as 'old fool', persisted with his threat, 'he should be locked up until he comes to his senses'.

The immediate cause of the conflict was Churchill's insistence that resistance soldiers disarm, an order they were willing to obey if it was applied equally to the Greek army's Mountain Brigade and the Sacred Battalion, a commando-style unit composed almost entirely of Greek officers who had liberated most of the Aegean islands. The resistance leaders wanted the slate wiped clean: they believed that a new national army should be formed under the direction of an elected Greek government rather than, as was happening, according to the dictate of Churchill and his Athens commander, General Scobie.

The debate in the House of Commons obliged Churchill to give his views on the resistance. 'It was not against the Germans [that resistance soldiers] were trying to fight to any great extent,' he claimed. 'They were simply taking our arms, lying low and awaiting the moment when they could seize power in the capital by force, or intrigue, and make Greece a communist state with the totalitarian liquidation of all opponents.'

Churchill made no mention of his secret deal with Stalin – secured in October 1943 during a visit to Moscow by Anthony Eden and shortly afterwards cemented at Yalta – that after the war, the Balkans would be carved up between the great powers: Greece going to Britain, Bulgaria to the Soviet Union. Stalin would do his worst in Bulgaria and elsewhere in eastern Europe and Churchill, and later the Americans, were damned if they were going to loose their Greek prize.

At the end of the Commons debate, Churchill's final words on his betrayal of the Greek resistance revealed his essentially romantic view of the country. 'I turn from the pink and ochre panorama of Athens and Piraeus, scintillating with delicious life and plumed by the classic glories and endless miseries and triumphs of its history,' he said, moving on to other business.

Defeat for the resistance was total. Churchill instructed Scobie to act in Athens 'as if you are in a conquered city where a local rebellion is in progress'. From November 1944 to January 1945 when they were forced to capitulate – ultimately blasted into submission by Royal Air Force dive bombers – the resistance sought an honourable compromise.

As partisans struggled to retain the city, often in street by street fighting against the overwhelming odds of 50,000 British troops, Britain simultaneously re-built the Greek army and police by inducting into them collaborators from the Security Battalions and X Bands. Some 5,000 collaborators awaiting trial were released from prison to help crush the men who had liberated Greece from the Germans. Mountain Brigade and Sacred Battalion royalists and known collaborators were given key appointments in preference to partisans. There were inevitable outrages on both sides. Partisans took hostages; the British rounded up some 28,000 people at random and deported them.

The resistance leader, General Sarafis, a lawyer and pre-war career army officer, lamented Britain's conduct. In his memoirs (published in 1946 and banned almost immediately by the Greek government), he disclosed a message sent to Scobie as the fighting raged. 'It is regrettable that in Athens fighting is now taking place between allies,' he told the British commander. 'The struggle which is in progress today is not a struggle of anarchists, but a struggle of free people who desire their liberty and independence.'

But on 15 January 1945, Sarafis bowed to the inevitable and gave in. Under an agreement signed the following month, all ELAS troops were banned from Athens and Salonika, and those not normally resident in the Peloponnese instructed to evacuate the area. Service personnel captured by partisans were to be swapped for an equal number of partisans held by the British. Scobie, who signed the agreement on behalf of the British army, did not keep the deal, according to Sarafis. Immediately after it was signed, ELAS soldiers handed over around 1,100 prisoners but received in return only 700 of its own men and 300 civilians.

Exactly one month later, the resistance signed a demobilisation agreement under which those who had taken part in the fighting were granted an amnesty and laws limiting free expression of political views were to be repealed. Sarafis issued the order for his men to surrender their arms. Almost 50,000 rifles and pistols were handed over to the British and the newly formed Greek National Guard, along with almost 2,000 machine guns, 100 pieces of artillery, over 200 mortars and communications equipment. In a morale boosting message to his defeated troops, Sarafis praised their bravery in fighting the Germans and urged them to play a useful role in the emerging country.

'On returning to your homes,' he said, 'you must be the best citizens and continue to work peacefully for your happiness and for the complete restoration of democratic freedom, so that it may be possible for our country to become, by its people's resolve, a modern and happy state with a truly democratic constitution.'

The agreement that ended hostilities also saw the demise of George Papandreou as prime minister and brought a compromise from Churchill on the question of the monarchy. General Plastiras, the nominal leader of the defunct National Democratic League, was installed in Papandreou's place. In September 1946, the issue of King George was put to the people in a referendum, held in an atmosphere of intimidation following the defeat of the resistance. To no one's surprise, a majority – 68 per cent – of those who voted supported his return to the throne.

The new government quickly abandoned clauses in the peace treaty that were supposed to guarantee the sort of democratic freedoms expected of a country within the western sphere of influence. During an eighteen month period after it was signed and ELAS had given up so many of its weapons, thousands of former partisans were arrested at random and interned, branded as communists. By July 1945 alone, some 80,000 members of the Liberation Front and its army, and their assumed sympathisers, were jailed, most of them held in island camps for 're-education'.

Britain failed to achieve stable government in Athens, however. Elections in March 1946 – fought amid right wing bully-boy tactics in rural areas – produced a succession of conservative governments but little stability. In a major tactical blunder,

the Communist Party and several other politicians from the
centre-left boycotted the poll, thereby cementing the very
isolation about which they complained so bitterly. Between
this election and another in late 1952, there were no less than
nine governments before stable rule was established, and only
then at a cost of a full scale civil war in which thousands of
Greeks died.

Chapter Three

Cheap Insurance for
the United States

'I just have to make up my mind what I think is best for
Greece. I hold all the cards.'
Dwight Griswold, US ambassador to Greece
head of President Truman's aid to Greece programme

Four months after President Harry Truman announced a programme of massive US military aid to Greece in March 1947,
more than 36,000 Greeks were arrested by their own government. They were sent into exile or imprisoned, many on island
detention camps where they were tried by kangaroo courts, if at
all. A further 37,000 people were dealt with by courts martial,
of whom 20,000 were convicted. Some were to remain in jail for
almost two decades.

Over the following three years, about 7,800 people were
sentenced to death. They included the young man who during
the German occupation scaled the walls of the Parthenon to
tear down the Nazi swastika. Others included members of
the Jehovah's Witnesses religious sect which the government
in Athens – and the US ambassador, Lincoln MacVeagh –
regarded as 'under communist domination'. Mercifully, only
3,136 of the execution orders were actually carried out.

American aid to this campaign of terror was orchestrated on
the ground by Dwight Griswold, a poker-playing, gum-chewing
former governor of Nebraska, who articulated vividly the client
state nature of the relationship between Greece and the US. 'I
just have to make up my mind what I think is best for Greece,' he
told a contemporary interviewer, who described him accurately

as the most powerful man in the country. Griswold characterised the Greeks as people 'to whom deviousness, subtlety and complexity are second nature' but consoled himself with the thought that he had the stronger hand. 'I hold all the cards. When you've got a lot of money, you're in a strong position,' he said.

Griswold arrived in Athens with instructions from the US secretary of state, George Marshall, that if necessary he was to cause a 'reorganization of the Greek government . . . indirectly through discreet suggestion and otherwise in such a manner that even the Greek political leaders will have a feeling that the reorganization has been effected largely by themselves and not by pressure from without'.

American involvement in Greece coincided with a growing fear in Washington that the post-war Greek government installed by the British was about to be overthrown. The US regarded anti-government forces as communist insurgents, aided by the Soviet Union. Although Britain still maintained some 6,000 troops and support staff in Greece, the Americans saw their presence as symbolic. London's decision to pull out this token force coincided with a proposal in Washington put forward to President Truman by his under-secretary of state, Dean Acheson. Acheson suggested that the United States intervene on the side of the government in Athens, opining that 'unless urgent and immediate support is given to Greece, it seems probable that the Greek government will be overthrown and a totalitarian regime of the extreme left will come to power'.

MacVeagh shared the assessment. In a telegram to Washington he said: 'If Greece falls to communism the whole Near East and part of north Africa as well are certain to pass under Soviet influence and to prevent this and the world-wide complications it would entail, a premium of not only five but many times $5 million would seem cheap insurance for the US.'

American intelligence agents reinforced the point. One reported quite simply that Greece was 'a battleground for US security interests'.

Truman responded swiftly. Within days of Britain's declaration of intent to withdraw, the Greek *chargé d'affaires* in Washington was summoned to the State Department and ordered to 'request' US aid. He obliged and gave Truman the pretext for launching, on 12 March 1947, the most significant post-war initiative undertaken by the US: the Truman Doctrine of intervention to protect the free world from communism.

'The very existence of the Greek state is today threatened by the terrorist activities of several thousand armed men, led by communists, who defy the government's authority at a number of points, particularly along the northern bounda-ries,' Truman told a special joint session of Congress. 'Greece must have assistance if it is to become a self-supporting and self-respecting democracy.'

He went on to appeal for some $4 billion immediate aid for both Greece and Turkey and to enunciate the domino theory. 'Collapse of free institutions and a loss of independence would be disastrous not only for them but for the world. Discouragement and possibly failure would quickly be the lot of neighbouring peoples striving to maintain their freedom and independence.'

Within three months, an American Mission for Aid to Greece was established in Athens to oversee the flow of US money and equipment. The Mission was followed swiftly by US military advisors whom Truman told to provide the Greek army with 'stimulating and aggressive assistance'. Soon an initial group of 170 US military advisors was in Greece, rising to about 400 within a year. They were followed by millions of dollars worth of fighter bombers, rifles and ammunition, communications systems, transport vehicles and even railways, roads, bridges and docks.

The target for the fledgling Greek army and its US suppliers was a left-wing partisan force of some 20,000 men and women. In October 1946, they responded to the repressive activities of the Greek government by forming an army in the mountains of northern Greece. Although eventually outnumbered six to one by a hastily expanded Greek Army, the rebels held the initiative at the start of the civil war.

American aid – 50 shiploads – tipped the balance in favour of the government. The crucial battle came late in 1948 in the

Grammos Mountains on the Greek–Albanian border. In an appropriately titled offensive called Operation Torch, thousands of gallons of American supplied napalm were dropped on guerrilla strongholds, followed by artillery shelling and hand-to-hand fighting as government troops advanced, village by village.

Prior to Operation Torch, both sides had steadily evacuated children from disputed territory. About 15,000 were moved out by the government. A further 28,000 were moved by the rebels to camps along Greece's northern borders. This action by the rebels gave rise to one of the most enduring myths of the civil war: that communists kidnapped children and took them into Albania, Yugoslavia and Bulgaria where they were brainwashed into becoming Marxist revolutionaries, waiting to swarm back over the border to establish a totalitarian dictatorship in Greece.

The truth is that the US embassy in Athens saw the evacuation as ideal material for propaganda against the rebels. The success of the propaganda may be judged by the fact that to this day, many in Greece believe all 28,000 children were indeed kidnapped. But at the time, both Dwight Griswold and George Marshall accepted that the vast majority of children evacuated were moved with the consent of their parents.

In secret dispatches from the US mission in Athens, Griswold wrote that 'relatively few children have in fact been kidnapped by the guerrillas'. He referred to them as refugees. Marshall concurred. 'There is inadequate evidence . . . that any substantial number of children were forcibly taken,' the Secretary of State acknowledged.

Nonetheless, the US charge in Athens, Karl Rankin, advised that the evacuation of rebel children was 'a major psychological blunder [by the rebels] which we should exploit by [the] widest possible publication in [the] US and abroad'. He believed the issue could be turned into 'useful anti-communist propaganda' and noted later, after the CIA took up his advice with gusto, that the child abduction story was 'proving unusually effective psychological warfare'.

CIA support was hardly surprising since the agency had by now come to the view that were the government in Athens to lose the civil war, there would be 'international panic'. An agency assessment of the situation in February 1948 said bluntly that if the Greek government was defeated, 'Italy would probably go communist within a few months . . . The future of Greece rests with the USSR and the US.'

Underpinning American involvement in the civil war was the publicly held belief that the rebel army was being supplied by the Soviet Union and its Balkan allies, who wanted to impose a communist dictatorship in Athens as it had done elsewhere in eastern Europe. But according to a retired US diplomat who served with a United Nations commission that investigated the claim of Soviet military support for the rebels, the evidence for this was at best 'very circumstantial'. Although the rebel army received some arms from Yugoslavia, Stalin told the government in Belgrade bluntly that the Soviet Union wanted nothing to do with the Greek communists. 'The uprising in Greece must be stopped and as quickly as possible,' he said, according to Tito's deputy, Milovan Djilas. The marginal involvement of the Soviet Union was confirmed by a CIA agent who was active in Greece at the time. 'The Soviets for some reason were standing by the Churchill–Stalin agreement [carving up the Balkans] and really didn't get involved in Greece, although they had their dupes and stoops – what Lenin called the useful idiots.'

The rebels lost the crucial battle for the Grammos Mountains and, in the winter of 1948/49, about 100,000 of them and their children fled across the border to Albania. From there, most were dispersed throughout the Eastern Bloc. For 30 years, successive Greek governments banned many of them from ever returning to their homeland.

By the end of the war in March 1949, 29,000 rebels had died, over 13,000 were wounded and 28,000 captured, according to government figures. On the government side, casualties amounted to over 23,000 dead and 3,700 missing. A further 4,000 civilians had been executed, murdered or died in crossfire. One historian's estimate, however, was that the total loss of life was as high as 158,000.

The end of the civil war meant total victory for the Greek Right and its patron, the United States. In 1952 under a new constitution and with the Communist Party outlawed, the right-wing Greek Rally Party won an overwhelming victory, taking 239 of the 300 seats in parliament. But the government in Athens could hardly claim to be running an independent country. It was utterly dependent for its survival on American military and economic support. According to recently declassified papers in Washington, from June 1947 to June 1957, 'all forms of US economic aid' to Greece amounted to $1,491 million. Over the same period, military aid accounted for $1,150 million, suggesting that a mere $341 million was spent on non-military projects, such as housing, health and education, which would have been of direct help to ordinary Greek people.

The extent to which the Greek army was influenced, and ultimately under the control of the US military establishment, can be gauged by the fact that between 1950 and 1969, a total of 11,229 Greek army personnel were trained in the US. The total officer corps of the Greek army in early 1971 was 11,000. In a gesture of admiration for their friends in Washington, the Greek military named their Athens headquarters The Pentagon.

During the 1950s, Greece became a major operation area for the CIA. The agency was established in Athens by Tom Karamessines, a Greek–American veteran of the Office of Strategic Services (the OSS), the World War II forerunner of the CIA. Karamessines was designated attaché at the US embassy in January 1946, one year before the agency itself was born. During the civil war, it was his job to liaise with British and Greek security officials. After the war, he built up a CIA station in Athens that became the hub of all CIA activity in the Balkans and Middle East, as far east as Iran.

As a regional centre, Athens station was responsible for ensuring that all stations under its umbrella and agents in the field were properly equipped and financed. A handful of the Greek-based agents worked out of the US embassy on Queen Sophia Boulevard but the majority were in the Tamion Building, a seven storey, pale pink monolith off Syntagma Square that would have looked at home among the Stalinist architecture of eastern Europe. The Tamion took up an entire block, with the CIA and US military advisors occupying most of the fifth floor, above Zonaras, a spacious café specialising in gourmet cakes and sweets.

The Athens station became the switching centre for all communications east and south of Greece that were relayed to Washington. The code pads for all stations reporting via Greece were kept in Athens. The station had its own C47 transport plane, supply warehouse and medical team, capable of being dispatched to anywhere in the region in the event of an emergency. Within a few years of being set up, the station had over 100 full-time agents, many of them Greek–Americans who remained in Greece well into the 1960s, as well as departments for communications (which alone employed some 30 people), logistics and finance.

The agency did not confine itself to running agents out of Greece and monitoring Soviet activity in the region. It helped establish an internal security organisation and took a hands-on interest in the Greek army's Hellenic Raiding Force, the elite unit set up by the British during World War II after the purge of anti-monarchists. The Raiding Force, sometimes known also as the King's Bodyguard, was developed into a quick-response, commando-style unit designed to put down any internal challenge to the government and harry an invader, always expected to be Soviet. During the civil war, the Force was used as shock troops against rebels in northern Greece and the Peloponnese.

In the mid-1950s, the CIA helped supply and equip the Force, and consciously re-modelled it on existing elite units in the US army and Britain – America's Delta Force and Britain's Special Air Service, the SAS. Under CIA direction, Raiding Force members were issued with green berets, long before the US army's own Green Berets unit came into being. The Raiding Force doubled as the Greek arm of the clandestine pan-European guerrilla network set up in the 1950s by NATO and the CIA which was controlled from NATO headquarters in Brussels by the Allied Co-ordination Committee. The idea behind the network was that it would operate as a 'stay behind' force after a Soviet invasion of western Europe. It would co-ordinate guerrilla activity between the Soviet occupied

countries and liaise with governments-in-exile. Those involved
would be members of the conquered nations' secret police and
intelligence services, plus civilian volunteers.

The Greek branch of the network was also known as Operation Sheepskin. But the sort of people who became involved in
the network and their political pedigree may best be judged by
what happened in Italy, where the local branch was known as
Operation Gladio. There is evidence that Gladio activists were
involved in neo-fascist terrorist outrages in the 1970s and 80s,
including the Bologna railway station bombing in which 82
people died. The outrages were an apparent attempt to destabilise
the country and thwart left-wing advances at elections.

The Greek Raiding Force was supplied initially by the CIA
with scuba diving equipment, parachutes and skis. American
agents built a complex of Nissen huts near Mount Olympus in
east–central Greece where Raiding Force recruits were tutored
by a CIA-hired Austrian ski instructor. A CIA specialist in
counter-insurgency was seconded to teach the Force the art
of mountain warfare. So keen was the agency to see that the
Force was adequately trained and supplied that, on at least one
occasion, senior agents circumvented the bureaucracy of the US
military mission in Greece and used their own confidential funds
to purchase equipment for it, in this case parachutes from a US
army base in north Africa that was about to close.

In the emerging US-dominated new order, internal Greek
security became the preserve of KYP, the Greek acronym
for the Central Information, or Intelligence, Agency. Tom
Karamessines, who later rose to become the CIA's Deputy
Director for Plans in Washington, was instrumental in establishing KYP. It was run by the Greek army with money
and equipment supplied by the US. Military control of the
organisation – which was responsible for internal security but
was used by the CIA as a virtual branch office – meant that the
highly politicised Greek army, dominated as it was by rightists
and royalists, was in an unrivalled position to spot and repress
anyone who spoke against the government.

According to a former senior CIA agent in Greece, the
relationship with KYP was 'very, very close'. Many KYP agents,

including some of the most senior in the organisation, were paid salaries by the CIA. They included George Papadopoulos, the former German collaborator who became a colonel in the post-war Greek army and eventually KYP's liaison officer with the CIA. Papadopoulos was on the CIA's payroll from 1952.

'There was enormous empathy of views between Greeks and Americans as to how the world was to be run,' claimed a former high ranking CIA agent who was based in Greece. 'With coinciding aims and purposes, and of course our money, it was easy to work with them . . . KYP were good at noodling out Greek communists and those who flirted with the Soviets.'

In order to assist KYP's poor technical expertise, the CIA supplied the organisation with weapons, transport, computers, tape recorders, bugging equipment and all such trappings of Cold War spying. 'We put KYP in the business of intercepting Bulgarian and Russian [radio] traffic because it's very expensive putting an American into that sort of job. They were able to man stations along the border [with Bulgaria] and we would take all the tapes and send them to America for decoding by the NSA [National Security Agency],' another former senior CIA agent revealed.

Once decoded and assessed, the Americans returned to KYP 'anything of interest to them'. Thus the Greek agency was wholly reliant on the CIA for information about the Balkans and anything happening there of consequence to Greece, as the CIA saw it.

While the CIA devoted most of its efforts to running agents in the Balkans and trawling for defectors, as well as monitoring Soviet activity in the Middle East and Greece itself ('there was a large embassy and trade mission used as cover by the KGB, we were always trying to recruit them'), KYP was given free rein over domestic Greek 'subversion' in the belief that it could be relied on to tell the Americans if anything cropped up.

KYP developed an extraordinary zest for gathering information. It was helped in this task by civil war legislation which remained in force long after the conflict ended. A special law had been enacted to exclude from positions of perceived importance anyone whose loyalty to the government was less than 100 per cent. The law required anyone applying for a job with a government office or company engaged in work on behalf of the government (no matter how tenuous the connection) to obtain a Certificate of Social Beliefs. These were issued by the police but before they were willing to oblige, applicants had to account for their political associations and those of their relatives. After the civil war, the law was extended to cover applicants for passports and driving licences. The effect was to encourage people to inform on others and, if the police expressed reservations about granting a certificate, it tempted them to fabricate information.

The information thus collected fell into KYP's lap when the agency was set up in the early 1950s and was energetically added to throughout the decade. The agency and the Secret Police eventually amassed fifteen tons of information – sixteen and a half million individual files on people regarded as a threat to the state. By 1961 when the accumulation amounted to details on about twenty per cent of the population, storage became a serious problem. It was solved when, as so often in the past, the CIA came to the rescue. The Americans presented their Greek friends with a computer system.

KYP was so proud of the equipment that after it was installed, the government held a press reception and demonstration. The head of KYP stood by the new machine and announced proudly: 'You in Greece may sleep peacefully because this marvellous accomplishment of American science never sleeps.'

To show how efficient the computer was at storing and retrieving data, he pressed a button and out flopped a file. Picking it up, he proclaimed with assurance that the file 'characterises an enemy of our country. Let's see who it is.'

To his embarrassment, it turned out to be one of the reporters present.

Chapter Four

A Whim of Iron

'Control was an absolutely unacceptable word when it
came to Frederika. Nobody could control her.'
Former Athens-based CIA officer

In all that they did in Greece, the Americans were never short of
allies among the host population. Whether it was the right-wing
political establishment, the business community or the royal
family: all benefited from the link with the US. The palace
maintained a persistent interest in the minutiae of day to day
politics and the army, seen as the personal fiefdom of the king.
As regards the CIA, the relationship was so close that the agency
was able to install and maintain a vital radio station in the palace
estate at Tatoi, just outside Athens.

The CIA's most fervent admirer in the palace was Queen
Frederika, whose husband Paul ascended the throne in March
1947 on the death of his brother, George II. Frederika was the
granddaughter of the German Kaiser, Wilhelm II, who paid the
Greek royal family 40 million marks in gold for their support
during World War I. Paul was widely regarded as a good man
but he was no match for his domineering wife.

Prior to her marriage to Paul, Frederika was Princess of
Hanover and attended school in Austria where she joined the
female wing of the Hitler Youth movement, the Bund Deutscher
Mädel. Her brothers fought in the German army and an uncle
is reputed to have had connections with the SS. When it came
to Frederika's position as Queen of Greece, she was not short
of the sort of grand vision so beloved of the Kaiser and Hitler.
She liked to think of the Greek royal house as descended from
the rulers of the Byzantine Empire.

She was extraordinarily strong willed and adept at using her intelligence, beauty and charm to outwit her opponents and those reluctant to give her what she wanted. Her opinions were held with intensity and articulated with force. They reflected the unreal world in which she lived, a member of a dwindling band of European royals whose members had a propensity for indulging themselves in obscure obsessions. Hers was Pantheism in particular and philosophy in general.

She believed in life after death not as a metaphysical concept, a kernel of some religious faith, but as an actual reality for which she had obtained personal proof. Following the death of King Paul, she told courtiers that he came to her at times with instructions as to how the country should be run. One staff member advised that she would be better not disclosing such information, as ordinary people might not understand. Undeterred, at Paul's memorial service in Tatoi she wondered out loud why a service was being held at all. It seemed there was nothing to mourn as the dead king had come to her in the night with the news that she must rule the country in his stead. While the service was going on, she left the church and returned after some minutes with the news that Paul had just told her 'Constantine [must] do as you say'.

Only the brave or care free would dare challenge Frederika's many pronouncements. In conversation, she would flit from subject to subject, able to hold forth on the merits of organically grown tomatoes ('Try them!') and vegetarianism ('I never eat anything that loves its mother'); space travel (she once urged Wernher von Braun, Hitler and NASA's rocket scientist to put her into orbit. 'After all, they might as well put a spare Queen into orbit as anyone else.' NASA declined politely.); exotic liquor concoctions ('Give me a huge champagne cocktail with peaches marinaded in wine'); President Richard Nixon's rapprochement with China ('a gimmick!'); and intellectuals ('I don't like intellectuals. They're all weak and they have no courage. When my husband and I were fighting the communists to save Greece, they sat in the cafés. They're still there and they're all against me.').

Some years after Paul's death and when she was living in

exile, Frederika encountered an Englishman who recorded the experience in his diary.

> After lunch, I sat with Queen Frederika and she began to talk to me about her life, politics and then philosophy ... The full force of her charm and power was being played on me and it was an astonishing experience. She is still at 53 a startlingly beautiful woman. The smile is dazzling and when, towards the end of our conversation, she mentioned this [man] who was godfather to Princess Irene and another of her 'great friends' who had said to her 'strong men will love you and others will fear you', my God I could see what the man had meant.
>
> She told me of her withdrawal from public life after the death of King Paul and the problems she had had with bad press, blaming the communists for it ... Her vigour, brilliance, sharp tongue and arrogance are simply too rich a brew for us ordinary mortals and at one stage I found myself blurting out quite spontaneously, 'But Your Majesty is absolutely magnificent!' Having begun, I saw that she expected me to continue in the same vein and it was certainly no lie to say that her combination of beauty and brains are simply overwhelming.
>
> From this point, the liquid look in her eyes, the radiance of her charm became even more intense and, as she rose, she turned those gorgeous blue eyes on me and said, 'You have impressed me.' I saw instantly how she managed the government-in-exile when King Paul was at the front. As she stood up ... she turned, fixed me with one of those liquid gazes, hoped that we would meet again and swept from the room with her blue beach kimono fluttering.
>
> I was utterly flabbergasted. I have no idea how long we talked. It could not have been more than 15 minutes but, in this short time, I felt as if I had been flattened by a steam-roller.

Frederika prided herself on the role she played during the civil war, visiting stricken villages on the government side and comforting the bereaved. She needed no encouragement in her dislike of communists but the civil war gave her views a sharp focus. She accepted without question the propaganda that the rebels had kidnapped a generation of Greek children.

'They're coming back!' she told an American author who interviewed her in Athens. 'Those youngsters are returning according to the plan, full-fledged brainwashed adult communists, a great fifth column attack, a phalanx in the scheme to make Greece communist. The families from which they were stolen have long since forgotten them. They've had other children and are not pleased at the invasion of these troublemakers.'

With the palace deeply involved in running the army and keeping a tight rein on government, Frederika eschewed dealing with staff at the American embassy. Diplomats, she pronounced, were 'fairies and half-wits'. The CIA, on the other hand, was something else.

According to a former diplomat, the agency went out of its way to create in Frederika the impression that it had a direct line to the White House. A retired senior agent confirmed that throughout the 1950s the agency was 'really riding high' with the palace. While much of the rest of the country languished in poverty, the Queen made sure her own needs were met through Post Exchange, the US government's system for supplying its staff abroad.

'There was enormous contact with Paul and Frederika,' revealed the former agent. 'She was constantly being gifted. She liked Post Exchange things, ranging from laundry soap to large electrical goods like refrigerators . . . She made known her likes and dislikes and since it was not very difficult to accommodate her, it was done. Control was an absolutely unacceptable word when it came to Frederika: nobody could control her.'

The quantity of goods which it was found necessary to hand over to the royal family to retain its favour (the CIA annually received what it euphemistically termed Frederika's 'Christmas list') grew so enormous that at least one ambassador complained to the agency. As one former agent put it, Frederika 'had a whim of iron'. The queen's rapaciousness extended to prominent members of the Greek business community. On one occasion she tried to extort a yacht from the shipping magnate Stavros Niarchos for King Paul's birthday. This was too much for the king and when he heard about it, he stopped the order.

Greek manufacturers and retailers, especially those dealing in food and drink, vied with each other for the cachet of being able to print on their labels a notice proclaiming themselves to be suppliers to the royal household. 'Being a supplier to His Majesty meant His Majesty got it for free. Everything that came into the palace came free,' according to Philip Deane, a senior palace official in the mid-1960s.

Deane saw for himself the full expression of the attitude that the world – or least the Greek people and the US government – owed the royal family a living. While working in the palace, Deane became aware of a relationship between the royal family and one of Greece's larger car dealers that allowed both parties cream profit from the dealer's customers. The royal family was able to buy cars duty free, a considerable saving as Greek import duties were among the highest in the world. The dealer supplied the palace with cars which the king would use for a brief period, perhaps as short as a month or two. Returned to the dealer, the cars would then be sold way above the normal retail price, being described as formerly owned by His Majesty. Profits were split 50/50 between the dealer and the palace.

Deane once witnessed the pettiness of the corruption. A foreign photographer approached him with a request to do a portrait of Queen Frederika. Deane obtained the queen's permission and arranged for an appointment. To the photographer and Deane's amazement, Frederika suggested at the sitting that she could arrange for the photographer to do the whole of Athenian society, if he agreed to share his takings 50/50 with her. The photographer leapt at the opportunity and told Deane that he would quietly bump up his portrait fee.

In the early and mid-1960s, Frederika was paid a bribe of $1 million and an annual 'retainer' of $250,000 by a Greek–American businessman, Tom Pappas. Pappas was trying to obtain government approval for a vast industrial complex in Salonika, the centre piece of which was an oil refinery joint venture with the Exxon corporation. According to reliable sources, Pappas correctly identified Frederika as a woman of great influence who could help smooth the way if she was paid. Pappas eventually built his complex – in the face of severe opposition from the Centre and Left – and refined oil on terms unfavourable to the Greek economy. As a result of his deal with the government, Pappas obtained monopoly rights over the manufacture of 29

products and, according to contemporary analysts critical of
the deal, stood to exercise effective control over 54 per cent
of Greece's exports.

Frederika's greed knew few bounds. In September 1964, the
wedding of her son, King Constantine, to Princess Anne-Marie
of Denmark provided a heaven-sent opportunity to make
money. As the wedding approached, the Greek shipping magnate Aristotle Onassis went to Tatoi to ask for Frederika's help
in selecting a diamond tiara for Anne-Marie. Onassis opened
a box containing two and, tilting them towards the queen
for her to see, asked which one she thought her prospective
daughter-in-law would prefer.

'Both,' said Frederika, smiling as she took the pair.

A silversmith was commissioned by the palace to craft small
boxes, each to be engraved with Constantine and Anne-Marie's
signature, as token gifts for heads of state invited to the wedding.
Behind the scenes, however, the smith was told to knock out
dozens of extras to be sold, at vastly inflated prices, to Greek *hoi
polloi*. As with the car dealer, profits were to be split 50/50 with
the royal household. In the run up to the wedding, the tone set
behind the scenes was perhaps best exemplified by the attitude
of the many Athenian hoteliers who begged Philip Deane not
to place guests with them. They implored him because at an
earlier royal celebration – Constantine's coronation in March
1964 – palace guests lodged with them had eaten, drank and
generally whooped it up day and night before returning home,
leaving their bills unpaid.

The wedding was an excuse for 'Joy throughout the land',
said George Athenassiades-Novas, a renowned loyalist and
president of the parliament, who wrote a poem marking the
occasion.

> Voicing the nation's joy,
> Of all Greeks throughout our land,
> My wish for the Princess from the North: bring happiness
>   to Constantine,
> That, with you, our people be happy,
> And with our glorious throne at the apex,
> May Greece, spirited and soulful, prosper for ever and ever.

Frederika's conduct cannot be explained by pleadings of poverty. Compared to all but a handful of Greek businessmen, the royal family was infinitely better off than everyone else in the country. Its wealth was based on family estates and a charity, the Royal National Foundation. Founded in 1946, the Foundation, was established ostensibly to distribute money to worthy causes such as schools and hospitals. It was funded by a special tax on cigarettes and further money was derived from a special tax on cinema tickets and imported cars. By 1968, it was estimated that the Foundation received $20 million a year but nobody in government or outside the close confines of the royal family knew where the money went. The charity was immune from government control and was administered entirely by the Queen.

Neither did the royal family pay income tax on the allowance given to it by the government (in 1962 the king received $567,000 a year) or on the revenue from the estates. Apart from the palace in Athens and the estate at Tatoi with all its farmland, royal property included some 5,000 acres of forest in central Greece, a summer palace (called Mon Repos) on the island of Corfu, a villa in Psychico (the most fashionable suburb of Athens), a hunting lodge on Mount Hymettos and villas on the islands of Petali and Rhodes. In 1962, Frederika asked the government for, and was given, the Byzantine monastry of Asterios. At the same time, she also indicated her wish to have palaces built for herself in Salonika, Ioannina, Corfu and Rhodes. The family also convinced the government to pay for a jet (cost: $1.5 million), two Dakota DC3s, a helicopter, several ships and eighteen cars, including two Rolls Royces.

Queen Frederika's relationship with the CIA was conducted not through minions or middle grade agents but with those at the very top of the agency in Greece. She developed a special liking for Laughlin Campbell, the CIA station chief from 1959 to 1962.

Campbell was a six foot plus, strikingly handsome CIA veteran with a broad smile that lit up his whole face and a sharp intellect behind it. Like many of the men and women who rose to post-war positions of prominence in western intelligence agencies, he did not begin his career as a spy. He was initially an academic, having studied philosophy in Canada, and his early interest in the subject was to serve him well in Greece.

In the two years after his appointment in Greece, Campbell cultivated a high profile, establishing close ties with several key figures at the heart of right-wing power bases. He shared many of their political views and saw himself as a link between the palace, the prime minister, Constantine Karamanlis, and the army general staff. He had Karamanlis' private telephone numbers giving him the sort of access to the head of government denied to all but the most important ambassadors. But then, Karamanlis owed his position to the Americans.

In October 1955, when the then prime minister, Field-Marshal Alexander Papagos died, US diplomats and CIA agents in Athens advised King Paul whom he should choose as a replacement. At the time, Karamanlis was only minister for public works, not a post from which would-be prime ministers regularly leap to the top job. But the American preference and advice to the palace was clear: Karamanlis was plucked from relative obscurity and became prime minister. The Americans had no illusions about their role in promoting Karamanlis. As one retired US diplomat said years later: 'He was our creature, our creation. We took him out of obscurity and moulded him.' It would be wrong, however, to suggest that Karamanlis had no popular mandate: in 1956 and 1958 he won two of the fairer elections fought since the end of the civil war and was returned to office.

Laughlin Campbell's access to the prime minister was nothing compared to the closeness of his relationship with the palace. It reflected an apparent meeting of minds with Queen Frederika. It was well known that the queen had little time for the embassy diplomats, preferring instead to deal direct with the CIA. But with Campbell, the empathy was personal.

The tall American believed strongly that Greece was held together by the crown and the cross, a coalition of the monarchy and the church that would keep the country stable and a friend to the west. The view that Frederika and her husband were crucial to the nation's survival was music to the queen's ears. Campbell met her privately at least twice a month.

On each second Tuesday evening, the CIA chief would journey to Tatoi, a modest Victorian hunting lodge style home with a whiff of Bavarian architecture about it. There, in the privacy of the royal home, he would speak to King Paul and Queen Frederika about the ancient Greek philosophers and the minutiae of Catholic theology: everything from Plato to Thomas Aquinas. If the queen didn't exactly sit at Campbell's feet, enraptured and in awe, the CIA man had just such a relationship with one of her heros, Panayiotis Pipinelis, the diminutive guru of Greece's right-wing establishment.

Pipinelis was extraordinarily conscious of his petite stature. His face was level with his Swedish wife's breasts, an observation that much amused Athenian society, and in order to increase his height, Pipinelis wore special platform shoes. The legs of his office chair were extended by several inches so that when he sat down, his head and shoulders were not below his underlings. But the effect was diminished somewhat because when he sat down, his feet dangled just above the floor.

Like other small men before him, Pipinelis had an appetite for power. He began his public service career as a foreign ministry civil servant but rose to be permanent under-secretary and, at various stages during his life, an ambassador, government minister and political advisor to the royal family. Like Campbell, he was a strong believer in the stabilizing influence of the monarchy and he wielded influence by tentacles stretching from the civil service to the palace and the military and back again via the political establishment.

Queen Frederika frequently sought his advice and confided her thoughts to him. Pipinelis was a passionate advocate of the Platonic ideal for society: government by an oligarchy of the great and good, loyal to the crown but co-opting onto itself others whom it judged capable of making an equally selfless contribution to the established order. He had little time for democracy and went along with it only so long as it produced right-wing governments – the sort he could tolerate.

Campbell admired Pipinelis and looked upon his as a scholar.

In the troubled years of the early 1960s, Campbell would go to
the old man, asking him to fill in those aspects of Greek history
– ancient and modern – missing from his own knowledge and
seeking advice on more contemporary matters. Campbell would
sit there listening, spellbound.

Campbell's bi-monthly sorties to Tatoi were not always
dominated by ancient philosophy and theology, however. For
example, the queen expressed interest in nuclear power: its
potential fascinated her. She also wanted to know everything
that was going on in government and military circles and did
not shrink from taking an active role.

In the year that Campbell took over the CIA station in
Athens, a controversy erupted that brought back some of the
bitter memories of the German occupation. It concerned a West
German tourist, Max Merten, who was arrested in Salonika,
where he had been stationed during the war. Merten had been
no ordinary German soldier, however. He had been responsible
for the transportation of Jews from Salonika. In 1959, when he
was an official in the West German justice ministry in Bonn,
Merten felt confident enough to make a nostalgic trip back to
Greece. But he was recognised and a diligent Salonika prosecutor
insisted that he be tried in Greece for war crimes. The German
government objected, arguing that only it had the right to try
him. A furious row ensued between Athens and Bonn which
came to a head after an intervention by Queen Frederika.

She told the government that she didn't want anything done
to damage business with Germany. The cabinet caved in and
Merten was released into German custody.

The antics of the queen were of course unknown to all but
a few of her subjects. The network of cosy relationships that
linked the palace, the army, the political establishment, the CIA
and the US embassy suited each and produced stable government
for most of the 1950s. The Left was defeated and in disarray,
its advocates either in exile, prison or too cowed to have much
of an impact on the life of the nation. But while Constantine
Karamanlis' government was prudent economically and brought
about a gradual increase in prosperity, the seeds of unrest were
everywhere.

Chapter Five

Pericles Betrayed

The result of the 1961 general election is 'proof positive of the Greek faith in the ideals of individual freedom and human dignity.'

Ellis Briggs, US ambassador to Greece

In the dry, dusty mid-summer heat of 1961, two of the CIA's most important men in Greece set out from Athens to conduct an opinion poll. It was a quiet affair without fuss or razzmatazz. They just got on with it, tramping the by-ways of mainly rural areas, asking key people in the community a few precise questions: The challenge from candidate so-and-so, is it serious? Are many people leaning away from the government candidate? What are the key issues here? Are there many communists? What is the likelihood of this or that candidate winning?

Laughlin Campbell and his helper did a lot of homework before they left their offices for the small towns and villages of key marginal constituencies. There was no point bothering with those areas where voting intentions were fixed, with a large majority guaranteed for one or the other party, and the outcome predictable. The crucial constituencies were those where a swing of just one or two percentage points – perhaps even less – could determine the outcome of the general election, due to be fought in October.

To ensure they had indeed correctly identified the key marginals, Campbell and his colleague visited each in turn. They booked into inexpensive hotels and set out to speak to people – local police officers, school teachers, priests, taverna owners: people whose assessment of small town popular opinion was as accurate as any Gallup computer, probably more so.

In the evenings, the two CIA men returned to their room and tried to relate what they had heard during the day to what they knew of the candidates. They drew a large chart using different colours and pinned it to the wall. It showed the likely outcome of the election in each of the marginals, assuming their was no interference with the polling.

A remarkably similar exercise was conducted by a right-wing cabal in the army, a group known as the Military Co-ordinating Committee. Their work was part of a plot to subvert the election, a plot that involved an alliance of the palace and the political right, and was christened – without a trace of irony – the Pericles Plan, Pericles being the hero of ancient Greek democracy. At meetings of the co-ordinating committee, members used the word 'enemy' to describe not only communists and their fellow travellers but anyone deemed to be neutral between the two.

Just like Laughlin Campbell's wall chart, the military con-spirators had a map of Greece on which key marginal con-stituencies were identified and shaded in colours, making the map appear for all the world like the theatre of a full-scale military campaign. Enemy areas (those tending to the left-wing EDA party) were coloured red, friendly territory (areas tending towards the ruling ERE party of Constantine Karamanlis) was coloured blue, and territory thought not to matter (those tending towards the recently formed liberal Centre Union of former prime minister George Papandreou) was coloured yellow. But as the election campaign progressed and the Centre Union gained in appeal, its colour became red and EDA was relegated to less threatening yellow.

It is not known if the CIA compared notes with their close friends and allies in the army conducting the same exercise but it would have been odd had they not. The military committee's method of ensuring the safe return to office of Karamanlis was crude but effective: people in the marginals were either paid in cash for their vote or terrorised into supporting their local ERE candidate. Part-time soldiers led by regular army officers and members of local gendarmerie, called on voters – many of them ill-educated peasants – and told them that if they did not

support the Right, they would be sent into exile. Those showing
reluctance were further intimidated, those expressing opposition
– the 'anti-national ones' – were beaten up.

The co-ordinator of the Pericles Plan, the man who provided
the crucial link between the military and the palace, was
Constantine Dovas, a former army general who was King
Paul's chief military adviser. Dovas, a rumpled, balding man
with a limp, was a confidant of Queen Frederika and a kindred
spirit of Panayiotis Pipinelis. He shared Pipinelis' vision of a
Platonic utopia for Greece. Dovas wanted the monarchy to
have powers similar to those of an American president, though
without the counterbalance of a Congress or Supreme Court.
The only function for parliament would be to debate and
approve decisions of the king and his advisers. In certain
extremely limited situations, parliament would be allowed to
disapprove the monarch's proposal.

As the October general election loomed, King Paul made
Dovas caretaker prime minister. Dovas' obligation under the
constitution was to ensure that the contest was a fair one,
carried out according to the law. As one of the leading Pericles
conspirators, he was singularly unsuited for the task.

The conspiracy was in full swing by August. Some of the
army officers involved worked for KYP, the Greek intelligence
agency. Many, however, were members of an organisation
within the army called IDEA, the so-called Sacred Bond of
Greek Officers. This rump which proved so attractive to extreme
right-wing military conspirators began life as a secret ginger
group of middle rank royalist officers based in Egypt during
World War II. They characterised themselves as 'nationally
minded' and maintained that their interests were identical to
the interests of Greece as a whole. Thus those who opposed
them – liberals and democrats – were against the country and
had to be treated as allies of the communists. Members of IDEA
had to be prepared to use 'forceful or dynamic action' to achieve
their ends: this included the use of arms against communists or
'those who naively co-operated with them'.

Those who enrolled and paid their 20 drachmas' monthly
dues had to swear allegiance to the 'national idea' and vow

to oppose anyone who would 'diminish the national feelings'. Members supported the notion of a 'just territorial expansion of the country for the creation of a greater Greece' and the 'need for purging the officer corps of all those who had internationalist ideas or who were of doubtful national feelings'.

IDEA was a natural home for former Nazi collaborators and immediately after the war the organisation began to attract them. Among the 2,500 mostly middle-rank officers who had joined by the end of the 1940s were 228 former collaborators. They included General George Grivas, head of the collaborationist X Bands who became so involved with IDEA that at one stage he was its leader. Among its other notable members was George Papadopoulos who revelled in the opportunity for plotting and conspiring provided by a command structure and communication system which IDEA set up inside the army, parallel to the official systems.

IDEA kept intelligence files on fellow officers who were not members, which, because of the organisation's influence, it was able to use to deny them promotions. This body of negative information – often based on no more substance than that a man displayed 'non-nationalistic feelings' – was used against real and imagined communists. They included officers who had not joined IDEA, others who had been purged from the armed forces by the Metaxas dictatorship and men deemed by IDEA to lack 'moral qualification'. By contrast, the Security Battalion collaborators and pro-fascist X Band members were regarded by IDEA as 'good nationalists' and given the protection of the organisation.

The Pericles Plan was run largely by officers with long-standing links to IDEA. They included General Nikolas Gogoussis, the director of information in Constantine Karamanlis' office, who was a leading member of the organisation; General Vassilios Kardamakis, chief of the army general staff who had close ties with it; General Alexander Natsinas, the director of KYP and a member of IDEA; General G Vardoulakis, chief of the gendarmerie; and two colonels, Odysseas Angelis and George Papadopoulos, each of them active IDEA members. Papadopoulos was secretary to the Military Co-ordinating

Committee orchestrating the plan even though, as an inquiry years later would demonstrate, he was barely literate.

After King Paul appointed Dovas prime minister on 20 September 1961, the intimidation of voters in key marginal constituencies grew in tandem with the plotters' confidence. One of the key figures on the committee, Lieutenant General Yannis Gennimatas, went so far as to give written instructions that 'not only should the communists be beaten but the neutrals as well'.

Fake electoral registers created an extra 200,000 ERE voters in Athens. The Right could also count on the support of the 200,000, mostly pro-government, members of the armed forces. (Army vote support for the government actually rose from a norm of between 70 and 80 per cent to a unbelievable 100 per cent.) In addition, anti-communist hysteria had been easy to whip up in the Surveillance Zone, the 650-mile-long strip across northern Greece where one million people lived beside Albania, Yugoslavia and Bulgaria. Support there rose from around 80 per cent to over 90 per cent. Instructions given to supposedly independent electoral officers contained emotive words and phrases, like one ordering them to 'supervise (voting) . . . for the national interest'. Everyone knew what national interest meant.

At polling stations in some rural areas, many people asked for the voting papers of the ERE candidate only, not bothering even to mention candidates in other parties. Requests were made pointedly in front of soldiers, just so the authorities could see for themselves who was loyal. In some small villages just before voting began, callers to homes reminded mothers in menacing terms that they had children or that their husbands had jobs. The implications were clear. In one village in Crete, the local ERE candidate polled more votes than there were people eligible to vote.

For Laughlin Campbell, the result of the election was a foregone conclusion which he was able to predict accurately. In a report to CIA headquarters about two weeks before voting, he said the result would depend on between 30 to 40 key constituencies and the extent of the swing to or from the government in each. He said he reckoned that ERE would win by around 49 per cent with the Centre Union getting some 32 per cent. The CIA man was just one per centage point out.

On election day, 29 October 1961, ERE got just over 50 per cent and 176 seats in the new parliament – a clear overall majority. The Centre Union won a little over a third of the popular vote and got 100 seats. The party rejected the election as a fraud and its leader, George Papandreou, announced a relentless struggle against the government. His only consolation was that EDA, his rival on the Left, dropped dramatically to take just 24 seats in the new parliament.

The result delighted the United States, the Greek military and the palace. The American ambassador declared that it was 'proof positive of the Greek faith in the ideals of individual freedom and human dignity'. As for the royal family, the result suggested no great change – life would go on much as before. But Frederika's hubris soon brought her into conflict with the new government. Few could have foreseen that she would provoke not one, but two international incidents, leading to the resignation of her own prime minister and the murder of one of Greece's best loved politicians, the left-wing peace activist Gregory Lambrakis.

In April 1963, Frederika made a private, nine-day trip to London for the wedding of Angus Ogilvy to Princess Alexandra, the daughter of the Duke of Kent, a cousin of Queen Elizabeth II and twelfth in line to the throne. In the social calendar of European royalty the wedding in Westminster Abbey was a relatively minor affair, but Frederika felt it was important to attend. She did not realise, however, the strength of feeling in some British quarters at the fact that fourteen years after the end of the Greek civil war, almost 1,000 political prisoners remained incarcerated in Greek jails and a further 900 were held in internal exile.

Assessing the situation from Athens, Constantine Karamanlis said he expected that if she went to London, she would be confronted by anti-royal protesters. He cautioned against making the trip but Frederika rejected his advice out of hand.

The day before the queen arrived in London with one of her daughters, Princess Irene, and Crown Prince Constantine, the criticism began. It came from an unusual quarter, the right-wing *Sunday Express* newspaper, which reported prominently on Frederika's past association with the Bund Deutscher Mädel. If that wasn't embarrassing enough, from the moment the royal party checked into Claridge's, the hotel was picketed day and night by Betty Ambatielos, a 45-year-old Welsh woman pleading for the release of her 49-year-old Greek husband, Antonios, imprisoned in Greece since 1947.

Tony Ambatielos' case was similar to thousands of others who had fallen foul of the post-civil war Greek establishment. A seamen's union leader and communist who spent World War II fighting the Nazis on the side of the Greek resistance, Ambatielos had spent almost fifteen years in jail for his political beliefs.

When the Greek resistance liberated Athens only to have British guns turned against it, Ambatielos fought back and, in the ensuing civil war, took the communist side. In 1947, he was sentenced to death for what were described as 'anti-nationalist activities'. He was never allowed to appeal against the conviction but the sentence was commuted to life imprisonment after the intervention of the Secretary General of the United Nations, Trygve Lie. Like thousands of others, Ambatielos remained in prison as successive Greek governments refused to honour promises of amnesty.

His case remained a live issue, however, because of his campaigning wife who lost no time taking up her position outside Claridge's. Mrs Ambatielos and a small group of determined protesters outside the hotel (including, on occasion, senior members of the Labour Party like Barbara Castle and Fenner Brockway) provided unwelcome, bad publicity for Greece.

On the queen's first Saturday in the city, she decided to go shopping with Irene. At about the same time, Mrs Ambatielos went into the hotel hoping to give her a written request to release her husband and other political prisoners. An official of the royal party refused but Mrs Ambatielos decided to wait in the lobby. When the queen and princess eventually appeared, Mrs Ambatielos stepped foward.

'Are you the Queen of Greece?' she asked. 'I would like you to take this letter about the release of my husband.'

'I don't talk to strangers,' Frederika snapped, as two large security men intervened.

Precisely what happened next is a matter of dispute but some of Mrs Ambatielos' supporters outside broke into a chorus of anti-royal chants terrifying Frederika. The queen and her daughter, who wanted nothing more than a day's shopping in some of London's up-market stores, found themselves reduced to scuttling down an alleyway to escape. They entered a mews and banged on the door of a house. A startled woman responded to the queen's cries for help and, once inside, Frederika had her telephone the police.

The Greek embassy insisted that the queen had been assaulted and accused Mrs Ambatielos of a being in a state of 'uncontrolled emotional agitation', supported by communist fanatics. Mrs Ambatielos denied that anyone touched the queen and said the verbal exchange with her in the hotel had been 'normal and polite'.

In a separate incident a few days later, Frederika was once again greeted by protesters outside the hotel. They held placards with slogans demanding 'RELEASE ALL POLITICAL PRISONERS IN GREECE', and 'GENERAL AMNESTY IN GREECE'. The protesters included a 16-year-old boy whom the police arrested and charged with disturbing the peace. If the queen hoped the British courts would show some solidarity, she was to be sadly disppointed. A local magistrate freed the youth, declaring: 'We have free speech in this country. I see no insulting behaviour.'

News of the protests spread quickly to Greece where they caught the attention of Dr Gregory Lambrakis, a professor at Athens University and left-wing member of parliament for Piraeus. Lambrakis flew to London immediately to support Mrs Ambatielos. He went to the hotel in the hope of speaking to the queen but had to make do with Major Michael Arnaoutis, Prince Constantine's aide-de-camp. Arnaoutis told Lambrakis bluntly that there was no chance of him being granted an audience. Besides, he said, the queen was in bed resting.

Members of the royal circle had little time for Lambrakis – either for his political views or his peace campaigning, which they saw as a front for communism and undermining the army. They also regarded Ambatielos as a common criminal, properly convicted.

Rebuffed by Arnaoutis, Lambrakis left the hotel empty-handed but was nonetheless able to score a propaganda point. 'It was a very great disappointment,' he told reporters outside the hotel, 'but I shall raise the matter in parliament when I get back to Athens.'

Lambrakis' approach was the last straw for the queen. She was apoplectic with rage and left palace officials in no doubt as to her feelings. Lambrakis did not know it at the time, but his action in London sealed his fate. Frederika was able to draw temporary solace from a grovelling apology sent to her by Britain's Foreign Secretary, Lord Home. Referring to the Ambatielos incident and the placard demonstration, Home told her that his government 'greatly regret that Your Majesty should have been subjected to such an experience'. Home, describing himself as the queen's 'respectful and obedient servant', said the protests had caused him 'deep distress'.

Back in Athens, Frederika gave full vent to her rage against Lambrakis. She demanded explanations from the British ambassador and gave press and television interviews attacking Mrs Ambatielos. With palace insiders, she was quite open as to her desire: she said she wished that someone would get rid of the offensive MP.

In Salonika, one of the queen's loyal subjects was prepared to grant her wish. He was Lieutenant General Mitsou, regional commander of the gendarmerie and a former member of the palace guard. Lambrakis was due to address an anti-nuclear rally in the city almost a month to the day after his encounter in London with Arnaoutis.

Mitsou had contact with an extreme right-wing organisation calling itself the Fighters and Victims of the National Resistance of Northern Greece, which was led by Xenophon Yosmas, a former Nazi collaborator. It was linked in turn to the grotesquely ill-named Directorate of National Enlightenment, a body connected to elements within Constantine Karamanlis' ruling party, ERE. The Directorate believed its function was to infiltrate and disrupt any organisations to the left of the government. Yosmas and Mitsou cloaked their shared opinions with a neo-fascist contempt for all ideologies, a distrust of Jews and foreigners, and a belief that the moral fibre of Greece was being destroyed by the likes of Lambrakis.

In May, one month after the queen's visit to London, the Salonika MP was due to speak to his local branch of the Union for Peace and Nuclear Disarmament, an organisation campaigning for a general demilitarisation of the Mediterranean. Yosmas arranged for a hostile demonstration and for some of his thugs to attack the MP with clubs. Mitsou arranged for the police to see nothing.

As the time for the meeting approached, a mob gathered outside the hall and jostled people trying to get inside. Lambrakis was staying in a hotel opposite and, in order to get to the meeting, he had to run the gauntlet of the mob. Despite a self-evident need for protection and the presence of a large number of police, no effort was made to ensure his safety and he was beaten as he crossed the road.

The atmosphere outside the meeting was considerably more hostile when it was over and Lambrakis left to return to his hotel. He was in the centre of the road, being taunted by youths as the police stood back watching, when a three-wheeled motor scooter sped towards him. As it passed, a heavy club was brought down onto his skull with a crash. Several in the crowd surged forward and administered further blows. The police did nothing as Lambrakis fell to the ground fatally wounded and the scooter sped on. Some of his supporters reacted differently, however, and caught one of the attackers – the pillion rider. The driver was arrested soon afterwards. Lambrakis died of his injuries four days later.

As attention focused on the conduct of the police, officers excused their inaction by claiming that had they sought to arrest the attackers on the spot, they would have succeeded only in making a tense situation worse. General Mitsou blamed the peace campaigners for staging the meeting. Their 'anti-national propaganda' had provoked the attack, he claimed. He said that Lambrakis' death was the result of a 'tragic road accident'.

There was widespread revulsion at the murder. Lambrakis, idolised by his supporters, was also popular with many of his fellow MPs who did not necessarily share his socialist views. His funeral in Athens was attended by over 100,000 people. Around the country, youth organisations dedicated to his ideals began to spring up in his name.

An investigation by a Salonika magistrate, Christos Sartzetakis, and the local public prosecutor, Stylianos Boutis, gradually revealed the truth behind the murder. The roles of Mitsou, Yosmas and his band of thugs plus several other senior gendarmerie officers were unearthed by Sartzetakis. But the lawyers' efforts to get at the truth were hampered by a palace ally, a man uniquely well placed to obstruct justice: Constantine Kollias, chief prosecutor of the supreme court in Athens.

Kollias was close to palace insiders like Constantine Hoidas, King Paul's chief political adviser. As Sartzetakis gathered evidence that senior gendarmerie officers were implicated in the murder, Kollias tried to dissuade him from interviewing people and to curtail the scope of the investigation. Kollias, who shared Yosmas' views about the need to 'regenerate the national spirit', eventually appointed a council of hand-picked magistrates who absolved the gendarmerie conspirators of murder in favour of lesser charges, including moral instigation of the crime, criminal negligence and abuse of authority.

The scooter driver and pillion rider were convicted of murder but given maximum remission of their sentence when the military dictatorship came to power in 1967. The authorities were also prevailed upon to return the confiscated scooter. Six key witnesses died in mysterious circumstances. Mitsou, who was retired early in the wake of the affair, was restored to duty by the junta, promoted and allowed to retire a second time, with an enhanced pension and an honourable discharge.

The Lambrakis case was remarkable for the breadth of arrogance and corruption it suggested existed inside the palace, among politicians on the Right and within the justice system – from local officers of the gendarmerie right up to the Supreme

Court. In the aftermath of the murder there was an air of triumph in the palace combined with barely concealed contempt for Lambrakis' mourners, who staged protest demonstrations throughout the country. Palace views were ably reflected some years later by Constantine.

'Do you realise what that shit did?' he responded to an aide who asked why the royal family so hated Lambrakis. 'He tried to break into my mother's hotel in England.'

The Lambrakis affair outraged Karamanlis. In public, he deplored the killing and, in private, expressed his anger at the manipulation of the investigation. 'Who the hell runs this country anyway?' he asked a friend. He later acknowledged to a biographer that the murder would ignite 'a great fire, sparks from which would be scattered beyond the frontiers of Greece'. He was right.

In Britain, where protests during the queen's visit for Princess Alexandra's wedding had already heightened awareness that Greek jails were filled with aging political prisoners, the Lambrakis murder aggravated anti-royal feelings. Although the protests had been minor, they focused attention on Greece with the result that many people became aware of the political prisoners issue, plus the fact that, in Greece, the royal family wielded real political power. Frederika's departure after the royal wedding had not been an end of the matter: Lord Home's sycophantic apology had drawn protests in parliament from the Labour leader, Harold Wilson.

It was against this background that Paul and Frederika planned to make a long-standing three-day state visit to Britain in July 1963. Karamanlis had no hesitation in advising once again that the king and queen should stay at home, as they were likely to be greeted by far greater protests than three months previously. Postponement was not a matter of royal protocol, in his view, but a case of simple political necessity given the potential for further damage to Greece's international reputation.

King Paul, at the urging of Queen Frederika, flatly rejected the prime minister's advice. Their view was that the invitation had been extended (and accepted) a long time ago and that it would be bad manners to back out at such a late stage. The queen was more acerbic. She was not going to be intimidated by people she regarded as hoodlums and fellow travellers of communist convicts.

The difference of opinion over the state visit brought to a head the serious issue of principle that lay behind the tension between the palace and Karamanlis. It was a straight question of who governed the country. Could an unelected head of state do what he wanted, irrespective of the views of the elected government? Was the monarchy a figurehead institution, above politics, or did it seek to arrogate to itself the authority to do what it wanted? Either the king and queen heeded the advice of the prime minister or there wasn't much point in being prime minister.

During hectic negotiations aimed at resolving the impasse, the four chiefs of staff of the armed forces shuttled between the palace and the prime minister. The officers were not uninterested in the outcome to the dispute as they knew Karamanlis had decided on a shake-up of top army posts in which they were to lose their jobs. Karamanlis had disclosed his intentions to the Chief of the General Staff, Lieutenant-General Constantine Sakellariou. After one meeting in the palace, the four men returned to the prime minister and suggested that he ought to resign.

A month before the visit was due to begin, the prime minister met the king at Tatoi. It was their second discussion on the subject and, after Karamanlis again outlined his objections, he got the impression that Paul accepted his view. After a morning's discussion, they agreed to resume in the afternoon when a letter of explanation for the postponement would be drafted for Crown Prince Constantine to take to London and present to Queen Elizabeth, in the absence of his parents.

Karamanlis left Tatoi confident that a crisis had been avoided. But just before he was due to return to finalise matters, he was telephoned by the king's political adviser, Hoidas, postponing the meeting for 24 hours. The following day, 11 June 1963, the prime minister went back to Tatoi and learned the truth: the

king had changed his mind, there would be no postponement
of the state visit.

In that case, said Karamanlis, he would resign. He suggested
the king dissolve parliament and appoint a caretaker cabinet to
oversee elections. The king demurred on the question of dissolving parliament (Karamanlis detected the hand of Frederika) and
instead appointed Pipinelis to head a new government. On the
Lambrakis affair, Pipinelis once confided bluntly to a colleague
that the MP 'deserved to die'. With his appointment as prime
minister, Karamanlis flew to Paris and self-imposed exile. The
state visit to Britain was back on the agenda.

Barely had the royal party set foot in London when the
protests began. As they rode from Victoria railway station in
open, horse-drawn carriages accompanied by Queen Elizabeth,
a nondescript-looking woman rushed from the crowd.

'Release my husband,' shouted Betty Ambatielos.

Five thousand police had been placed on alert. Demonstrations were promised by several organisations including
Lambrakis' former associates in the Campaign for Nuclear
Disarmament, a group calling itself Save Greece Now and
the League for Democracy in Greece, which dated back
to the civil war and was linked to the Greek communist
party. Protest organisers vowed that it would 'follow the
king and queen everywhere they go. Every time they appear
in public we shall be there.' Bertrand Russell, the eminent
philosopher, Nobel laureate and peace campaigner, declared
that if the government did not allow people to indicate their
disgust at the situation in Greece, then it would have to
accept responsibility for any 'unfortunate incidents during
the royal visit'.

On the first night of the visit, around 2,000 people gathered
in Trafalgar Square and attempted to march down the Mall
to Buckingham Palace where the king and queen were being
entertained at a state banquet. Amid shouts of 'Sieg Heil'
and 'fascist', 94 people were arrested during clashes with
the police. On the second night, Paul and Frederika were
escorted by Queen Elizabeth and the Duke of Edinburgh to
a performance of Shakespeare's *A Midsummer Night's Dream*.

For the first time in living memory, a chorus of boos greeted a British sovereign in her own country.

Dwarfed only by the annual CND marches, the demonstrations were the largest and most vociferous protests on a specific issue – political prisoners in Greece and the role of the Greek royal family – that London had seen since the 1930s. The protests shocked and provoked a vitriolic attack on the protesters by the American magazine *Time*.

'The anti-Greek chorus', it wrote, 'is made up of a motley collection of communists, socialists, anti-monarchists, vague crusaders in search of new causes, ban-the-bombers (including that foolish sage Bertrand Russell), all of them joined in the London streets by joy-riding beatniks. Amazingly, they were also joined, in spirit, by Labour Party Leader Harold Wilson and Deputy Leader George Brown, who chose to boycott a banquet for the visitors – which could only raise questions about the mental health and stability of British politics.'

The visit turned out exactly as Karamanlis had feared. But Frederika had no regrets. She declared the decision to go to Britain had been absolutely right. 'I am not worried about these few people who demonstrated. The memory I have is of the warm reception we were given on our arrival,' she said, safely back in Athens.

There was very little that appeared to worry the palace. Although the prime minister had resigned, he had been replaced by a trenchant royalist and with what looked like seamless efficiency. The government was being run by a loyal and energetic supporter of the monarchy, a man who shared Queen Frederika's contempt for the vagaries of democracy.

But Pipinelis and Frederika were in for a shock.

Chapter Six

Palace Intrigues

'My Strength is the Love of My People.'
Motto of the kings of Greece

Since the rigged 1961 general election, George Papandreou and his Centre Union party had waged a vigorous campaign of opposition not just to the government's policies but to the legitimacy of the government itself. The collapse of the Karamanlis government in the wake the controversy over the royal visits to London and its replacement by the supposedly interim regime of Panayiotis Pipinelis did not bring stability.

Neither King Paul nor Pipinelis showed any inclination to call an election following Karamanlis' resignation in June 1963 but the weight of pressure from the Centre Union eventually prevailed. The elections were fought in early November in an atmosphere considerably different from the 1961 contest. This time there were no allegations – or indeed convincing evidence – of widespread ballot rigging or intimidation of voters and the result seemed to justify Papandreou's campaign since the 1961 contest. The Centre Union won 42 per cent of the popular vote and 138 seats in parliament. The ERE could only manage 39 per cent and 132 seats, even with the help of Karamanlis who returned from Paris to assist his old party. Although short of an overall majority in the 300-seat parliament, Papandreou nevertheless headed the single largest party and was able to form a government.

In February 1964, he called a snap re-run and, buoyed by a number of public spending measures that increased his popularity, secured his overall majority. For the first time since the end of the civil war in 1949, the Right faced the prospect of having to come to terms with a loss of political power and all that went with it. The fact that the Centre Union was able to win not one but two elections was due in no small measure to the attitude adopted by Henry Labouisse, the new US ambassador appointed by President Kennedy.

Labouisse was posted to Athens in 1962 and quickly became unpopular with most of the top people in the CIA station. As far as the station chief, Laughlin Campbell, was concerned, Labouisse epitomised the 'bleeding heart liberals' he so despised. For his part, Labouisse was horrified when he learnt of Campbell's *modus operandi*: his intimate relationship with the palace – Queen Frederika in particular – and members of the right-wing political hierarchy.

Labouisse ordered Campbell to modify his behaviour and, by August 1962, the CIA man was out, transferred to Paris. He was in America on leave when told to move, much to his dismay. Campbell had little time for the French, preferring Athens with its ubiquitous reminders of a glorious past, plus the cut and thrust of a turbulent present.

Not long before the second general election, a number of army generals approached the ambassador. They asked how the US would react to a coup to forestall a Papandreou victory. Labouisse said the US would be against such a move and cabled Washington with a copy of his answer. The state department supported his position.

Papandreou's double victory, and the uninterrupted four years or more in government that it guaranteed him, sent shock waves through the right-wing establishment. Many, including several key palace advisers, believed it signalled that the country was well on the road to a communist take-over. That was something they were determined to stop.

A month later, the establishment Right lost its figurehead when King Paul died of cancer. His death had the twin effect of removing a comparatively sane and restraining voice from within the palace while at the same time catapulting Crown Prince Constantine onto the throne, too young to shoulder the responsibility with the required degree of wisdom.

The handsome, 23-year-old prince was an accomplished athlete, winning a gold medal for yachting in the 1960 Rome Olympics. He was also an expert in the martial arts and an enthusiastic squash player. Outside the world of sport, however, he was an average performer. His first formal tuition was at a school set up specially for him by his father. Paul contrived that the young prince shared his education with a supposedly representative cross section of Greek society. Constantine's nine classmates included a shipowner's son, a baker's boy and the son of a beggar. But this experiment in egalitarianism had its limits: the other boys were instructed to address the six-year-old prince as Your Royal Highness.

Queen Frederika insisted that her son receive no formal training for the task to which he was born. 'We didn't educate our son to become king in any special way,' she said in an interview two and a half years after his coronation. 'Tino started by listening to the daily chats between my husband and myself about what was going on.' When he was twelve, the prince began attending meetings with King Paul and his ministers and staff to listen to their discussions on the affairs of state.

'I was present at many of his meetings and conferences,' Constantine recalled during the same interview. 'But I was never allowed to say anything – just to sit in the corner and listen. After meetings my father would explain in detail what was going on.'

For all his grooming for the job, Constantine turned out to be the wrong man in the wrong place and at the wrong time. What Greece needed in the mid-1960s was a head of state who remained above politics but who could, by his example, help calm an increasingly hysterical political and military establishment. Constantine could have been an icon for his generation, a catalyst for change in a decade when young people throughout the western world were making themselves heard. He might have been a force for good, helping loosen a little the dead hand of the old conservatives, the people who wanted to keep Greece frozen in time, untouched by the changes taking place everywhere else. Instead, he was a disaster for his country, a man of limited vision, putty in the hands of his mother and other manipulative palace advisers.

Within days of Constantine's accession in Athens, Philip Deane, then in Washington, received a letter bearing the Greek royal insignia. Its message was clear enough. The new king said how much he admired Deane's work as a journalist, how he wanted him to come to Greece and help 'liberalise the palace'. Curious, Deane left his desk at the United Nations information centre, took a plane to Athens and found himself shortly in Constantine's spacious, high ceilinged office with its large easy chairs and thick pile carpet. The room struck him as something of a cross between an old fashioned gentlemen's club in London and a Victorian salon.

As soon as perfunctory chit-chat was dispensed with, Constantine came to the point. Would Deane like to join the royal household as his secretary general? The position was equivalent in rank to the head of a department in the civil service but had a great deal more status.

Constantine told Deane he wanted a right hand man who could act as a link between himself and the outside world: the intelligentsia, the media, trade unions and anyone else of importance in society.

The two agreed that Deane would want a day to think the offer over but he was hardly back in his hotel room when the phone rang. It was Frederika summoning him to the palace in Tatoi. Once there, she berated him. Why was he delaying? What was there to think through? Deane found it difficult to concentrate on what she was saying – he was struck by her piercing blue eyes and the magnetic force of her personality.

It was not the first time that Deane had been dazzled by the queen. When he was a young, acting sub-lieutenant in the British navy during the war, Deane was at a ball in Alexandria hosted by Greek army officers in exile and attended by the king and queen. To the amazement of his colleagues, Deane had the temerity to ask Frederika to partner him in a dance. She warmed to such cheekiness and the pair of them waltzed gayly across the floor.

But it was one thing to flirt with royalty, another thing

to work for it. Deane held his ground against Frederika's
entreaties but only for a day. 'I took the job for a mixture
of reasons – curiosity, political ambition. I also felt flattered,'
he recalled later.

Recruiting Deane to the palace was not as odd as it might
appear. Although he had never sought to curry favour with
royalty or advance himself via royal channels, Deane had
impeccable credentials and was much admired in royalist and
military circles. They thought they were hiring one of their own
but they were in for a surprise.

Deane was born in 1923 and christened Gerassimos Gigantes.
His father was Lakis Gigantes, a distinguished Greek army
officer who commanded the Sacred Battalion in World War
II and fought in north Africa alongside Montgomery at El
Alamein. Using commando-style guerrilla tactics, men under
Lakis' command liberated the Aegean islands. The Battalion was
the only section of the Greek army, as opposed to the resistance,
to play a major role in driving the Nazis out of Greece. Members
of the Battalion achieved folk hero status among many Greeks,
partly due to the antics of their flamboyant leader, who would
go into battle flying a lace pennant made from women's knickers.
After the war, however, Lakis' strongly held democratic views
made him easy prey for the extreme right-wing IDEA clique
in the reconstituted Greek army. Having survived Winston
Churchill's Cairo purges of 1943 and 1944, he was forced out of
the army in 1947. It mattered not one jot that at the time his military career was brought to an end, Lakis Gigantes was the most
decorated officer in the army. Luckily for Deane, the opprobrium that was attached to his father did not extend to him.

Deane's uncle, Yannis Gigantes, was a resistance fighter sent
from Cairo to Athens by the British to attempt to unite the
two main resistance organisations. While in the city, he was
betrayed and subsequently confronted in his apartment by a
German soldier and five Italian intelligence officers who came
to arrest and almost certainly torture him. Yannis had only
a revolver and six bullets yet he refused to give up. After a
furious battle, he fell dead with no less than 42 wounds, but
those who came to the apartment to find his body are reputed

to have had to step over the corpses of his six attackers, one
bullet in each.

With such a distinguished lineage, it was not surprising
that Deane was steered towards a military career. He parents
enrolled him in the British Royal Navy's officer training college
in Dartmouth, England. When World War II was over, Deane
resigned his commission and began a career in journalism.
He worked part-time for the *Observer* newspaper in London
which decided it could not cope with a by-line like Gerassimos
Gigantes and bestowed on him the pen name Philip Deane that
stuck for most of the rest of his life. In July 1950 at the age of
26, he went to Korea to report the war but after being there
for barely a week, he was captured when the soldiers he was
with were taken prisoner by north Korean troops. For five
days, Deane and several others were force marched, hands
bound behind their backs with telephone wire, until they
found themselves in the headquarters of the communist army.

For almost three years – until the spring of 1953 – Deane
was held as a prisoner of war, despite his status as a reporter.
He survived sustained efforts to brainwash him and force him
to broadcast communist propaganda denouncing the West. He
was released shortly before the formal cessation of hostilities and
later wrote a book, *Captive in Korea*, describing his experiences.
A contingent of the Greek army took part in the war and Greek
interest in the conflict was thus higher than it might otherwise
have been. Deane's bravery and tenacity were not in doubt but
his ordeal was transformed in the eyes of royalists into an
exaggerated struggle of good against evil in which the young
hero triumphed.

After his experience in Korea, Deane resumed his journalistic
career and continued to work for the *Observer* in London
and Washington until he joined the UN information service
in 1961. Within days of arriving back in Greece as a servant
to Constantine, he was disabused of any illusions he had that
the young king would act as a new broom. Two things quickly
became obvious: corruption was rife and the influence of the
extreme Right unbridled.

Deane got off to a bad start with Constantine's chief political adviser, a young lawyer and economist named Constantine Hoidas. Hoidas shared the palace's view of itself that the monarchy bound the nation together. The royal family had a right to the position it held, a right not bestowed upon it by the people. People were subjects and power did not derive from them. As a consequence, parliament was an irritation, something that got in the way of royal rule. In fact, there is anecdotal evidence to suggest that Hoidas may even have believed the king had a divine right to rule.

The evidence comes via his Scottish-born wife and the conversation she once had with an Englishman, whom she thought worked for the British embassy in Athens. The man called to her home one day with a package for her husband and was invited inside. Over tea, Mrs Hoidas, apparently anxious to extol her husband and emphasise what an important man he was, said that Yes, he knew many people at the embassy. His chief associate there was the head of intelligence, she said.

'My husband has had a revelation,' she went on. 'Constantine, you know, is the second coming!'

Her guest burst out laughing, assuring Mrs Hoidas that Constantine, whom he had recently seen, did not seem like the son of God. Mrs Hoidas was outraged and accused her guest of mocking the royal family. She was so agitated by the incident that she reported it to her husband who made a formal complaint to the British embassy. The luckless deliverer of the parcel, who was not a member of the diplomatic corps, subsequently found himself being carpeted by an embassy official for damaging relations with Greece!

Hoidas was a tall, urbane, if slightly ascetic looking man, and his attendance at parties was much sought after by Athenian society hostesses, though he was dogged by ill health and forced regularly to go abroad for kidney treatment. He also had a fiery temper and a few days after Deane moved into his office, they had a public row over where their respective secretaries should sit.

In his official capacity as the designated link between the palace and the government, Hoidas appeared to operate without restraint. He was in the habit of bypassing the prime minister and making direct contact with Petros Garoufalias, the ultra loyal, sycophantic defence minister appointed by George Papandreou as a sop to the palace.

The other senior figure in the royal household was Constantine Dovas, the Pericles conspirator who stayed on as Constantine's chief military adviser after King Paul's death. When Deane began work at the palace, Dovas was slightly in awe of him because of his Korean War experience and status as a minor national hero.

These were the men who, in the weeks following Constantine's coronation, became embedded in a conspiracy to destroy the Papandreou government. Their chief associates in the palace were Queen Frederika and Major Michael Arnaoutis, the king's private secretary and supervisor of his military training since Constantine was sixteen. Deane was a witness to their activities.

He was first alerted to what was going on by his father who had been head of military intelligence in the 1930s and retained many of his old contacts. Lakis warned his son that if he joined the palace staff he should beware of a Colonel George Papadopoulos. And he reminded him that through a network of valets, chauffeurs and the like, the CIA had its sources in the palace. Deane had not heard of Papadopoulos, the KYP/CIA liaison officer on the CIA's payroll, secretary to the Pericles Plan committee and habitual conspirator known to his army colleagues as 'Nasser'. But before he left the king's service, Deane would be more than familiar with him.

The military leaders of the plot were army generals: the chiefs of staff and their senior colleagues. Their handmaidens were middle rank officers of mixed distinction – Papadopoulos and his associates. During the months that he worked for the king, Deane noticed that these officers were regular callers to the palace to see both Dovas and Arnaoutis. Prompted by his father's cautioning and his own journalistic instincts, he began to note their names: apart from Papadopoulos, the visitors included Colonels Ioannidis, Roufogalis and Nicholas Makarezos, who were also KYP officers; Brigadier Dimetrios Ioannides and

Colonel Yannis Ladas, both members of the military security
police; and Brigadier-General Stylianos Pattakos, the commander of the armoured training centre and the most senior officer
among the handmaidens.

They were a close knit group. Papadopoulos, Ioannides,
Ladas, Makarezos and Roufogalis were all members of IDEA.
Papadopoulos and Makarezos were also close because they
had graduated together from the Greek Military Academy in
1940. Despite Papadopoulos' apparent lack of intellect, he and
Makarezos graduated in the top half of their class.

When the handmaidens came to the palace, Dovas and
Arnaoutis would talk to them behind the closed doors of Dovas'
office. Arnaoutis, who shared Hoidas and Dovas' political
views and their general contempt for politicians, certainly
made no effort to hide his association with the Papadopoulos
group. In telephone calls to General Yannis Gennimatas, the
former Pericles conspirator who was promoted to chief of the
general staff at the insistence of the palace, Arnaoutis discussed
Papadopoulos and his associates. Dovas too was quite blatant.
'We've seen to it that loyal officers hold key positions,' he once
told Deane. Loyal in this context referred to men who were
obedient to the palace and who could be relied upon to carry out
royal commands, even if they went against the constitution.

It soon became apparent to other members of the royal household that Deane did not share their view of the world. About a
month after he began working for the king, he travelled with
Constantine to Salonika for a ground breaking cemerony at an
industrial complex owned by Tom Pappas, a Greek–American
entrepreneur and US Republican Party fund-raiser. The event
was of great local importance and the area's dignitaries were out
in force, but among them were two officers, Lieutenant General
Mitsou and a colleague, who were shortly to be indicted for the
murder of Gregory Lambrakis. This was well known to the
palace because of the efforts of its faithful servant in the Supreme
Court, Constantine Kollias, to obstruct the investigation.

Far from avoiding the two officers, Constantine sought them
out and chatted amiably to them. Deane was upset: Lambrakis
was a friend, someone with whom he had played basketball in

his youth, yet here was the king associating publicly with men suspected of having organised his murder. Perhaps Constantine didn't know. Deane had a quiet word in his ear but the king rounded on him. 'He spoke of Lambrakis with massive and venomous contempt. In his eyes he had no right to live,' Deane recalled later.

Deane's evident sympathy for Lambrakis prompted Panayiotis Pipinelis to have a chat with him. On a sunny summer evening in his villa overlooking the sea outside Athens, Pipinelis dispensed with the Lambrakis affair: why should 'loyal officers be persecuted for exterminating vermin that insulted the Queen Mother?' He then proceeded to try to recruit Deane to an inner circle.

Pipinelis outlined his political philosophy and spoke of the sort of people who one day might rule Greece. Deane could be one of the chosen few, he said. As Pipinelis explained his Platonic vision for his country, he became more and more enthusiastic, at one stage drawing himself up from his chair, his voice rising with him. Rigid and filled with patriotic fervour, Pipinelis stretched his right arm forward, his open palm facing down in the manner of the ancient Greek salute and the more recent Nazi gesture. Standing thus, he recited the oath of allegiance taken by recruits to the armed forces. He pledged himself to the 'fatherland' and summoned as witnesses the spirit of Zeus, the mythical supreme god of ancient Greece who lived on Mount Olympus, and Ares his son, the god of war.

Pipinelis told Deane of his 'grand design', of building a 'third Greek civilisation' to follow the classical and Byzantine ones of old. He suggested that Deane was the sort of bright young man who might be offered an initial position as junior minister of the navy, or information perhaps . . . one day even Foreign Minister. The choice was Deane's. The king's secretary general demurred.

Deane's attitude did not go unnoticed. Less than three months after joining the king's service, he learnt that he was the subject of secret police surveillance. In June 1964, his driver and bodyguard with whom he had become friendly told him that he was under constant watch. The man, a KYP agent called

George whose main function was to spy on Deane, showed him where eavesdropping bugs had been hidden: in the posts of his bed, in chandeliers, table lamps, under the passenger seat of his car, in the steering column and under the back window shelf.

As the palace plotters went about their business planning the destruction of the Papandreou government, memos between them referred to 'the day', and detailed which buildings in Athens would have to be taken over in the event of a coup: the radio station, telephone exchange and the like. The correspondence reflected what was clearly a two way process: those from the colonels and their associates would begin 'I have the honour to respond to your command at our last meeting . . .'

Despite the appearence of a close working relationship between the king, Dovas and Arnaoutis on the one hand, and the Papadopoulos group on the other, it would be wrong to assume there was any affection or camaraderie between the two camps. Rather, the king and his staff were wont to show their contempt for the middle rank officers behind their backs. When they left the palace after their meetings, Constantine and his courtiers would refer to them as 'the smelly feet' – *vromopotharee*, in Greek – and the ladies of the court, pandering to the school boyish humour of it all, would giggle and spray perfume in the air.

The palace preferred to associate with those in the army whom it saw as its own. Among them was Lieutenant General Grigorios Spandidakis, one of the senior plotters who in early 1964 was due to retire. The palace, the United States embassy and the CIA intervened in a sustained campaign of lobbying to ensure that Spandidakis remained in the army, despite the recommendation of an army review board. Dovas and Arnaoutis said that those who were trying to 'victimise' Spandidakis would not be allowed to get away with it. US embassy officials told the foreign ministry 'the facts of life' about the relationship between Washington and Athens, as one former embassy official puts it. The fact was that what the Americans wanted, the Americans got.

The same view was conveyed directly to the Greek chiefs of staff by the US army attaché in Athens, Colonel Oliver K

Marshall. Jack Maury, the man who replaced Laughlin Campbell as CIA station chief, made the agency's views crystal clear. To Deane and others, he said that Spandidakis was considered 'essential to the security of NATO' and, in a clear indication that the US would exercise a veto over certain appointments the Greek government might try to make, added that Washington was 'not about to give aid to people it does not trust'. Maury was a force to be reckoned with and Spandidakis remained in the army.

As soon as he arrived in Athens, Maury adopted a high, even ostentatious, profile. He lived and acted in a way that drew attention to himself, something that the head of the local CIA station might have been expected to avoid, but not Jack Maury. Unlike many of his fellow countrymen, Maury came from a family long established in America, in his case in the southern state of Virginia. He was intensely proud of his background and particularly fond of his memories as a Marine Corps major. He gained firsthand experience of the country that was to be his sworn enemy for most of his working life when, during World War II, he spent time in the Soviet Union helping administer the $11,000 million lend-lease aid which the US extended to the Russians.

As soon as he got into his stride in Athens, Maury was able effectively to ignore the ground rules laid down by Ambassador Henry Labouisse. He re-established the contacts set up by Laughlin Campbell that were so frowned upon by the ambassador. He indulged high level politicking and was soon dealing direct with the palace – with Frederika and Constantine in particular – while leaving some of the more mundane affairs of the station to his underlings. However, the ambassador's insistence that the station reduce the number and extent of its dealings with local politicians resulted, according to one former CIA man in Athens, in several agents being transferred to Vietnam and the agency's activities in Greece being run down.

'Relations with KYP were not the same any more,' lamented another former CIA agent. But others, like Kay Bracken, the State Department expert on Greece and the Near East who served as political counsellor at the embassy in the late-1960s, recalled a station that was as feverish and secretive as any.

'Agency types had a habit of invoking the "we are so secret syndrome" and telling people they were not entitled to know things,' she said in an interview. 'They were obsessed with secrecy. They paid newspaper editors for information. I would go to lunch with an editor or senior journalist and be told things that I would pass on, but later I would find out that the agency had got the same information from the same person but had had to pay for it.'

Despite all the secrecy, Maury liked people to be aware of his position and the elevated status he bestowed upon himself. He drove a large American car ('bigger than the ambassador's', he was fond of pointing out), wore loud suits and large rings and, among embassy staff and at social functions, would not hesitate to drop names. 'I have 60 full-time members of my staff which makes me more important than the ambassador, I guess,' he told Deane. The king's secretary general found Maury to be 'incredibly self-satisfied'. At one social function, Maury was with his colleague OK Marshall, when the army attaché made the remarkably prescient observation that Colonel George Papadopoulos would one day govern Greece and govern it well. Deane was disgusted at the way diplomats would simper over him and attempt to fawn their way into his favour in the hope of ingratiating themselves into the company of the king. Even someone of Labouisse's stature and access asked Deane from time to time to arrange lunch with Constantine, saying it helped his standing with the State Department.

As the weeks went by, Deane's horror grew as he became familiar with the *ancien régime* mentality that pervaded the palace and the contempt the king's advisers had for the norms of democratic behaviour. It is perhaps surprising that it took as long as fifteen months before the inevitable clash took place between the king and Prime Minister Papandreou. When it came, Deane had no doubt where the blame lay.

'The hostility between the king and George Papandreou began in the palace,' he said years later. 'The prime minister made repeated attempts at a rapprochement, direct as well as by not reacting in kind to insults and impediments placed in his way.'

Matters began to come to a head early in 1965 when Papandreou presented to parliament the results of a government appointed military inquiry into allegations that the 1961 elections had been subverted. The credentials of the investigators appeared to be impeccable: they included a general and senior officers of both military intelligence and KYP. But the information they disclosed about the Pericles Plan and the involvement of the military in it, and in particular the role of General Yannis Gennimatas, chief of the general staff, was sensational.

When Papandreou revealed the findings to parliament, he was accused of aiding communism by undermining the army. Constantine charged that he was stimulating communist infiltration of the armed forces and destroying morale. The king said that the five investigating officers were unfit to remain in uniform and ought to be dismissed. The opposition encouraged him by launching a campaign of vitriolic abuse against the government. The royalist defence minister, Petros Garoufalias, took the side of the palace, to the extent even of forbidding one of the investigators to defend himself in a libel action.

Papandreou reacted to the findings of the inquiry by resolving that Gennimatas had to resign. It was not acceptable in a democracy that an officer, against whom evidence existed of a such a determined effort to subvert an election, should be allowed to remain as head of the army. The Right had already reacted to the Pericles allegations by producing a conspiracy of its own. It was called Aspida, meaning shield, and became ammunition for the palace and its supporters to deflect attention away from Pericles.

Aspida began as an allegation by General George Grivas, the former World War II collaborator and IDEA leader who commanded the Cyprus-based Greek National Guard. Grivas was an extreme right winger who in the 1950s led a Cypriot independence movement, EOKA. After a bloody military campaign against the British, EOKA had to settle in 1959 for Cypriot independence rather than its ultimate goal, *enosis*, or union with Greece. In late 1964, Grivas plunged headlong into Athenian

politics when he travelled to the city with a tidbit of information
which the Right seized upon as their way out of the Pericles
nightmare.

Grivas told defence minister Garoufalias that Andreas
Papandreou, the prime minister's son, was leading a left-wing
cabal inside the army. Andreas, a demagogue and political
opportunist, was loathed and reviled by the Right. He had
recently resigned from government after attacking the US
for its policy on Cyprus. Not long after leaving the cabinet,
Andreas went to Cyprus where he was treated as something
of a hero. Grivas claimed that during this visit to the island,
Andreas consulted with his alleged co-conspirators. Grivas told
Garoufilias that Aspida aimed to effect a communist take-over
of Greece.

George Papandreou's determination to get to the bottom of
the Pericles affair was met head on by right-wing demands that
Aspida – rapidly referred to by American diplomats and military
advisers as a 'plot' – should also be investigated. To make
matters worse, Andreas Papandreou returned to government
in April 1965, at the request of his father, to help re-shape
the economy. In the succeeding weeks, the Pericles and Aspida
affairs became enmeshed in a nightmare of assertions, claims,
lies and conspiracies that brought the country to the brink of
disaster and helped ultimately to push it over the edge.

It was at the behest of the ubiquitous Colonel Papadopoulos
that the row moved beyond the realm of an otherwise knock-
about political conflict. Papadopoulos' efforts to foment right-
wing activities within the army had been discovered as recently
as the late 1950s. However, efforts by Constantine Karamanlis
to have him removed were thwarted by the combined efforts
of the IDEA organisation and the palace. Karamanlis simply gave up. When Papandreou took over, he insisted that
Papadopoulos be transferred to what he hoped would be
harmless oblivion on Greece's north-eastern border with Turkey. The move did not go unnoticed in the palace. When he
heard the news, King Constantine is alleged to have telephoned
the under-secretary for defence, Michael Papaconstantinou,
and asked, 'Are you trying to destroy the armed forces?'

Papadopoulos spent his time in the wilderness as commander of the 117th Artillery Squadron of the 11th army division stationed at Evros. But he was not idle. Though far from Athens, the colonel – still in the pay of the CIA and controlling his network of KYP cronies – whipped up propaganda about Aspida, eagerly accepted as fact by the palace and the political Right. At the same time he was up to even more sinister activities.

In May 1965 he provoked chaos by claiming a communist conspiracy within the armed forces, citing as evidence the fact that some artillery equipment had 'broken down'. Dozens of military personnel were detained, apparently on orders issued by him. Papadopoulos personally arrested a private, had him beaten up and immersed in water after which he 'confessed' to being a communist saboteur. A subsequent investigation discovered that soldiers had failed merely to maintain gearboxes properly.

In a separate smear, Papadopoulos alleged a communist conspiracy against his troops when rifle ammunition was discovered to be defective. An investigation revealed, however, that out of all the ammunition at the disposal of Papadopoulos' troops, just three bullets had faulty charges and thus would not fire properly. Papadopoulos didn't stop there. In yet another effort to foment unease, he alleged a further communist conspiracy, this time to sabotage military tanks. The truth was that Papadopoulos himself had manufactured the 'evidence' for this conspiracy by pouring sugar into the fuel supply.

Truth mattered for little, however, and Aspida became the catalyst for a barrage of criticism directed at Papandreou. The row would ultimately destroy his government.

Chapter Seven

The Elephant and the Flea

'Fuck your parliament and your constitution . . . If your
prime minister gives me talk about democracy . . . his
parliament and his constitution may not last very long.'
President Lyndon Johnson to the Greek ambassador
to the United States, June 1964

About the last thing George Papandreou needed in 1964 was a
crisis over Cyprus. The island was the most emotive issue in the
periodically explosive relations between Greece and Turkey, and
was seen as crucially important to Western intelligence interests.
But at Christmas 1963, communal warfare broke out between
the 80 per cent Greek majority and the 20 per cent Turkish
minority. Any government in Athens that handled Cyprus
matters wrongly could expect to be swept from office. For
the US and Britain, upheaval on the island threatened valuable
installations used to spy on the Soviet Union. In addition, the
island contained one of Britain's largest remaining overseas military outposts. According to a March 1960 assessment prepared
for President Eisenhower by the then-director of the CIA, Allen
Dulles, a British base on the island constituted 'one of the largest
air bases in the Middle East and [the British] are in the process of
establishing there the headquarters of their unified Middle East
Command'.

Under the island's 1959 constitution when Britain granted it
independence, the United Kingdom retained sovereignty over
two military bases on the south coast, Akrotiri and Dhekelia.
The Royal Air Force retained part of Nicosia airport for its use
and British military and defence ministry employees continued
to operate a highly valuable electronic spying facility in the
Troodos mountains.

In the early 1960s, Troodos was able to probe deep into the Soviet Union using over-the-horizon radar (OHR) which gave access far beyond the natural obstacle of the earth's curve by bouncing signals off the ionosphere. OHR was relatively new and Cyprus, by its very location, was one of the West's most forward stations for eavesdropping on the Russians as well as anyone else of interest in the eastern Mediterranean, Middle East and as far as Iran. The eastern Mediterranean also happened to be a particularly good area for intercepting certain types of electromagnetic waves in the Soviet Union, according to a senior source in the United States National Security Agency.

What was gathered at Troodos was relayed to GCHQ, the British government's communications headquarters at Cheltenham, England. From there, it was sent to the much larger NASA electronic intelligence gathering and analysis operation in the US.

Neither the US nor Britain would easily give up such treasured military facilities and any Greek government whose actions over Cyprus threatened such assets would find itself under massive pressure. When the communal violence of Christmas 1963 spread over into 1964, British, Greek and Turkish soldiers made an initial joint effort at restoring order before United Nations troops were called in. Although the violence subsided, diplomatic activity remained furious, with Athens pressing for a solution that would satisfy the island's majority population as well as domestic Greek opinion.

Cyprus was not an issue that the palace felt it could ignore. King Constantine and his advisers believed that Greece's position was not being put across adequately where it mattered most – in Washington. In mid-1964, Constantine and his cousin the Duke of Edinburgh discussed the Cyprus problem. The Duke suggested that Greece needed an information campaign to highlight Athens' position. Constantine ought to initiate one, he said.

The king thought about the idea and decided he liked it. The best man to act as a lobbyist was someone who knew Washington well. Constantine chose Philip Deane, who despite the reservations some in the palace may have had about him, knew the American capital very well. Apart from any other considerations, the job got Deane out of the palace. Constantine told Deane that his work in Washington would serve as a good example to the much disliked Papandreou of 'what the palace could do'.

Deane's starting point was the belief that President Johnson, facing re-election in November and already embarked on a diplomatic initiative on Cyprus, was vulnerable to Greek–American voter pressure in some of the larger cities. As he devised a strategy paper suggesting how a campaign might be launched, he came into increasing contact with the prime minister and his controversial son, Andreas. Deane admired the elder Papandreou whom he regarded as a democrat and statesman of stature, and developed a liking for Andreas whose politics he equated with much of what the US Democratic Party stood for. Deane's encounters with the Papandreous and other liberal politicians of the Centre Left served to reinforce his growing conviction that, by working for the king, he was in effect on the wrong side.

The perception that the relationship between Deane and the king was not all that it should be soon spread beyond the confines of the palace. The right-wing press in Athens began to give Deane a hard time and the ubiquitous CIA station chief, Jack Maury, remarked to him one day, 'We're going to have to put some interesting items in your dossier.' The interesting items included the entirely false allegation that, during his incarceration in Korea, Deane changed sides and made pro-communist propaganda broadcasts – an allegation that originated with Maury's colleagues in KYP, the Greek intelligence service.

By the time Deane decided to resign from the palace, the prime minister had been forwarded a draft of his plan for selling the Greek line on Cyprus to the Americans. Papandreou liked what he read and resolved that Deane ought to be working for the government. His offer to Deane, which the king's erstwhile secretary general accepted, was the position of ambassador extraordinaire, based in Washington and with a status equivalent to that of a junior minister in the government.

By the time Deane arrived in Washington and began proselytizing the Greek case, relations between Greece and

Turkey had become white hot. A proposed Turkish invasion and forcible divison of the island in early June 1964 was postponed after President Johnson intervened personally with the Turkish prime minister, Ismet Inonu. However, when Papandreou and his son, Andreas, arrived in Washington a few days later, the President pushed for Greek acceptance of partition with a Turkish military base on Turkey's side of the island.

Such a 'solution' had for some time exercised the mind of George Ball, Johnson's under-secretary of state who visited Cyprus in the spring of 1964 and eagerly told British officials that partition was the only option. Ball's preference was well known to his colleagues in the State Department. On one occasion while in his office discussing the island's future, he pinned a large map of Cyprus on the wall. As he stared at it, his eyes fell on the Karpas Peninsula, a 50-mile-long panhandle stretching north-east into the Mediterranean. Could it be made larger to accommodate a Turkish military base? he asked his officials. Such a move would almost certainly be fought tooth and nail by the Greek Cypriot authorities. But Ball thought that if he could physically enlarge the island, then at least no territory would have to be taken from the Greeks to give the Turks their base, whatever other objections would be raised to a base.

At a time when the State Department had no less than twelve separate solutions to the Cyprus problem, the idea of creating more land probably didn't seem very bizarre. Ball decided that an expert assessment ought to be made and so an Air Force general was summoned and told to produce an analysis of the number of troops Turkey would need to base on the island in order to quell an attack on their community by the local Greeks. Once the size of the base was thus determined, engineers were to estimate the amount of land it would be necessary to reclaim from the sea in order to build it. This idea was to copy the Dutch by reclaiming land in the sparsly populated upper end of the peninsula and keeping the sea at bay with dams. The new land would house the base, below sea level in what the Dutch call a polder. Not surprisingly, the idea didn't get very far. It was concluded at an early stage that such a grandiose scheme would take too long and cost too much.

When George Papandreou met President Johnson in June 1964, the Greek prime minister told him he would never be able to convince his parliament to approve a US plan to partition the island. 'Maybe Greece should rethink the advisability of a parliament which could not take the right decision,' Johnson responded.

Refusing to bend, the Papandreous left America, but Johnson continued to pressure for partition – to the amazement of Deane and the Greek ambassador, Alexander Matsas. On one occasion, Matsas was summoned to the White House and presented with a plan devised by Dean Acheson, the former secretary of state lately become presidential adviser and mediator on Cyprus. Under Acheson's scheme, not only would Cyprus be divided but Greece would be expected to surrender another of its islands, Castelorizo, a tiny outcrop east of Rhodes, to its arch enemy. Matsas repeated Papandreou's earlier reply, adding that the Greek constitution didn't allow the prime minister to give away bits of the country.

'Then listen to me, Mr Ambassador,' Johnson thundered, 'Fuck your parliament and your constitution. America is an elephant. Cyprus is a flea. Greece is a flea. If those two fleas continue itching the elephant, they may just get whacked by the elephant's trunk, whacked good . . . We pay a lot of good American dollars to the Greeks, Mr Ambassador. If your prime minister gives me talk about democracy, parliament and constitution, he, his parliament and his constitution may not last very long.'

'I must protest your manner,' Ambassador Matsas spluttered but Johnson continued shouting.

'Don't forget to tell old Papa-what's-his-name what I told you. Mind you tell him, you hear.'

Matsas reeled away from the White House and back to his embassy. He told Deane exactly what the president had said. Deane wrote everything down immediately – and wondered what he should do. The pair resolved that a full and explicit report should be cabled immediately to Athens. Not long after it was dispatched, the phone rang.

'Are you trying to get yourself into my bad books, Mr Ambassador,' asked the US President. 'Do you want me to get really angry with you? That was a private conversation me and you had. You had no call putting in all them words I used on you. Watch your step.'

Click! The line went dead before Matsas had time to utter a response. He remarked to Deane that the cable encoding machine had been provided by the Americans. From then on, he and Deane delivered important messages to Athens by hand.

By early 1965, the Pericles–Aspida affairs were overshadowing the Cyprus issue and dominating domestic politics in Greece. Papandreou had appointed a senior military officer to lead the inquiry into Aspida. Lieutenant General Ioannis Simos was a royalist and head of the army advocate general corps, a position equivalent to that of president of the military court. After Papandreou returned from Washington, Simos presented his findings to the government.

He confirmed the existence of a loose association, among some junior and middle rank officers, called Aspida. He recommended disciplinary action against fourteen men, including four colonels, and that no further sanctions were necessary. It appeared that Aspida numbered at most about 100 members who proclaimed, in a manner more appropiate to a boys' adventure club, that they would defend Greece against communist and what they called anti-popular forces – hardly the stuff of a communist conspiracy. Simos' report said that Aspida was led by a group of 'vain and excited officers' seeking personal advancement.

The report, which Papandreou accepted, noted that a particular captain boasted of his relationship with the prime minister and his son but that there was, in fact, no evidence of any involvement by any political personality – a coded reference to Andreas. But the report was grist to the mill of those in the royal entourage determined to see George Papandreou removed from office. For Queen Frederika and the king's advisers, along with a number of American diplomats and the CIA station chief Jack Maury – all of whom wanted to see the back of the Centre Union prime minister and his son –, the controversy was too good an opportunity to miss.

Those who counselled that Papandreou needed to be confronted found a receptive audience in the king. Constantine declared he was not satisfied that the Aspida matter should be laid to rest with the Simos report. He demanded a further inquiry – one with a view to criminal proceedings. Papandreou conceded, directing simultaneously that further investigations be made into the involvement of senior military officers in the Pericles Plan, General Gennimatas in particular.

On the day that Papandreou allowed the further investigation into Aspida, Constantine held discussions at his summer retreat on Corfu with Garoufalias. The defence minister subsequently ensured that the officer appointed to the investigation, Colonel Laganis, was a trusted royalist and a member of the IDEA organisation to boot.

Within a matter of days, the two affairs were brought together in a perfect synthesis: the new Aspida investigation resulted in the arrest of some 28 officers on charges that they were involved in a communist conspiracy to take over the armed forces. Among those detained was Colonel Alexandros Papaterpos, the deputy head of KYP and the man who had led the five-strong team that investigated the Pericles affair. Papaterpos faced the fantastic allegation that he was the 'military leader' of Aspida.

On 23 June 1965, the cabinet decided that General Gennimatas had to be removed and replaced by an officer whose loyalty was to the elected government, the law and constitution. Immediately after the decision was taken, Garoufalias tipped off the palace by briefing Constantine Hoidas. Garoufalias told him everything, prompting Hoidas to write the next day to Papandreou saying bluntly that the king was not prepared to countenance any changes to the upper echelons of the armed forces. The king's view, explained Hoitas, was that by trying to sack Gennimatas, Papandreou was laying the armed forces open to what he called 'communist penetration'.

For Papandreou the issue was more fundamental. There could hardly have been a more blatant challenge to the authority of a prime minister. It was more fundamental than the row between the palace and Karamanlis over the government's advice to cancel the second royal visit to London. An unelected king was telling a democratically elected prime minister that the writ of his authority did not run to control of the nation's armed forces. On the day that Hoidas' letter arrived in Papandreou's office, the prime minister decided to sack Garoufalias and take over the defence ministry temporarily. Garoufalias remained at his post, ignoring his dismissal and continued to issue instructions in the name of the government. He declared that he had been appointed by the king and could thus be removed by him only. Papandreou was a 'national danger', he added.

Constantine insisted it was his duty to protect the constitution. For him, the issue was a moral one. 'It was not morally correct for George Papandreou to take over the defence ministry when it was investigating Andreas Papandreou. I just didn't think that it was right, proper,' he remarked some years later.

The king's advisers persuaded him that the time was ripe to embark on a course of full-blown confrontation with Papandreou. Throughout the following days, Constantine was counselled by his mother and Jack Maury. According to a senior source in the US State Department who was familiar with Maury's actions at the time, the CIA station chief 'worked on behalf of the palace . . . He helped King Constantine buy Centre Union deputies so that the George Papandreou government was toppled'.

But while Maury was aiding and abetting Constantine, embassy diplomats were trying to engineer a compromise. At the end of June, a situation report was cabled to Washington. It said: 'Embassy remains hopeful that a head-on collision will be averted through realisation by both sides that a confrontation is not in their best interests, and we are taking every opportunity to point out that a confrontation would be damaging to the nation's interests.'

The diplomats were over-optimistic, however. On 8 July, the first of several letters from the king's summer retreat on Corfu was delivered to Papandreou's house shortly before midnight. It was a rambling attack by the king, charging Papandreou with responsibility for allowing KYP to launch 'a revolutionary conspiratorial organisation within the armed forces with the sole object of overthrowing the constitution of the country and imposing a dictatorship of an abject nature, abhorrent to every free person'.

The king went on to accuse the prime minister of conspiring personally to destroy the armed forces, of threatening him and trying to blackmail him. Constantine said that Papandreou was encouraging a campaign to undermine the army. In a sly reference to Andreas Papandreou's alleged involvement in Aspida, Constantine noted the prime minister's position 'has for some time been very delicate indeed'.

'This is my last warning,' wrote Constantine.

The prime minister replied, saying that he was surprised and distressed by the king's missive, but pointing out that a judicial inquiry into Aspida had been launched on the foot of the Simos report and that the king now appeared to be challenging the prime minister's right to run the government.

'You lay claim to the right to determine yourself both the Minister of National Defence and the leadership of the armed forces, even contrary to the decision of the responsible government,' wrote Papandreou. 'I address to Your Majesty an appeal that, in the interests of the nation and the throne, you do not persist in these views. I enclose for your signature the decree for the assumption by me of the ministry of national defence.'

On 10 July, the king dispatched his reply. It was another letter, more intemperate and incoherent than the last. Two things were clear, however. The king was opposed to the removal of General Ginnimatas, and he was not about to accept the role of a constitutional monarch. He, and not the elected government, would be the final arbiter as to who would hold what position in the armed forces. It was a view of his role shared by no other reigning European monarch.

'As far as concerns the replacement of the chief of the army general staff,' Constantine wrote to the prime minister, 'it was you who notified me of your decision and I sent you a message, through my private secretary, that I could not accept a procedure whereby I was merely informed of a decision which, as I was given to understand, was being made without my having the opportunity, according to the constitution, to express an opinion. And I added that *in the present circumstances*, judging the matter from a national viewpoint, I was not in agreement with your decision . . . as guarantor of the preservation of the constitution . . . I am obliged to take a special interest in the armed forces, which exist to protect the nation from external and internal dangers . . . The solid establishment of the principle that the armed forces belong only to the nation is not achieved merely by proclaiming that principle. That principle must be carefully and constantly applied in practice. I, standing above politics, have the duty of exercising an objective vigilance over the faithful application of the principle . . .'

The king's missive threatened the prime minister with dire consequences if he did not remove the alleged Aspida conspirators from the army and KYP. Constantine concluded with the declaration: 'I rest on the indestructible strength which is the love of my people', an adaptation of the royal motto, My Strength is the Love of My People.

In a further letter dated 15 July, the king appeared to concede the dismissal of Garoufalias but refused point blank to allow Papandreou to take over the ministry himself. The prime minister was quick to point out the flaw inherent in the king's logic.

'Thus the principle is established that I may be prime minister but not also minister of a certain ministry,' he wrote to the palace. 'I would therefore be a prime minister under prohibition. But if I do not inspire confidence, I must stop being prime minister. It is inconceivable that I will be able to remain as prime minister but not as minister of national defence . . . I address to you Your Majesty an appeal that you do not insist in your refusal but rather respond to the claim of the legitimate governor of the country.'

That evening, Papandreou went to see the king in Athens. He told him that if the palace did not accept that the prime minister had the right to appoint ministers and senior army officers, he would have no choice but to resign and have the people decide the issue in the ensuing general election.

The idea of elections did not appeal to the king. He had

been advised by the professor of constitutional law at Athens University, whom he saw an hour before Papandreou's arrival, that if the prime minister sought elections, the king would be honour bound to dissolve parliament. But technically, said the professor, he could simply ask someone else to be prime minister and see if that person could win a vote of confidence in parliament.

Constantine decided that honour could wait. As Papandreou outlined his position, the president of parliament and one of his erstwhile Centre Union colleagues, George Novas, was waiting in an ante-room. He had been summoned earlier at the behest of Queen Frederika and without the knowledge of the prime minister. Papandreou stayed for just fifteen minutes. He asked the king to sign the decree removing Garoufalias and installing him in his place. There was little discussion – the argument had run its course and there was nothing more of substance that either man could say. The king's reply to the prime minister's request was brief and to the point.

'No,' he said.

In that case, replied Papandreou, I shall resign tomorrow.

The king leapt at the declaration of intent. Determined not to let an opportunity slip from his grasp by an overnight change of mind, Constantine took the initiative. As Papandreou walked out of the room, the door had barely closed behind him when Novas was ushered in through another entrance. Then and there, the king asked him to be prime minister, the best offer of his political career. By the time Papandreou reached home, the radio was broadcasting the appointment of his replacement. There would be no elections. It was all over.

Chapter Eight

Squash in Malta

'The Americans know everything that goes on in the army.'
King Constantine

About a month before King Constantine engineered the down-fall of George Papandreou and his government in July 1965, the CIA station in Athens filed to Washington a report disclosing the existence of a 'rightist Greek military conspiratorial group' within the army. The report was the first of fifteen dispatched over the following eighteen months. Gradually these reports established a picture of the group and its main co-ordinating figure, Colonel George Papadopoulos. Although the reports gave the initial for his Christian name as D, instead of G for George, there was no doubt as to whom they referred. The last was dispatched from Athens on 23 January 1967. The sum of the reports proved that the CIA were not only aware that conspirators were planning to overthrow the government and institute a military dictatorship, but that it knew the group included the very man who would eventually lead the coup, a man who had a long established relationship with the agency itself, a man who was on the CIA's own payroll.

US knowledge of Papadopoulos and his penchant for creating conspiracies was long standing. According to an assessment of the period which remains surpressed by the State Department, as early as 1963 the US government was aware that Papadopoulos and two of his associates, Pattakos and Makarezos, 'had formed a group which began to consider the possibility of an eventual take-over of government'.

With the demise of Papandreou, Papadopoulos' star was once again on the ascent. Almost immediately after the prime minister

was ousted, he was brought back from the wilderness of his
provincial posting and installed in the offices of the general
staff in Athens, once again working directly for KYP. His
specific task was psychological warfare – propaganda – but
he continued in his capacity as a liaison officer for the CIA.
Others from the group of conspirators who visited the palace
so regularly in 1964 and who were now likewise restored to key
positions included Nicholas Makarezos, who was given a staff
job in KYP, and Stylianos Pattakos who was placed in command
of the armoured training centre at Goudi, a large barracks just
outside Athens.

The king's delight at getting rid of Papandreou gave rise to
only a short lived celebration, for it ushered in a period of
chaotic instability with parliament unable to elect a government and mass protests on the streets. The young activists
of Papandreou's Centre Union came into their own. Nicos
Constantopoulos, the party's student leader, launched a wave
of protests, having restrained himself for several months at the
request of Papandreou. The deposed prime minister had pleaded
with him that continual agitation only played into the hands of
the palace and the Papadopoulos cabal. Now, with the prime
minister out of office, Constantopoulos was released from any
such constraint. He and other leaders organised a series of rallies
with thousands of students. Their chant was 'One-One-Four,
One-One-Four' – a reference to Article 114 of the constitution
under which sovereignty was said to derive from the people,
not the palace.

It was September 1965 before a government managed to obtain
a vote of confidence in parliament, and only then by the barest
of majorities. It was headed by Stephanos Stephanopoulos,
Papandreou's former deputy who defected with a number of
Centre Union MPs, including Constantine Mitsotakis, and was
supported by the ERE. Their betrayal created a deep rift in Greek
politics that persists to this day. But the Americans were relieved
that, at last, a government was in place. In the middle of
the crisis, the embassy had informed Washington of growing
pressure for a military take-over to resolve the impasse.

The temporary resolution of the crisis also gave the king

time to make a number of military appointments. The most important of these concerned the chief of the armed forces general staff. General Yannis Gennimatas, who helped subvert the 1961 election with the Pericles Plan but managed to escape the vengeance of Papandreou, finally retired. He was replaced by General Grigorios Spandidakis, one of the senior officers with whom the Papadopoulos group had been in contact since at least 1964, a man saved from recommended retirement by the CIA. General Spandidakis literally owed his career and high office to Jack Maury.

The installation of an apparently stable government and his ability to exercise unfettered control over the army gave Constantine renewed confidence. In a highly political New Year message that could hardly have been designed to lower tensions and project the monarch as a unifying figure, the king implied that those who were against him were communists. The address was written by his adviser Hoidas and in it Constantine denounced his opponents as 'filth'. But with a supine government to his taste, the king believed the opposition had been seen off. The fact that February 1966 saw the largest demonstration in Athens for over two decades, when up to 700,000 people gathered to cheer their support for Papandreou, seemed to matter little. Constantine's friends in the press said the protest was the deposed prime minister's swan song and charged that it was orchestrated by communists.

Two months later the king went abroad on a trip which showed those outside Constantine's close circle the extent of his relationship with the American military establishment and the CIA. The occasion was a five day visit to Malta for a squash tournament between a Greek team and an opposing team comprised of Maltese and British Royal Navy players.

The focal point of Constantine's day to day relationship with the CIA was a US army colonel, Joseph Lepczyk, with whom he played squash. But Lepczyk was in reality Constantine's minder, placed in that position by the CIA for whom he worked. Far from being the innocuous squash partner the king liked to pretend, the 49-year-old American was a spy whose role was to penetrate the palace and relay information not just to the CIA but to the Defence Intelligence Agency as well.

Lepczyk was a Polish–American from Michigan who was posted to Greece in 1959 where he worked undercover as a member of the US army attaché's staff in the Athens embassy. His function was described officially by the euphemism that he was engaged in 'foreign area special training detachment'. With this entrée to the royal circle, Lepczyk kept himself well informed about what was going on in the palace and passed interesting bits of information on to his superiors. He wasn't the only CIA functionary close to Constantine, however. When the king saw his brother-in-law, Juan Carlos of Spain, practise karate and express an interest in martial arts, the agency provided a tutor for him.

Lepczyk's role and usefulness was confirmed by a senior US diplomat who served in Greece at the time. Lepczyk, he said, 'was CIA and he was important because of his access to the king. He probably had better access than anyone.' Another man with deep access to palace affairs for a time, Philip Deane, said that Constantine once confided that he, the king, knew all about the Aspida plot because Lepczyk had told him about it. 'The Americans know everything that goes on in the army,' said the king.

Constantine became fond of the CIA man and was blind to any malign explanation for his friendship. 'He was not politically motivated,' Constantine confided to friends years later. 'He was a very straightfoward man.'

Tha Malta squash tournament was suggested by a Royal Navy player and the Greek team accepted. At the last minute, however, the team leader informed the British that Constantine had requested Leyczyk be included. Admiral Sir John Hamilton, the commander of the Royal Navy base at Valletta, was irritated. He asked colleagues who Lepczyk was. The reply – that he was close to the king and almost certainly worked for the CIA – did not please him. Whatever Lepczyk's pedigree as a spy was, Hamilton felt that the tournament was between British naval officers, Greeks and Maltese. Lepczyk, an American, should not be invited, he told colleagues. But pleadings with the Greeks were to no avail. Constantine was determined that Lepczyk would come.

In due course the king flew in to the Mediterranean island and was confronted immediately with an embarrassing reminder of events back home. Newspaper billboards throughout the island proclaimed ΕΝΑ ΕΝΑ ΤΕΣΣΑΡΑ – Greek for 114. 'Oh God, not here too,' the king remarked glumly as his car swept past the first billboard on the way out of the airport. George Papandreou's main supporter on Malta happened to be Dom Mintoff, the former Maltese prime minister and head of the Maltese Liberation Movement, and the sympathetic local media duly gave their support to their countryman's campaign. One declared in an editorial: 'Games or no games, private visit or not, the majority of the Maltese people are not keen on having in their midst persons who stifle democracy and, in the eyes of the world, King Constantine is the head of state who went against the will of his people when he removed the prime minister because he did not go about according to his wishes.'

Ignoring Admiral Hamilton's directive, Constantine was followed to Malta by Lepczyk who arrived in his own plane, courtesy of the CIA. There followed several days of subterfuge as Royal Navy officers and the Maltese tried to keep Lepczyk away from the tournament by giving him incorrect times and locations of matches and sending him on wild goose chases. Initially, the king thought it was an hilarious joke but soon he realised, with some embarrassment, that it was not.

The social highlight of the tournament was a banquet hosted by Admiral and Lady Hamilton in Villa Portelli, their official residence on the island. Lepczyk's name was not on the invitation list, conspicuous by its absence. Constantine took a Royal Navy officer aside and pleaded with him to have Lepczyk included. He said the CIA man was upset. More important, he had been informed, he said, that if Lepczyk was not invited, 'Greece would suffer for it.' Admiral Hamilton rejected the last minute plea. Lepczyk was on no account to turn up at the banquet, he ruled.

By now, resentment about Lepczyk was so high among other members of the Greek team, they announced that if the

American came to the banquet as a team member, they would boycott it. In desperation, Royal Navy officers and some of the Maltese players arranged for Lepczyk to be kidnapped and deposited somewhere on the island far away from the reception. The plot worked but the ensuing meal turned into a frosty affair with the king and his wife, Queen Anne-Marie, exchanging barbed comments, to the embarrassment of those within earshot. During one incident as Constantine was regailing those around the table with a family tale, he was interrupted by the Queen. 'Be honest for once,' those present recall her saying with irritation. 'The real reason you did it was because your mother told you to.'

When the royal party left the island, Lepczyk flew back to Athens on board the king's plane, while the rest of the Greek team made their way home by ferry and road. The CIA man had been humiliated. He believed his treatment was part of a plot by British intelligence to prise the king away from the Americans and into the control of the British. Lepczyk, the American spy, told the king on the way back to Athens that he should be wary of one of the Royal Navy officers, whom he denounced with indignation as a British spy.

Back in Greece, the controversy generated by the king's ousting of George Papandreou refused to go away. What kept the issue alive was the fact the governing party had been removed and replaced without a general election. Neither the palace nor its sycophants in parliament were eager to see their popularity tested at the polls. For the Right, the focus of attention was Andreas Papandreou. It would be difficult to understate the degree to which the former prime minister's son was loathed by the Right and the CIA. By the mid-1960s, the CIA file on Andreas described him as corrupt, morally sinful (his extra-marital affairs were legendary) and said he posed a danger to US interests in Greece.

The antipathy went back a long way. In the 1930s, Andreas fled Greece to escape the repression of the Metaxas dictatorship. As a student, he had flirted with a Trotskyist group (hence the CIA's suspicions) and fallen foul of the authorities. He went to America where he became a US citizen, embarked on a flourishing career as an economist and academic and, during World War II, served in the US Navy. His reputation made, he returned to Athens in the late 1950s at the invitation of the Karamanlis government and set up an economic research institute. He later entered politics at his father's request and renounced his US citizenship, prompting President Johnson to quip, 'You can't trust a man who breaks his oath of allegiance to the flag of the United States.'

Another explanation for the CIA's dislike of Andreas was given by a retired senior official of the State Department's Intelligence and Research (INR) section. Andreas was used by the CIA as a source of information during the 1950s, notwithstanding his earlier flirtation with Trotsky, or perhaps because of it. During that period, Andreas was also co-opted by the CIA onto a covert study group for Mediterranean policy making. According to the INR official, the relationship was severed by Andreas when he returned to Greece. Having prospered in America, Andreas then did a classic about-face and proceeded to carve a political career in Athens by being a most vitriolic, demagogic critic of the US. Cold War warriors in the CIA and the US diplomatic service found that very difficult to take.

There were others in the State Department who regarded Andreas as suffering from mental illness. In an unpublished analysis prepared for academic consumption, John Owens, a political counsellor in Athens and later a member of the Greek desk team back in Washington, advanced the theory that the prime minister's son suffered from 'paranoid neurosis'. Owens attributes the decision of Constantine Mitsotakis and others to defect from the Centre Union to their intense dislike of Andreas, who had been promoted over their heads by his father and who placed himself at the head of a cabal of young radicals within the party. In his paper, Owens argued that Andreas' 'extreme partisanship, even fanaticism . . . [and] tendency to make sweeping statements, frequently of an extreme nature, against those opposing him' made a significant contribution to the eventual military coup.

'It is my belief that, by his actions, Andreas Papandreou

created the psychological atmosphere which made the coup possible. By his inflammatory speeches, by his divisiveness within his own party, by his attacks upon the king, the conservative parties, the United States and NATO, and the Greek establishment generally, Andreas aroused the fears of his opponents – and they were many – that an electoral victory for the Centre Union, which would enable him to play a major role in governing the country, would create a situation in Greece which they considered beyond the limits of toleration.'

Whatever the merits of such a view, Owens' explanation for Andreas' conduct at the time is that he suffered from a 'neurosis . . . which seemed to drive him compulsively towards conflict and even defeat'. Andreas' later career provided ample ammunition for those who would charge him with being untrustworthy and impossible to work with. However, Andreas' predilection for explaining events in Greece in the mid-1960s in terms of conspiracy had a basis in fact.

Throughout 1966, the royal and military establishment strained to produce evidence that would implicate him in the Aspida affair. In May, all those charged in connection with the Pericles Plan to subvert the 1961 election were acquitted by a military court, but the judicial investigation into Aspida rumbled on. In October, the trial of the 28 officers began with witnesses including a pimp who claimed to have heard some of the accused assert that George Papandreou supported them. Two of the accused gave evidence of being offered bribes ranging from $33,000 to $100,000 if they implicated Papandreou senior and junior in a plot to establish a communist dictatorship. A statement, later retracted and for which there was no supporting evidence, claimed that Andreas told a clandestine meeting that Aspida would act as a scalpel in removing the monarchy and the Right from Greece. Curiously, surgical imagery was later employed by Colonel George Papadopoulos to explain his own operation on Greek society.

The Aspida trial ended in March 1967 when fifteen of the accused were given prison sentences ranging from twelve to eighteen years. Thirteen were acquitted. The only senior officer to characterise the proceedings as the witch hunt they were was removed immediately from his post. In May 1967, a month after Papadopoulos and his associates staged their coup, the body of the Aspida defence lawyer, Nikiforas Mandilaras, was washed ashore on Rhodes.

The Aspida affair was not the unqualified victory which the palace and many on the Right believed it to be. The combination of a sham trial and the king's eighteen-month-long failure to dissolve parliament and call a general election eventually proved too much for some right-wingers.

Panayiotis Kanellopoulos, the successor to Constantine Karamanlis as leader of ERE, decided late in 1966 to with-draw his party's support for the Stephanopoulos government. Kanellopoulos concluded after a party investigation that the case against Andreas was non-existent. He wrote to the king saying the real danger facing the country was the spate of rumours – fed by the palace and extreme rightists in the military – of an imminent communist take-over. In his memoirs, the ERE leader said there was 'not even the smallest indication [of guilt] on the part of Andreas Papandreou'.

The pressure on the palace was too great. At the end of the year, a new interim government was appointed, headed by Kanellopoulos, and elections set for the following spring. By this stage, however, plans were well under way to see to it that if the courts failed to prevent a return to power by the Centre Union and the Papandreous, subversion and brute force would. Opinion polls, corroborated by secret surveys carried out by the CIA, predicted an overwhelming victory for George Papandreou and everyone knew that would mean the return to office also of his son.

Chapter Nine

The Wrong Coup

'The first rule of coups is there is always one being plotted. The second rule is that the one that happens is the one you don't know about.'

US State Department Greek affairs analyst

The plan by the palace and senior army officers to stage a coup – Constantine preferred to use the term 'extra parliamentary solution' – was well advanced by the end of 1966. At the turn of the year, the last of the key men who would carry out the orders, Colonel Yannis Ladas, the commander of the Military Security Police, began work on the wave of repression that would be necessary to secure the coup in the vital moments after the take-over began. For the next several weeks, Ladas worked out how to arrest 10,000 people in a matter of hours. The CIA, and through it the US ambassador at the time, Phillips Talbot, was aware of the thinking among the army's generals, who met several times in March and April 1967, dithering over the precise date on which they would seize power.

There were many in the agency who believed that something had to be done to subvert a Centre Union electoral victory. Among them was the Athens station chief, Jack Maury. Early in 1967, Maury drew up a scheme for a $100,000 covert operation aimed at influencing the outcome of the poll. Maury's plan was designed specifically to undermine Andreas Papandreou. He wanted the agency to fund the campaigns of ERE candidates and selected Centre Union politicians known to be against Andreas Papandreou.

A constituency by constituency analysis, similar to that drawn up before the 1961 election by Maury's predecessor, Laughlin

Campbell, identified key marginal seats where a judicious dispersal of cash might help tip the balance in favour of right-wing candidates. A black propaganda campaign was also to be run through well disposed newspapers. As one former diplomat put it, Maury's plan was 'to raise the seeds of opposition' to the Centre Union. According to a State Department source, the head of the CIA station believed that 'Andreas had to be stopped'.

'Maury was real worried about Andreas,' confirmed Kay Bracken, one of the US embassy's political counsellors in Athens. 'In the run-up to the coup, some in the embassy argued that the political chaos was normal and that things were like this all the time in Greek politics. Others, however, regarded Andreas as the problem and as a dangerous threat to stability. These people said darkly that he had associates who were on the communist fringes. [Maury] never seemed to take account of what Andreas actually could do, as opposed to what he said he would do.'

Bracken was against Maury's plan for another reason. For some time, diplomats in the embassy had been trying to shed their image of inveterate interference in domestic Greek affairs. According to Bracken: 'We had been struggling to convince the Greeks that we were not interfering. If we had done something like this, they would have found out and there was no guarantee of success. It was too dangerous.'

That view was shared by Ambassador Talbot and Maury's plan was eventually rejected by Washington, much to the irritation of the station chief and his close colleagues. When Talbot, an old newspaper man and academic inducted into the foreign service by President Kennedy, arrived in Athens in place of Henry Labouisse, he also inherited titular responsibility for CIA activities. Some in the agency felt that the new ambassador was yet another 'bleeding heart liberal' come to make life awkward for them. They would have preferred a man whose view of the world was as black and white, as sharply defined in its certitude, as their own.

As one former agency stationed in Athens at the time of the coup put it: 'Talbot was a slow guy in a bang bang job. Dealing with him could be like playing tennis with a marshmallow – you just didn't know whether he was going to stick or spin.'

When Talbot was drafting his report on Maury's plan, the CIA station chief showed his hand. Talbot wanted to tell Washington that an electoral victory by the Centre Union would be preferable to a coup. Maury objected. He argued that to state this 'would arouse too much interest in Washington', according to a former embassy official privy to their discussions. At Maury's insistence, the line was deleted from Talbot's report, something the ambassador would later regret.

Despite Maury's intervention, Talbot's substantive recommendation against any covert operation by the CIA was forwarded to Washington otherwise undiluted. It was considered by a committee comprising representatives of the National Security Council, the CIA, the State Department, the Defence Department and the White House. Known as the 303 Committee after the number of the room in which it met inside Washington's Old Executive Building, it discussed the plan in February 1967. According to CIA information which was considered at the meeting, the agency stated bluntly that a coup was being planned with the active participation of the king, or at least his knowledge. Talbot's recommendation against the plan was supported by the ambassador's boss, Secretary of State Dean Rusk, though not out of any great defence of the principle of non-intervention. According to one State Department source, Rusk was against the plan 'because he didn't think it would work, that it would be discovered and that, in any event, the military would intervene'.

In the face of such opposition, Committee 303 decided to do nothing. Walt Rostow, a White House adviser on national security, reputedly closed the meeting with a cryptic comment: 'I hope you understand, gentlemen,' he said, 'that what we have concluded here, or rather have failed to conclude, makes the future course of events in Greece inevitable.'

Elsewhere in the Washington bureaucracy, others were becoming alarmed about what appeared to be going on in Greece. The series of CIA reports about the Greek military conspirators that had stopped after fifteen instalments aroused the interest of Charley Lagoudakis, a Cretan-born analyst in the State Department's Intelligence and Research section (INR). The reports had ceased without explanation in February 1967 and when Lagoudakis found them, he drafted a memo to his boss, Phil Stoddard, urging further information as fast as possible. Lagoudakis was particularly interested because, apart from his natural curiosity in Greek affairs, the reports mentioned individuals who did not dominate other CIA dispatches, which concentrated on the palace and the generals.

INR's job was to evaluate intelligence provided by the National Security Agency, the CIA and the departments of state and defence. In the mid-1960s it operated out of the fifth, sixth and seventh floors of the State Department's headquarters in Washington and, with a staff of about 360, was the second largest section in the building. According to a retired senior analyst, INR worked on the basis that 'intelligence was too important to leave to any single agency'. But INR apparently had limited clout. Lagoudakis' requests for more information were fobbed off.

When he asked for further biographical details on the officers named in the reports – particularly Colonel Papadopoulos and Brigadier-General Stylianos Pattakos – the CIA response 'wasn't much good', according to the retired analyst. Lagoudakis was told the information was categorised as coming from an F6 source which meant, according to the CIA, that it was impossible to evaluate either the source itself or the veracity of the information provided. The CIA told INR what was already common knowledge within US diplomatic and military circles at the time: that senior Greek army officers had been discussing a coup.

'We began to develop a little picture and it was the generals we got information about. It was they who were plotting,' revealed the retired analyst. 'The reports Charley [Lagoudakis] got spoke of coup plots but nobody takes these reports seriously. The first rule of coups is there is always one being plotted. The second rule is that the one that happens is the one you don't know about.'

But Lagoudakis took the information in the fifteen reports

seriously and pressed his case. At least one request from him
was passed directly to the CIA station in Athens. Lagoudakis
asked quite simply to be updated on the series of reports that
had suddenly stopped. He never got a reply.

In Greece, as the date for election drew nearer, King
Constantine began to get nervous. About two months before
voting, finally scheduled for 28 May 1967, the king approached
Ambassador Talbot. What would be the US response to a
military take-over to avoid an election or a Centre Union
victory? he asked. Constantine tried to distance himself from
what he was proposing by saying the military was agitated.
He claimed he could hold them off for a limited period but
that he could not guarantee their reaction if the result went
against the Right. At about the same time, the king made similar
overtures to Constantine Karamanlis, the retired former ERE
prime minister, with a view to Karamanlis returning from exile
to lead any resulting government. Karamanlis, wedded to the
ideals of democracy, gave him a dusty reply.

There was an equally unequivocal answer from Talbot. The
ambassador said it was essential for elections to take place
and that the US would not support any so-called 'extra-
parliamentary solution'. The king did not press his case and
when he left, Talbot cabled Washington with a report of their
conversation, seeking backing for his response. The reply was
swift. A cable was dispatched urging Talbot to 'warn the king
more strongly against a possible deviation from the constitution'. This advice was followed up by a longer explanation of
Washington's view.

'The United States in principle is opposed to non-democratic
actions in Greece as elsewhere,' Talbot was told. 'This is
based both on the traditional US support for the concept of
governments based on the consent of the governed, and on our
conviction that such "solutions" seldom solve constitutional
crises and generally worsen the situation they were designed
to improve . . .

'Public opinion here and throughout the world would
undoubtedly react unfavourably to the imposition of a dictatorship in Greece. The failure of democracy to work in a NATO

country – as demonstrated by a resort to extra legal means – would also tarnish the image of the entire Western alliance . . . It is difficult to speculate on what the official US reaction would be (other than it would certainly be unfavourable) and to outline what specific measures the US might feel constrained to take, since that would depend on the circumstances at the time . . .

'You should continue to impress upon His Majesty the perils of such a course and at the same time stress the other alternatives open to him.'

On 10 April, Talbot cabled Washington with the news that he had seen the king and told him that 'the United States considers dictatorships to be wrong in principle and rarely work yet create many difficulties'. According to Talbot, Constantine did not make any substantive reply but observed rather ominously that a constitutional crisis could arise before the election in mid-May.

United States policy as enunciated to the Greeks was now seriously divided, with the king receiving conflicting advice. On the one hand, the embassy had expressed its unambiguous opposition to a coup; on the other hand, the CIA, with which the palace maintained such close relations, was saying that a Centre Union victory was so inimical to US interests that it ought to be avoided. There were some in the CIA and US military establishment in Greece who believed that a Centre Union electoral victory had to be avoided at all costs. In some cases, these were men whose careers in Greece stretched back to the civil war – Greek–Americans, some of them brought into the service by Tom Karamessines, who had become indistinguishable from their native Greek counterparts. It was they who worked on a daily basis with the Greek KYP agents and army officers and with whom the CIA had developed a symbiotic relationship. The Americans were not reluctant to express their views and the Greeks knew how to please their masters.

As the date of the elections drew nearer and the political temperature rose, Constantine's senior military officers identified 16 April as a possible date for the coup. The take-over was to coincide with a so-called 'Peace March' from Marathon to

Athens, in reality a left-wing anti-US, anti-NATO protest rally
that was guaranteed to enflame the Right. Inside the palace, the
date was favoured by Queen Frederika on the spurious grounds
that the march was in effect an assault on the constitution. But
the date was abandoned when the march was called off. An
alternative date, 24 May, was chosen to coincide with a rally
in Athens by the communist-dominated EDA party, the Union
of the Democratic Left. Almost immediately, however, this date
was also cancelled, for reasons never disclosed.

Among the military, the cancellation was communicated to
Colonel Papadopoulos by General George Zoitakis, commander
of the 3rd Military Corps in Salonika, which represented the
bulk of the army. Papadopoulos, as co-ordinator for putting
the proposed generals' coup into effect, had close contacts
with two other generals – chief of the general staff, General
Grigorios Spandidakis, and deputy chief of the defence staff,
General Odysseus Angelis. The three generals each had contacts
variously with Papadopoulos and two others from the colonels'
group – Pattakos and Makarezos.

Zoitakis' message that the coup date was postponed yet again
came as stale news to Papadopoulos. After almost a lifetime's
association with the CIA, Papadopoulos was not without his
sources inside the Athens station. A friend there communicated
to him the fact that the generals had decided at a meeting of the
Supreme Military Council not to move on 24 May. The CIA
had detailed and intimate knowledge of the plans being made
by the generals because the agency had a source among them.
The source was so effective that within minutes of the Council's
meeting – held on 20 April – the agency was confident it knew
what decision had been taken.

'We found out by very good means that [the generals] had
no intention of stopping the elections,' a senior CIA source
disclosed. 'We, that is the agency, the embassy, were relaxed
in a very real sense.'

In fact, the generals had every intention of stopping the
election. The question wasn't would they try, but when? The
CIA's position was flawed in two other respects. First, the
agency's knowledge of what the generals discussed at their 20

April meeting was dependent on what was said openly during the main discussion. The agency had no means of knowing what was said during intervals or between smaller groups of generals, unless their source was privy to those particular discussions. Secondly, the agency failed to plan for precipitate action by the lower rank officers geared up by the generals.

The fact that a coup did take place, though not the one expected in some quarters, appears to have been a cock-up within a conspiracy. Just before the 20 April meeting, the wife of a Greek army Major-General who was not due to attend it received an anonymous telephone call. 'They will strike tonight,' said a voice before ringing off hurriedly. The message was passed to Spandidakis who ordered that Pattakos be alerted immediately. Pattakos in turn told Papadopoulos.

Thus the colonels were getting conflicting information: the generals were saying no coup date would be decided until after further discussions the following week, a view communicated separately to the colonels by a CIA source. But the anonymous telephone caller, whose information was passed on by Spandidakis, was apparently suggesting that it would happen on the night of the very day that the postponement was apparently decided upon.

Papadopoulos decided enough was enough. The coup would take place that night – with or without the generals. Spandidakis, who had wanted a further delay to consult the king, Zoitakis and Angelis were presented with a choice and quickly threw their lot in with the colonels.

As Pattakos prepared his tanks in Goudi barracks, a member of the US embassy's political staff was drafting yet another memo about the possibility of a coup. It was intended for Kay Bracken on the Greek desk in the State Department, and warned of the imminence of a military take-over. The ink was barely dry when the tanks were rolling down Queen Sophia Boulevard, passed the embassy gates and on towards parliament.

The first units to move, however, were members of the CIA-trained Hellenic Raiding Force. Around midnight on 20 April, they took over the Athens headquarters of the Greek defence forces, the so-called Pentagon. They were under the orders of Lieutenant-Colonel Costas Aslanides, operations chief of a brigade of paratroopers. Once the building was secured, Aslanides alerted Goudi barracks and Pattakos let his tanks roll.

With binoculars strapped around his neck, the Brigadier-General with a penchant for order and religion stood upright in the turret of the lead tank as he directed the column towards Syntagma Square and the seat of Greek democracy. He followed the same route into the city taken by the Germans when they conquered Greece in April 1941. Pattakos stopped occasionally to look around for any sign of opposition. There was none. He radioed his co-conspirators that there was no enemy in sight and he was proceeding to the square, the royal palace nearby, the radio station and communications centre.

The take-over was based on the Prometheus Plan, a NATO-designed scheme to be put into action in the event of communist insurgency. Throughout the early hours of 21 April, it served well as an instrument to throttle Greek democracy. In the event of opposition, Prometheus was unequivocal: 'Smash, without hesitation, any probable enemy resistance,' it instructed.

In the Parnis mountains about 25 kilometres north of Athens, all was quiet inside the royal residence of Tatoi. Constantine had just gone to bed after watching a film with his sister Sophia, the wife of Prince Juan Carlos of Spain. The phone woke him at 1 a.m. It was Major Arnaoutis, his secretary and trusted aide. In a whisper barely audible to the king, Arnaoutis said there was gunfire outside his house in Athens. Did His Majesty know what was happening? His Majesty said he didn't.

The king's immediate reaction was to call Dimitrios Bitsios, director of his political office in succession to Hoidas. Constantine was anxious lest Bitsios knew something that he, the king, didn't. Constantine's anxiety was caused by his earlier overtures to Talbot and Karamanlis. Had someone made a move without first obtaining royal approval? Bitsios said he knew nothing.

Prime Minister Panayiotis Kanellopoulos was woken in the early hours when the captain of an army patrol shouted through the keyhole of his apartment in the fashionable Kolonaki district of the city.

'You're under arrest for your own safety,' said the officer.

The prime minister retorted that he was in no need of protection. By the time the soldiers kicked his door down and rushed inside, the 60-year-old man had armed himself with a pistol. He picked up the phone and dialled, saying that he would do nothing nor go anywhere without first speaking to the king.

'Talking is not necessary. Put on your clothes and follow us,' said the officer.

As the weapon was snatched from his hand and the phone slammed down, Kanellopoulos had just enough time to hear Constantine shout, 'What's happening?' The prime minister was frog marched from the building, shouting ineffectually, 'Kill me here! I will not go with you.'

George Papandreou was asleep in his modest, white-washed villa in Kastri, just outside the city. The 78-year-old leader of the Centre Union woke to find a young army captain standing at the foot of his bed, gun drawn. 'The armed forces have assumed the governing of the fatherland,' said the captain. 'For your own protection, follow me.'

The old man was allowed to dress in his bathroom before being led away in one of two military vehicles that had surrounded the house.

At about the same time, Andreas Papandreou was also being arrested. Eight soldiers burst into his house, seven with fixed bayonets, one with a sub-machine gun. During the commotion, Andreas had time to rush onto the roof and hide. But a soldier found his 14-year-old son and put a gun to the boy's head.

'I surrender,' said Andreas, throwing down his own weapon.

He was driven away from the fashionable suburb of Psychico, past the villas and bungalows favoured by the diplomatic corps and the CIA.

In the operations room of the State Department in Washington, a cable machine snapped suddenly to life with a message from Athens. It was graded 'flash', the highest level of cable urgency.

'Understand prime minister has just been seized by military elements and tanks in Constitution Square.'

The department's Greek desk staff had gone home for the day but were alerted and within an hour, key officials had returned in time for a second message.

'Armoured road blocks established at Constitution Square and peripheral points. Telephones out. No information on king.'

Both cables were signed Talbot.

Like most other people in Athens on the night of the coup, Talbot had been in bed when it happened. The first he knew was when the guard at the gate of his residence near the embassy called to say a man was insisting on speaking to him. Panayiotis Kanellopoulos' nephew was agitated when he told Talbot that 'men in uniform' had taken his uncle away. Talbot tried to call the Marine guard at the chancery but the line was dead. He got into his official car and set out, the first time he had personally driven the embassy's Cadillac.

Guards at the embassy proper said they knew nothing of what was going on, despite the appearance of tanks on the streets. Inside the building, the only other person on duty was a communications officer but all his external phone lines were dead. He was reduced to monitoring incoming radio traffic. Talbot sent his flash to Washington but was unable to reach his own staff in Athens.

Kanellopoulos' nephew suggested they go to see the prime minister's wife. When the ambassador heard her story, he shot back to the embassy and sent his second, more detailed, message. It was received in Washington by a baffled State Department staff. They knew neither what was happening nor who precisely was dispatching the cables, as all such communications from the embassy were automatically signed in the name of the ambassador. As soon as Talbot identified himself, it was left to Washington to rouse other embassy staff in Athens.

The department was able to phone Hellenikon, a US air force base at Athens airport. From there, an army colonel used one of the few remaining lines that had not been cut to re-route the call to the home of Norbert Anschuetz, the number-two man at the embassy. Dan Brewster, head of the Greek desk, told Anschuetz as much as he knew and suggested he get to the embassy fast.

Harris Greene, deputy CIA station chief, was alerted sometime before 5 a.m. by one of his agency colleagues. Greene leapt out of bed and headed into the city. Confirmation that something was wrong came when he drove past the home of Arnaoutis and caught a glimpse of soldiers roughing him up. By the time Greene reached the embassy, traversing some of the city's back streets to avoid army road blocks, Jack Maury was already there.

The two CIA men conferred briefly and insisted to Talbot that they hadn't a clue what was happening. Talbot's military attaché, OK Marshall, claimed that he was equally in the dark about the unfolding events. Marshall had the king's number in Tatoi and somehow managed to get a call through to him.

'Sir,' said OK, 'What the hell's going on?'

'I don't know,' said the king. 'But whatever it is, I'm against it.'

From his palace in the mountains, the king could see the city below, its orange street lights glowing in the half light of an early dawn. From Tatoi, it looked silent and calm. Had the king been a little nearer, he would have heard the sound of sirens and the smashing of doors.

In the space of some five hours, over 10,000 people were arrested by military squads and taken to 'reception centres'. The officer behind the round-up was Colonel Yannis Ladas, the 47-year-old director of military police. Ladas used his position in the army to extort money from brothel customers and he nurtured a deep seated dislike of teenage boys with long hair and girls in miniskirts. He was involved in the capture of the Pentagon and it was his proud boast that he took the building with a squad of just twenty men.

'My plan was carried out with mathematical precision,' he said in an interview some years later. 'Within twenty minutes, every politician, every man and anarchist who was listed could be rounded up.' Ignoring the role of the Raiding Force commandos, he said that 'the army general staff was in my power within five minutes using only twenty military policemen, even though it was at the time guarded by 1,000 infantry men and 500 air force people . . . a very simple, diabolical plan'.

As dawn broke over the city, the radio station blared out martial music peppered with slogans. The coup leaders declared their take-over to be a revolution. 'Quiet, order and security prevail in the land,' said one broadcast. 'The revolution, carried out bloodlessly, marches forward to the fulfilment of its manifest destiny! Greeks, pure and of a superb race, let the flowers of regeneration bloom out of the debris of the regime of falsehood!'

Through propaganda that was more suited to Europe of the 1930s or Maoist China, the people of Greece were told that 'unity, work, peace, progress' was the key to their happiness. 'Our aim is the equal redistribution of national wealth,' said one military slogan. Another extolled the merits of 'Democracy unpolluted by foreign ideologies and propaganda!'

Shortly after 6 a.m., the radio broadcast a decree, allegedly in the king's name, proclaiming the revolution and suspending eleven articles of the constitution. People could now be arrested on the spot and without warrant, brought before military courts and dealt with. Homes could be searched with impunity. Meetings and strikes were outlawed, domestic news subject to censorship. The stock exchange was ordered closed, bank deposits frozen and foreign exchange banned. Borders and ports were sealed and communications with the outside world cut for ordinary citizens.

At about 7 a.m., Papadopoulos, Pattakos and Makarezos arrived at Tatoi to speak to the king. When Constantine was told by an air force officer that the men who had seized power were in the hall waiting to see him, he insisted that they be disarmed before he would receive them. Pattakos and Makarezos each removed their guns and left them on the hall table. Papadopoulos, cautious as ever, took off his gun but removed the bullets and placed them in his pocket as he walked inside. No one was going to burst in and shoot him with his own weapon.

Constantine told them their actions were 'unacceptable' and demanded to see the man he assumed was their boss, Chief

Hulton Deutsch

Hulton Deutsch

British troops arriving in Greek towns and cities in late 1944 after the Germans were driven out by the British-supported Greek resistance, were greeted by enthusiastic crowds (above). However, Churchill's determination to reimpose the monarchy, in the person of King George II (left), caused bitter resentment.

The British post-liberation commander in Athens, General Ronald Scobie (above centre), attempted to negotiate with the EAM resistance leader, General Stephanos Sarafis (above left), and the EDES leader, General Napoleon Zervas (above right), but within days, British troops shelled EAM's headquarters in the city and arrested their former comrades-in-arms (below).

In 1947, Britain handed over responsibility for Greece to the United States when Churchill (right, with President Harry Truman at the Potsdam conference) realised the UK's war-shattered economy could not sustain long-term involvement. Truman dispatched Dwight Griswold, former Governor of Nebraska (below), to dispense largesse as head of the American Economic Mission to Greece and help ensure a Greek government in tune with US strategic interests.

Press Association

Hulton Deutsch

Associated Press

Greek government troops in the Civil War were amply supported by the US, who even supplied napalm for the final assault (above) on the Grammos Mountains in the winter of 1948/49. The successful assault added to the government's total of over 28,000 prisoners of war (left).

Hulton Deutsch

Hulton Deutsch

Queen Frederika (above) and King Paul (behind her) made much in later years of how they helped boost the morale of government troops, seen here at a garden party in the Royal Palace, Athens, at the end of the civil war. A less warm reception awaited the couple in July 1963 when they visited Britain (right) to be greeted by crowds demanding an end to royal-supported repression in Greece.

Mogens Camre

Supporters crowded around Andreas Papandreou (left) as he campaigned in March 1967 for elections that his father, George Papandreou (below, left) was expected to win. Philip Deane (below) witnessed many of the palace intrigues that led to King Constantine sacking the elder Papandreou as prime minister in July 1965.

Hulton Deutsch

Photographer unknown

April 21 1967: junta tanks and troops outside parliament in Athens (above) brought the election campaign to an abrupt halt. Not long afterwards, King Constantine (below, on the left) found time to celebrate Easter with the man who commanded the tanks that day, Brigadier Stylianos Pattakos.

Photographer unknown

Associated Press

The junta leaders (above, left to right) Colonel George Papadopoulos, Brigadier Stylianos Pattakos and Colonel Nicholas Makarezos. The junta cabinet was sworn in (left) immediately after the coup by King Constantine, who hoped, despite his action, that his stony countenance would show people he did not approve of the new regime.

In June 1973, Papadopoulos appointed himself President, delighting in the role (left), and taking comfort in American support for his dictatorship, cemented with an early visit by US Vice-President Spiro Agnew (below, with his wife) who was met at Athens airport by the junta leaders.

Photographer unknown, photo supplied by Elias Demetracopoulos

Associated Press

Scan-Foto

The murder in May 1963 of Dr Gregory Lambrakis, (above, left) the left-wing MP and human rights campaigner, at the hands of palace-inspired thugs provided a taste of the terror to come in 1967, much of it at the hands of Inspector Basil Lambrou (above). The junta's reign of torture was exposed at the Council of Europe after a determined investigation by the Norwegian judge, Jens Evensen (left).

Steven Siewert, The Guardian

Author, The Guardian

Martin Packard (top left) led a British-based cell of Democratic Defence, working hand-in-hand with, among others, Roger Williams (top right). Nicos Leventakis ('Takis', left) took part in several of their escapades — and not a few of his own. Arne Treholt (above) aided the resistance from Norway but was later jailed for spying for the Soviet Union.

Eleftheroipa, Athens

Eleftheroipa, Athens

Vassilis Filias (top left) led Democratic Defence while living underground in Athens until his arrest in June 1968 and continued to help co-ordinate activities thereafter from his prison cell. Stellios Nestor (top right) led the Salonika cell until his arrest in May 1968 and subsequent torture. Gerassimos Notaras (left) helped organise a cell in the Greek navy until his arrest in October 1967. Dom Mintoff of Malta (above) advised British-based resistance activists.

Eleftherotipa, Athens

Eleftherotipa, Athens

Spiros Mercouris (above) helped co-ordinate
Democratic Defence anti-junta propaganda
from London. Costas Kalligas (left), the
journalist and resistance activist, introduced
Martin Packard to Vassilis Filias.

Hulton Deutsch

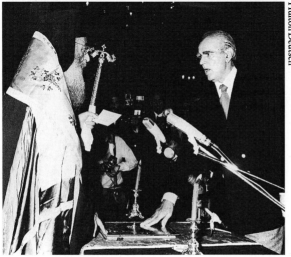

November 17 1973: an anti-junta sit-in by
students at the Athens Polytechnic was brought
to a bloody end when the regime met opposition
with tanks (above). But within eight months,
Papadopoulos was ejected from power by an
internal coup which in turn collapsed in July
1974, giving way to a return to power for
Constantine Karamanlis (left), pictured being
sworn in as prime minister.

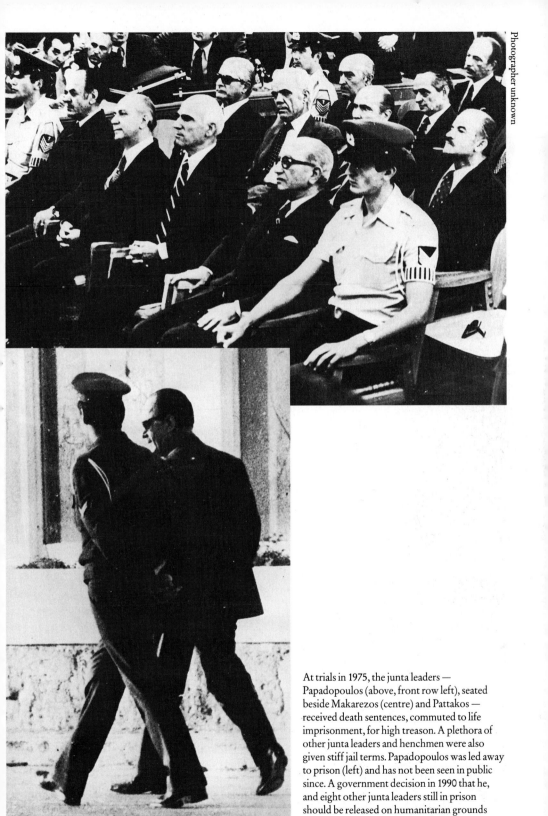

Photographer unknown

At trials in 1975, the junta leaders —
Papadopoulos (above, front row left), seated
beside Makarezos (centre) and Pattakos —
received death sentences, commuted to life
imprisonment, for high treason. A plethora of
other junta leaders and henchmen were also
given stiff jail terms. Papadopoulos was led away
to prison (left) and has not been seen in public
since. A government decision in 1990 that he,
and eight other junta leaders still in prison
should be released on humanitarian grounds
was abandoned after public protests.

August 29 1989: at a steel furnace outside Athens, 16.5 million personal files, amassed by the security apparatus of successive governments since the end of the Second World War, were set ablaze in a symbolic effort to break from the repression of the past.

of Staff Spandidakis. The colonels left saying they would
dispatch Spandidakis to Tatoi. Throughout the early morning
as Constantine waited in ignorance, officers loyal to him
telephoned Tatoi with suggestions but he rejected almost every
proposal that would have allowed him to seize the initiative.
Among the first to call with a proposal was Admiral Constantine
Engolfopoulos, chief of staff of the navy.

'The Fleet is under our control. It must not fall into the hands
of the mutineers,' said the admiral.

'Please do nothing. I want no bloodshed,' replied Constantine.
Engolfopoulos was arrested shortly after.

The palace phone rang again. This time is was a senior naval
commodore on behalf of retired Admiral Athanasios Spandis,
the former Greek representative to NATO and director of the
Greek Atomic Energy Commission. Spandis, who also served
as a political adviser to the deposed prime minister, was already
at the Skaramanga naval base and offered to take the Fleet to
Crete. He suggested that Constantine establish a base there and
set up a government in opposition to the coup leaders.

'I think you are running ahead of events,' said the king.
'Wait for my orders.' But the line was cut and the orders
never came.

The next suggestion for action was from George Rallis, minister for public order in the deposed government. He proposed
that units outside Athens be ordered to advance on the city and
crush the coup. Constantine dithered but eventually approved
an order telling the Salonika-based 3rd Corps to move on the
capital. But the commander of the 3rd Corps, General Zoitakis,
was already with the coup and, in any event, the radio message
was intercepted.

An alternative command was issued by Spandidakis. Cleverly,
he merely repeated the order to implement the Prometheus Plan
– the one already in operation effecting the military take-over.
Under the plan, the forces in the north, the Salonika 3rd Corps
included, were commanded to stand firm. Thus nothing was
done to stop the coup.

Rallis also advised the king, who was now surrounded by
tanks, to protect himself. In a pathetic gesture of defiance,

Constantine told some of the 30 men stationed at the palace
to order the tanks away. When they attempted to carry out his
command, they were promptly arrested.

When Spandidakis eventually arrived at Tatoi, Constantine
was in for a surprise. The chief of staff told the king that he,
not the cabal of colonels who had just left the palace, was
head of the new government. The claim must have given
the king cause for hope, in the belief that his generals whom
he knew had been planning a coup might, after all, be in
charge of events. Constantine ordered Spandidakis to drive
him to Psychico, to Queen Frederika's house. They arrived
to find tanks surrounding the building. The king instructed
Spandidakis to have them removed – an order that revealed
the true status of the chief of staff when he attempted to
carry it out. The soldiers replied insolently that they no longer
obeyed him whereupon Constantine leapt from the car and
shouted at the officer in charge that he had five minutes to
remove himself, his tanks and his men. The shock of a direct
command from the king had the desired effect and the tanks
moved off.

After seeing the queen, Constantine went to the Pentagon
defence staff headquarters to find out what was really going on.
At about 11 a.m., he walked into the building unchallenged and
to his office. He sat there for a while, alone. From time to time,
he opened the door to an ante-room. The people it in would fall
silent and once the door was closed again, their chatter would
resume. They were discussing the firing and promoting of the
king's officers.

Eventually, Papadopoulos and the others walked in to see
the king.

'I want to see my prime minister,' the king demanded
immediately.

'Your majesty, you don't have a prime minister,' said
Papadopoulos. But Constantine insisted and eventually Kanellopoulos was ushered in. The king asked to be left alone
with him.

'Three colonels and two captains have taken over the country,'
Kanellopoulos said. 'What are you going to do about it?' The

king replied by asking the deposed prime minister what he thought he should do.

'Arrest them,' Kanellopoulos said without hesitation.

The king brought him over to the window and showed him the tanks ringing the place. 'What other advice do you have for me?' he asked.

'You must order them to return to barracks,' Kanellopoulos said according to his own version of events, disclosed to a friend some years later.

'I cannot, I dare not,' replied the king. 'They are armed. If I tell them that, they will shoot us both.'

'You are young and you're armed. You are a young man and I am an old man. I shall stand by your side.'

Again the king demurred.

'The only alternative advice I have', said Kanellopoulos, 'is that you turn your weapon on yourself.'

The king said that he wanted to gain time so that he could eventually take over himself. In the meantime, it was imperative to have as many civilians as possible included in the new regime. When Papadopoulos and the others returned, the king told them that Constantine Kollias, the 66-year-old head of the Supreme Court, trusted palace ally and the man who helped frustrate the investigation into the murder of Gregory Lambrakis, should be prime minister. Papadopoulos said he wanted Spandidakis. As if to underline the weakness of the king's position, Pattakos informed him that the Americans were backing the take-over. The king responded by asking to be allowed call OK Marshall. Pattakos said no.

Constantine then demanded to be allowed speak to his generals, assembled in a room nearby, without the coup leaders being present. This request was granted. To those who had not already joined the coup, Constantine attempted to summon up all the authority of his status as commander in chief of the armed forces, not to say head of state. He reminded them that he was a Field Marshall of the Greek armed forces and said he was totally against the coup.

'Who is going to stand with me?' he asked. There was a moment of silence and then all the generals rose to their feet,

standing in emotional solidarity with their king. But they didn't
have a pistol between them.

The colonels demanded that Constantine sign the decree
giving royal approval to their rule and make a broadcast. The
king said he would do nothing yet, he wanted more time, and
he again requested that Kollias be appointed prime minister. This
time Papadopoulos agreed, apparently hoping to win the king
over by a small compromise and, in the sure knowledge that
regardless of who was prime minister, he, Papadopoulos, and
his friends would be the real centre of power. As Constantine
left the Pentagon, he saw Kollias being led in by a group of
soldiers. The king told him he had no time to talk but that he
would be swearing him in as prime minister that evening. It had
to be done to avoid bloodshed, said the king.

With that, Constantine returned to Tatoi for a shower and
change into his dress uniform for the swearing in ceremony.
When he drove to the royal palace in the city, he noted with
irritation that tanks around the building had their guns pointed
in at the palace, rather than away from it.

After swearing in the dictatorship, Constantine allowed himself to be photographed with the new cabinet – the most valuable
piece of propaganda he gave the colonels. The picture was
flashed around the world as proof that it was the king's men
who had seized power, that the head of state was a willing
participant in the destruction of Greek democracy. Years later,
the king sought to put a different gloss on his decision.

'Look at the picture,' he said on one occasion. 'Look at me.
See how angry I am. The people could see I disapproved and
they knew whose side I was on!'

But there is little disapproval evident in the picture.
Constantine, expressionless, is staring directly at the camera
while many of the others are looking elsewhere, almost all of
them equally expressionless. To the king's left is Spandidakis,
on his far right, Papadopoulos. Behind him is Pattakos and
Zoitakis. On the king's right is Kollias, looking up approvingly
at the young monarch.

Later in the day, the people heard from their new puppet
prime minister. 'We belong to no political party and are

not prepared to favour one political camp at the expense of the other,' Kollias declared on radio. 'Nor do we belong to the economic oligarchy, which we shall not permit to cause poverty. We belong to the class of toiling men and we shall stand beside our impoverished Greek brethren ... We proclaim brotherhood! From this moment there are no rightists, no centrists, no leftists. There are only Greeks who believe in Greece and in a noble, lofty and full ideal of genuine democracy, not democracy of the rabble.'

The new regime was installed by the time Phillips Talbot managed to speak to the king – something he had been trying to do most of the day. When the two finally met in Tatoi, Constantine was in a foul mood, according to what Talbot later told colleagues. The king spoke of the junta as 'a bunch of stupid right-wing bastards'. He asked whether Talbot could arrange for a helicopter invasion of US Marines from the nearby Sixth Fleet. Constantine said that if the Marines were sent to support him and the generals loyal to him, the junta could be crushed. Talbot said he would ask Washington. He returned to the embassy and cabled the State Department immediately. The king believes 'a deep rot has set in', he told Washington.

'The problem as the king sees it would be to restore control and command of the army to the proper general officers, and to reduce the power of the dreadful Nasserite colonels and brigadiers,' said Talbot. He reported that Constantine 'couldn't yet see whether it would be better for him to stay in Greece and fight "these fascists" or whether he should better leave with his family and return with a landing operation from which he could confidently call for the Greek armed forces' support'.

Talbot then mentioned the plea for help. He said the king had asked whether it would be possible to plan for a landing of US Marines should the need arise. 'He was not sure that this was a good idea, but as he envisaged it, the Greek army would readily accept the king's authority backed by the presence of the US Marines. I promised to enquire about this but added it seemed to me just not on the cards,' said Talbot.

Washington's reply was swift and to the point. 'As to the question of a possible landing of US Marines to help him and

the generals to reassert their control over the armed forces,'
said the State Department, 'we would hope that this was more
a rhetorical question than a real one. If the king should return
to this question you should disabuse him of any hope on that
score.' The reply cable added, however, that if 'humanitarian
considerations' justified it, the US would provide a helicopter
to evacuate the royal family. Throughout the day, Talbot looked
to his senior CIA officers for information but Maury and Greene
provided little help. They managed to establish radio links
with various contacts in the Greek military and passed scant
information about the coup leaders to the embassy's political
section.

Sometime after the coup, Talbot sought evidence that the CIA
had been instrumental in staging it. Despite the long association
between the agency and key figures in the junta, he could find
nothing that pointed conclusively to active CIA involvement in
the coup itself. While he believed that members of the junta who
were also members of Greek intelligence would not have acted
without at least the tacit approval of their contacts in the CIA,
the most he could determine was that 'the agency had not been
on top of its job'. He put his own lack of prior knowledge
of the plot partly down to the antipathy that existed between
the diplomatic staff and the CIA and a consequent lack of
communication.

As soon as Talbot knew what sort of regime had seized power,
he urged US Secretary of State Dean Rusk to make a tough
statement denouncing the coup. But Washington wanted to
hedge its bets. There was no immediate official public comment
from the US government and, 24 hours after the coup, Walt
Rostow, the national security adviser to the White House, issued
confidential instructions as to what inquiring journalists should
be told. He said the situation in Greece was 'still uncertain
enough that we don't want to take too positive a public posture
. . . While the facts are emerging, we still have a lot to learn
about the strength of the king and other factions involved. State
[Department] rightly fears that too quick a reaction by us could
precipitate something close to civil war.'

It was to be a full week before Rusk made any public statement about the coup and then only to say that Washington was waiting for some 'concrete evidence' of an early return to democracy. In the meantime, Talbot took unilateral action by ordering two shiploads of US military supplies steaming towards Greece diverted elsewhere. His decision, made on the spur of the moment in the immediate aftermath of the coup, was prompted by visions of the public relations disaster that would occur if the ships docked and disgorged their cargo into the arms of the junta.

Talbot had more immediate problems however. A row erupted in the embassy when he refused Maury permission to make contacts with the junta. CIA staff were not happy.

'These lads had taken over the government so they were *de facto* a government, even though the ambassador refused for the first few days after the coup to let anyone make any contact with the top people in government,' according to a retired CIA officer who was there. 'It was only after we pleaded and begged that he permitted a clandestine meeting with some middle-level types.'

By the time secret contact was made with the junta, it had consolidated its grip on power through a regime of imprisonment and torture, the like of which had not been seen in western Europe since the end of World War II.

PART TWO

Chapter Ten

Democratic Defence

'We have here a sick man, whom we have on the operating table, and if the surgeon does not strap him down for the duration of the operation, there is a possibility instead of the operation giving him the restoration of his health, it may lead to his death.'

George Papadopoulos, 1967 April 27

The security police and junta soldiers were too busy rounding up supposed subversives and 'communists' to notice the gathering that took place in central Athens the day after the coup. They were an unassuming lot, the young academics, sociologists, economists and lawyers who assembled in a house in the fashionable district of Kolonaki early on 22 April 1967. As they made their way to the rendezvous, the eerie, numbed calm of the morning after was broken by the sound of wailing sirens criss-crossing the city, police seizing the innocent and ferrying them away to uncertain futures. But it was the men on their way to the meeting, darting through the narrow streets around Mount Likavitos and Kolonaki, whom the authorities would soon want to capture. They were the core figures of the first organisation formed to resist the coup: Democratic Defence.

Their leader was Vassilis Filias, a swarthy, chain smoking 40-year-old sociologist and political analyst who worked at the Centre for Social Research. Other leading lights included Gerassimos Notaras, a tall 31-year-old ascetic looking political scientist who habitually wore dark glasses; Dionysius Karayiorgas, professor of economics and political studies at Athens University; Costas Simitis, a lawyer and friend of Andreas Papandreou; George Krimpas, a handsome 31-year-old economist who had resigned his post at Athens' Centre for

Economic Planning in protest at the king's overthrow of George Papandreou in 1965; Nicos Constantopoulos, the 25-year-old law student who was president of the Athens University students' union and general secretary of the Centre Union's student organisation; Costas Kalligas, the 39-year-old editorial writer for the conservative *Kathimerini* newspaper; Asteris Stangos, a columnist whose liberal views appealed especially to students; and George Mylonas, Papandreou's former education minister.

It was these men and their associates who were to do more than most over the next few years to irritate and undermine the junta at home and discredit it abroad. At the meeting they decided to form Democratic Defence, dedicating themselves to generating propaganda against the junta and whatever military action against it was possible. It was an ambitious project for a group of people whose careers had hardly trained them for the task they were about to undertake.

Most had come to know each other through a political debating group they formed shortly after George Papandreou was elected prime minister in 1964. It was called the Papanastasiou Club, after Alexander Papanastasiou, a social democrat in the Greek Liberal Party in the 1920s. The club was modelled on Britain's Fabian Society and sought to emulate the political pamphleteers of the eighteenth century. Those who joined represented much of the best and brightest that Greece had to offer in the mid-1960s. It was their hope that by stimulating debate they would push Greece further along the path of democratic reform.

Through open meetings, often in members homes, sometimes in halls or theatres in the centre of Athens, the Papanastasiou Club tried to promote a different approach to politics – away from the sloganising of entrenched positions of the post-war and post-civil war years and towards calm discussion, pluralism and tolerance. A declaration of intent spoke of the ill-effects of one-sided rule, the exploitation of the civil war to stifle opinions and the lack of rational discussion about the direction in which the country ought to be headed. Throughout 1964 and 1965, there flowed a stream of newspaper articles and pamphlets which began to have an impact on the political scene.

Almost all the key members of the club were academics but apart from that, they had one other thing in common: nearly all had received at least part of their education outside Greece. Many had taken further degrees or doctorates in universities in Britain, France, West Germany, Switzerland and the US, and had been exposed to more sober, and liberal politics than they found at home. Filias, the club chairman, had gone to universities in Britain and France, Notaras had studied in Switzerland, Simitis, the club's general secretary, in West Germany, and Krimpas and Karayiorgas in Britain.

On the morning of the coup, Filias was asleep at home in his parents house on the slopes of Likavitos. He was woken at 6 a.m. by his brother who told him what the radio was saying. He leapt from bed, dressed and ran to Simitis' house to tell him to destroy all the club's records. Notaras was in his house near Syntagma Square and was similarly woken in the early hours by a cousin who relayed the grim news. Notaras' first reaction was to call the other club members to alert them, and at 7 a.m. he tried to get a demonstration going but without much success – people were either too shocked or uninterested. It seemed that almost two years of political upheaval since the king sacked Papandreou had exhausted the capacity of ordinary people to react by taking to the streets. Filias and Simitis decided that dedicated activists such as themselves could not stand idly by, however, and they called a meeting to discuss what, if anything, could be done. The meeting was set up in Krimpas' house, available because its owner was trapped in Paris when the coup happened.

About 50 people turned up. Without exception, everyone was opposed to the new regime and agreed that all means, including military action, should be used to get rid of it. Filias, Karayiorgas and Simitis proposed that they form a resistance organisation. The name was devised later by Filias, amused that its initials in Greek, DA, were the same as those of the city council, thus giving Democratic Defence a profile on every litter bin in Athens and all other municiple property stamped with the council's initials!

It was decided that a committee of five, which included Filias, Simitis, Mylonas and, later, Constantopoulos, would run the organisation. Kalligas was given the task of recruiting people and initiating propaganda, especially through his foreign journalist contacts. Filias wanted to build a broad based organisation along the lines of the World War II EAM organisation. They faced more down-to-earth tasks, however.

The first problem was printing. It was critical that any resistance group should produce anti-junta posters and pamphlets to get its message across to people inside Greece and also to tell people outside the country what was going on. Such was their desperation for a printer in this pre-photocopy age, that Notaras even looked into the possibility of making crude letters out of wooden blocks. The problem was solved at least initially by Filias. Inside the Centre for Social Research where he had an office, there was a small Gestetner printing machine that could run off A4-size sheets of paper using a wax stencil. Filias stole the keys to where the machine was kept and material was printed there at night, mainly pamphlets and leaflets for the media. Small handbills denouncing the junta were also run off and stuck hurriedly on hoardings and kiosk walls around the centre of Athens during frantic night-time sorties running the gauntlet of the regime's agents and police. If no posters were available, walls were daubed with paint.

During the summer of 1967, the resistance managed to create its first explosions. Tiny quantities of industrial explosives or detonators obtained from sympathetic Greek servicemen were placed inside litter bins stuffed with anti-junta leaflets. When they went off – activists were careful not to injure innocent passers-by – propaganda was scattered all over the streets. Another tactic was to ridicule the junta. One ingenious method of doing this was devised by members of the left-wing Patriotic Front, founded the day after Democratic Defence by Mikis Theodorakis, the internationally renowed composer and folk-singer, and Rigas Feraios, a group of militant students. It was known as 'the talking fridge'. Electric appliance outlets in Athens were fond of displaying their wares on the pavements outside their shops. A tape recorder would be placed inside a fridge with a small quantity of explosives attached to a timing device. The timer would activate the tape and people nearby would suddenly hear a talking fridge.

'This is your talking fridge. Down with Papadopoulos! Down with the junta! Long live democracy!' messages would proclaim before the explosives went off, scattering leaflets about and infuriating the police but delighting onlookers.

The initial activities of the resistance were little more than pin pricks in the side of the junta but they demonstrated publicly the existence of opposition and the Security Police and military were enraged. All plotters against them were branded communist and hence all resistance activities were part of a communist conspiracy to overthrow the state, their state. The regime issued several edicts regarding personal behaviour, each one revealing more about the men in charge than the problems besetting Greece. Having banned miniskirts and long hair, the colonels went on to outlaw beatniks and foreigners with beards. Beggars were ordered to be rounded up and placed in asylums and street pastry sellers urged to wash their hands regularly. Such philosophy as the regime had was summed up by convoluted statements from spokesmen like the one which proclaimed that under the new order, 'the village will have the entire affection of the government'.

The junta went to great lengths to explain its action, predictably raising Papadopoulos' old bogeyman, the communist conspiracy. The coup leader likened the country to a sick patient, with himself playing the role of doctor. The patient needed some surgery, he was fond of saying, and had to be strapped down for the duration. A junta spokesman explained that the military take-over had been necessary because of allegedly widespread fears of violence erupting when George Papandreou held a rally in Salonika on 23 April, expected to be attended by some 100,000 people, to launch the Centre Union's election campaign. The spokesman claimed that Papandreou was going to call for a people's revolution and claimed it was well known that communists were going to attend the rally.

Not long after the coup, Brigadier Pattakos, whose tank sortie into the centre of Athens propelled him into the job of interior minister, ordered that all school children should attend confession and communion. Despite this apparent interest in the spiritual and intellectual well-being of Greek youth, some 1,046 books were banned. They included Greek classical authors such as Euripides, Sophocles, Aeschylus, Aristotle and Aristophanes; modern-writers such as Jean-Paul Sartre, Thomas Mann, TS Eliot, Albert Camus and Maxim Gorky. Also banned were hundreds of films, including *Zorba The Greek*, and all movies featuring Melina Mercouris, the Greek actress star of *Never on a Sunday*. Anyone caught listening to the music of Mikis Theodorakis, who wrote the theme music for *Zorba*, faced the prospect of a court martial. Theodorakis' crime was that he held left-wing views. Melina Mercouri was lumped in with him.

The junta sought to give its repression a veneer of legality. Unfortunately for their image abroad, they did so by resurrecting laws of censorship enacted during the period of Nazi occupation and which were aimed at combatting 'subversion of society, the monarchy and religion'.

All normal political activity was outlawed, transgressors risking immediate arrest. Parliament was dissolved and the activities of political parties suspended. One organisation, the left-wing EDA Party which had 22 seats in parliament, was outlawed completely. Political youth organisations and any trade unions with leftist leanings were also banned. In June, there was a purge of all university professors whom the junta decided showed 'disloyalty to the prevailing social regime'. Some 2,500 army officers were forced into retirement. They were drawn mainly from ranks that had the most experience but were seen to be less than enthusiastic about the junta. Some were simply victims of score settling. One result of these purges was that Greece's ability to meet its obligations to NATO was weakened. It is ironic that one of the main reasons for the lack of trenchant US condemnation of the junta was a wish not to damage Greece's position in NATO.

In tandem with its repression, the junta made sure to look after its own. In May, a decree raised the salary of the prime minister from $755 a month to $1,500 and that of all other ministers from $720 to $1,330. Cabinet members were also to retain any salary that they had been receiving for other state jobs – such as their positions in the military or judiciary. Papadopoulos, nominally just a minister in Prime Minister Kollias' office, looked after some of his old comrades from their Nazi collaboration days. One was retired General Kourkoulakos, who like Papadopoulos had spent the war years working in the collaborationist Security Battalions which the Germans set up, and who later, under American tutelage, served in KYP. Papadopoulos appointed him governor of the Agricultural Bank of Greece. Another was retired General Patilis, who also served in the Security Battalions. Papadopoulos made him a minister and he later rose to be deputy prime minister.

Within four months of taking office, the tax system was altered to attract foreign investment. Companies with head-quarters outside Greece were granted freedom from all Greek company taxation and their staff members in Greece absolved of the obligation to pay income tax. The state would not require account book audits for foreign companies and there were to be no foreign exchange controls on registered mail. Two-year renewable work permits were introduced and staff with foreign companies were allowed duty-free importation of cars, furniture and personal belongings.

Thus the new tax regime allowed foreigners to operate totally tax free in Greece and export all their profits without any examination by the Greek government. The government promised that all applications for inclusion in the new tax system would be given a yes/no answer within eight days of applying. The penalty for breaking the code – and it is difficult to imagine that anyone would disobey a system that gave them such advantages – was a fine of between just $1,000 and $5,000. American companies such as Ford, National Cash Registers, Union Carbide and Trans World Airlines rushed to take advantage of the opportunity, and the law was quickly extended to embrace Greek shipping merchants like Aristotle Onassis and Stavros Niarchos. Both opened offices in Piraeus, reversing a trend that had seen some eight and a half million of Greece's twelve million tons of shipping register outside the country.

Despite the clampdown and arrest of thousands, Filias and his associates were able to remain active. Democratic Defence cells were established outside Athens and contacts made abroad. In Paris, George Krimpas helped the cause by briefing journalists and lobbying for anti-junta newspaper comment. Shortly after the coup, he moved to London where he did the same. His father in Athens urged him to stay abroad and he installed himself in the Bayswater home of an old flatmate from his days at university in London. He called Greek exiles – George Yannopoulos, a lecturer in economics at Reading University, John Spraos, an academic at University College London, and others – all of whom were to play a crucial role in keeping the issue of the junta alive, if not in the minds of the British public, then at least in the newspapers.

Not long after Krimpas arrived in London, Filias and the others in Athens decided that Asteris Stangos should move permanently there to help co-ordinate Democratic Defence activities from Britain. At about the same time, Spiros Mercouris, brother of Melina Mercouris, the actress, arrived in London to visit his dying father in hospital. Unaware of the activities of Krimpas and Stangos, Mercouris also began writing letters to the newspapers. The others contacted him and asked him to join Democratic Defence. He agreed. Mercouris, a tall, 41-year-old cigar smoking businessman with a silver beard and Omar Sharif good looks, was an ideal recruit. As a youth, he had been a messenger in EAM while his father ran an obscure, anti-German group called RO. Mercouris was known to be a good organiser, clearly understood what resistance was about and, perhaps most useful in public relations terms, could help organise his sister to the cause.

In May, Mercouris rented a flat in Kilburn which quickly became the centre of Democratic Defence activities out of Britain.

Chapter Eleven

Doing the Right Thing

You are guilty of 'conduct prejudicial to good relations
between London and Athens'.
                British embassy official to Martin Packard, 1967

There were fewer people than usual on Kavouri beach just
outside Athens when Costas Kalligas led a young Englishman
onto it one day in late May 1967. Coups are not good for tourism
and most of the people there that day were Greek residents from
nearby suburbs. A few people were swimming. Kalligas pointed
to one in particular, a broad-shouldered muscular man with a
mop of jet black hair.

He told the Englishman to wade out to the man and introduce
himself. He did and the two stood for a while talking, chest
deep in water under a clear blue Greek sky. Vassilis Filias was
cautious and used a false name. He quizzed the man about his
background and his offer: Why should he of all people want to
fight for the cause of democracy in Greece? He, an officer in
the British Royal Navy.

When he first heard of him, Filias had been unsure whether
it was a good idea to meet Lieutenant Commander Martin
Packard, a 35-year-old Malta-based naval intelligence officer,
former peacekeeper with the British Army in Cyprus and holder
of the MBE. But to those who knew Packard, his burgeoning
involvement in Greek affairs came as little surprise.

Packard's connection with Greece went back to 1957 and
to a Greek woman, Kiki Tsatsoulis, whom he met that year
while on leave in the city. They fell in love and eventually
married. In the succeeding years, Packard learnt to speak
Greek, growing to love the country and its people. Kiki's

family had connections with Athens' liberal intelligentsia: her father was a successful businessman whose mentor had been a wartime political colleague of George Papandreou. Through the Tsatsoulis family, Packard had an entrée to some of the best and brightest that Greece had to offer in the early 1960s.

To his naval superiors in Malta, Packard probably appeared to be a model Lieutenant Commander: very much one of their own. His father, Kenneth Gordon Packard (after Gordon of Khartoum), was a Church of England vicar, a vocation he pursued after a successful career as a teacher of classics. He sent his son to the Royal Naval College in Dartmouth at the age of thirteen, straight from an idyllic childhood in rural Sussex. Packard passed through the college with ease and set himself on course for a life in the navy. Professionally he was keen, hard working and innovative. He saw combat in Korea in the first year of the war there. Later he joined the navy's Fleet Air Arm in which he saw front line carrier service before qualifying as an advanced jet flying instructor.

But Packard could also be unconventional in his approach and he had little time for the collective arrogance towards the rest of the world that characterised the attitudes of many in the British military. He had a natural liking of foreigners, their countries and cultures. Whereas the instinct of some of his colleagues was to view those outside England with a certain disdain, Packard felt enriched by cultural and racial differences and plunged into new countries with enthusiasm and vigour. He was naturally gregarious and it was typical of him that in Greece he found himself playing squash regularly with King Constantine. It was through Packard that Constantine came to Malta for the squash tournament with local players and the Royal Navy team.

After his spell of peacekeeping in Cyprus in late 1963 and 1964 (for which he was awarded his MBE), Packard returned to Malta and resumed his job of assistant to the Royal Navy's Fleet Intelligence Officer. It was routine work, shuffling through reams of military reports, diplomatic dispatches and newspaper clippings, and reducing them to succinct, readable assessments of what was said to be going on in the eastern Mediterranean. Being a naval intelligence officer in one of Britain's largest naval bases outside the UK was actually not very exciting, despite the mythology attached to such job titles. Naval intelligence was regarded widely in the service as something of a dead end and Packard's tasks were mundane. He received no specialist intelligence training from any of the British security services, MI5 and MI6, nor did he ever work for them. He was a desk bound bureaucrat with an office inside Lascaris, the admiralty buildings on Valletta's customs house jetty.

A combination of being bored in Malta and wanting the sort of challenge that peacekeeping in Cyprus had given him prompted Packard to seek a career with the United Nations. Packard had run joint British–Greek–Turkish patrols on the island and spent much of his time mediating between the warring Greek and Turkish Cypriot communities. His unconventional approach – he rarely wore full uniform, never carried a gun but was endlessly patient with gunmen on both sides – earned him a reputation with visiting journalists who likened him to Lawrence of Arabia.

When Britain washed its hands of the Cyprus problem and handed it over to the UN in mid-1964, Packard worked with UN personnel and envied the fact that they, unlike he, would be staying on the island trying to finish the job of reconciliation to which he had been dedicated. Friends at the UN encouraged him to try a career as a professional full-time mediator. Packard thought about the idea, liked it and approached the navy. His superiors agreed to sponsor him on a Arabic language course in the well-founded expectation that the Middle East would need trained mediators for some years to come.

On the day of the coup in Athens, Packard was on leave in London, part of the way through his language training and about to go to Beirut. He knew enough about what had been going on in Greece prior to the coup to suspect that the men taking over would want to drag the country into some sort of 1930s–type tyranny. He asked the Navy for further leave, explaining that he was concerned for his in-laws in Greece and wanted to visit Athens. The Navy suggested he use the opportunity to take a Greek language refresher course.

Before he left London, Packard began lobbying and propagandising against the junta. He adopted a false name to protect
his position with the navy (which maintained an absolute ban
on political activity) and fired off letters to the newspapers
denouncing the coup. He urged friends, Britons and Greek
expatriates, to do likewise and contacted journalists he knew
from his time in Cyprus. He tried to convince them that
the coup was an outrageous illegality, deeply oppressive to
the Greek people, that international opprobrium would help
weaken the new regime and that a continuance of the junta
would result in a severe weakening of NATO's eastern flank
rather than the strengthening of it. Packard's own instincts and
his father's connections led him to lobby, particularly through
Liberal Party members of parliament.

The response to his overtures was patchy, several people
saying they would wait to see how events unfolded before
condemning the new regime. Some Greeks who were outside
the country when the take-over happened took the same line. On
one occasion just a few days after the coup, Packard discovered
that a former Centre Union minister, Elias Tsirimokos, was staying at the Cumberland Hotel in central London. Packard went
to see him with a journalist from the *Economist* magazine.

Tsirimokos' credentials were impressive. He had been leader
of the Greek Socialist Party and on the war-time central
committee of the EAM resistance movement. Later he moved
steadily to the Right and eventually joined forces with George
Papandreou in the Centre Union and served as foreign minister
in 1964. After Papandreou was ousted by the king in 1965,
Tsirimokos sided with the pro-Constantine faction in the party
and served briefly as prime minister. He was probably the most
senior MP outside the country when the coup happened and
Packard thought he would be the ideal person to galvanise Greek
opposition abroad.

When Packard and the journalist met him in his hotel room
late one morning, Tsirimokos looked dishevelled. Packard
explained his background and his connections in Athens and
urged him to make a statement against the junta. But Tsirimokos
said he would say nothing until he knew precisely the position

of the king. It was a response that foreshadowed the extent to which many Greeks were willing to give the regime the benefit of the doubt after the chaos of the recent past.

As Tsirimokos gave his reasons for doing nothing, a small protest of Greek students wound its way down Oxford Street amid chants of 'Fascism will not previal', and 'Down with the junta'. Tsirimokos looked out the window as they passed the hotel.

'Idiots,' he said before showing Packard and the journalist out. In Athens with his in-laws, Packard let it be known that he wanted to help. He asked his brother-in-law, Aris, who had been a member of the Papanastasiou Club (dissolved by decree of the junta one month after the coup), whether there was anything he could do. He made little secret of his desire to become involved in any activities against the junta that might be taking place. He told Aris about his letter-writing to newspapers back in London and how he had tried to touch base with politicians and prominent Greek exiles to drum up support for the crushed forces of democracy.

Word of Packard's overture was passed around and the first person to approach him as a result was Agamemnon Koutsogeorgas, Andreas Papandreou's lawyer. Koutsogeorgas said that since Andreas had been arrested and imprisoned, he had been deputised to carry on his opposition to the junta. He asked Packard if he could help set up secure lines of communication to the world outside Greece. Packard said he would help if he could and overnight wrote a draft scheme which he gave to Koutsogeorgas the next day.

It included a system of placing advertisments in newspapers that were available in both Athens and London. All that was necessary was that people in either place monitor the classified columns each day. Simple notices, placed in, say, the births column of the *Daily Telegraph*, could be used to transmit crucial messages. All that was needed was for the sender and receiver of the message to have agreed on certain key words or a style of prose so that the ad could be distinguished from genuine announcements. In this way, people outside Greece could tell those inside of the pick-up details for a person who was to be smuggled out or the details of a covert delivery to Athens. Packard also said that a system allowing for safe telephone conversations could be devised using pre-arranged key words to convey information in such a way as not to alert any eavesdroppers from the Security Police.

Koutsogeorgas promised to get back to Packard within 48 hours but never did, apparently confiding to an associate that the suggestions were too professional for his needs. In the meantime, however, Aris had also mentioned Packard's offer to Vassilis Filias' friend, Costas Kalligas.

Filias took an instant liking to Packard that day on the beach and, while reluctant to involve an outsider in Democratic Defence, his caution was tempered by the knowledge that the organisation was so badly off, in terms of both personnel and equipment, no offer could be rejected out of hand. For half an hour or so, Packard and Filias swapped views – opinions about social philosophy, how the individual should react in the face of tyranny, and right and wrong – and it was clear they held much in common. Packard said he believed strongly in democracy, liberal, social democratic politics and human rights. He explained why he thought the coup had happened and what the forces were behind it. Filias asked how much he was willing to help. Packard said as much as he could within reason.

He offered to establish contacts abroad, saying he knew a number of British Liberal Party politicians and academics, the latter partly because he had a house in Oxford and was acquainted with several of the university's senior academics, including Sir Maurice Bowra, the warden of Wadham College who, as author of *The Greek Experience*, was one of the leading classicists of the day. He said that a number of backbench politicians interested in international affairs had already come out against the coup, as had other people – journalists, lawyers and people in the arts. Packard mentioned that through his time on Malta, he had become friendly with Dom Mintoff, a former prime minister but then leader of the island's opposition party which was campaigning for full independence from Britain.

Packard suggested that all his contacts could be used in an anti-junta propaganda campaign. He offered to liaise with

anyone nominated by Filias and do as much as possible of what
they asked. What he said was music to Filias' ears but he decided
to think on it and do some checking. After their meeting, he
discussed Packard with a number of other leading figures in
Democratic Defence. Some were anxious and a check was made
on Cyprus. Vassos Lyssarides, who was President Makarios'
doctor in 1964 and now a prominent member of the island's
parliament, confirmed that Packard had been a peace-keeper just
before the UN took over. He told of Packard's efforts to bring
the Greek and Turkish communities back together and how he
had negotiated with Makarios and other members on the secret
committee that co-ordinated the activities of the Greek–Cypriot
militia. In Lyssarides' view, Packard had done the right thing
and could be trusted.

Despite this confirmation, some people, notably Gerassimos
Notaras, remained wary of Packard but a compromise was
agreed whereby Filias alone would deal with him direct.
From his side, Packard insisted that he never be given the
real names of any resistance activists and, throughout the life
of the junta, he knew any that he dealt with, including Filias,
by their *nommes des guerre*.

Filias gave Packard an initial, simple task. Could he return
to England, buy a small printing machine like a Gestetner, and
bring it back to Greece? Packard said yes. He flew to London,
bought the printer, dismantled it, packed the bits into a suitcase
and flew back to Athens, passing through customs undetected.
Filias was delighted and, from then on, their relationship grew.

Packard told the Navy that he had retained a tutor in Athens
to help brush up his Greek. He applied for the allowance,
naming Filias and Kalligas as his teachers. Soon, Her Majesty's
government was paying what amounted to a small salary to the
two main leaders of resistance to the junta.

Packard and his wife Kiki spent much of the summer and
early autumn of 1967 in and out of Greece, setting up a route
across Europe – through Germany, Austria and Yugoslavia – so
that propaganda produced by the London cell of the resistance
(the first outside Greece) could be driven to Athens. George
Krimpas and others were involved in producing a resistance

newspaper, *Democratic Defence*, made possible in part by
175,000 drachmas of Filias' savings. Some of the material from
London was delivered to Greece by Kiki, who hurtled across
Europe in a pale blue Triumph Herald sports car with resistance
propaganda stuffed behind the seats and in false compartments.
Each time she arrived in Athens, she was met in woods outside
the city to hand the material over to anonymous activists.

Whenever he was in Athens, Packard became Filias' messenger, delivering letters from him to other resistance activists, all
the time trying to avoid the attention of the authorities. Unlike
senior figures in the organisation, Packard was unknown to
the police as he had no track record of political activity in
Greece. He could move about Athens, resonably secure in the
knowledge that he was not being watched.

Movement was not entirely impossible for leading activists,
however, and, in July, Filias went to Salonika to organise a
cell there. He had been told that a young lawyer, Stellios
Nestor, wanted to become involved. After Filias spoke to him,
it was agreed to form a cell and Nestor recruited leading local
politicians and academics. A young journalist, Lena Doukidou,
who had been a student in Salonika and whom Filias knew, was
recruited to liaise between activists in the two cities. For months
on end, Doukidou delivered resistance leaflets and posters from
Athens and returned with information about repression in
Salonika that formed the basis of reports sent to sympathisers
in Europe for use in the propaganda war against the junta.

Similar cells were organised in most provincial towns, as
well as in universities, and the army and navy. The army
group was poorly organised, however, and its members were
quickly arrested, one of them being severely tortured. Another
cell was set up inside the judiciary. Two key members, George
Kouvelakis and Spiros Plaskovitis, worked for the Council of
State – in effect the country's supreme court.

It was through Kouvelakis and Plaskovitis that the resistance
got one of its earliest and best scoops. Shortly after the junta took
over, it announced that a new constitution would be drawn up
as part of its ambition to recast Greek society in its own image.
Towards the end of the year, sufficient work had been done by

a committee for a draft to be submitted to the judiciary for its views. The two judges got a copy and gave it to Filias who asked Packard if he could think of any way that foreign opposition to the proposed new constitution could be promoted in advance of it being published.

Packard consulted Sir Maurice Bowra, who suggested he try Cedric Thornberry, a lecturer in constitutional law at the London School of Economics. Thornberry was also a legal adviser to the British Labour Party and a sometime correspondent for the *Guardian* newspaper. He had previously come to Packard's attention in August when he and Lord Gifford, a prominent human rights barrister from London, went to Greece to investigate the disappearance of Mikis Theodorakis who had been arrested. Gifford was connected to the League for Democracy in Greece, an organisation that for years had been campaigning for the release of political prisoners held since the end of the civil war.

When Thornberry and Gifford went to Athens in search of Theodorakis, the British embassy helped arrange a meeting with the new Public Order Minister, Totomis, a former employee of the Greek–American businessman Tom Pappas who allowed the CIA to use his Greek companies as a front for some of their activities.

Thornberry and Gifford met Totomis in the office of Interior Minister Pattakos and were presented with denials and little information, although they eventually saw Theodorakis in prison. Pattakos exchanged banter with the pair, denying that anything was wrong in Greece . . . now that the new government was in place. At the end of the meeting, he warned Gifford to look after himself back in London. 'Take care young man,' he said. 'Communists have infiltrated the House of Lords.' (Pattakos' view on this extended to other foreign parliaments. He once proclaimed that the US Congress was over 50 per cent communist.) Thornberry's eventual report in the *Guardian* about Theodorakis was picked up by the BBC Greek Service and broadcast back to Greece – Krimpas and the others in London made sure of that.

Packard took Bowra's advice and contacted Thornberry,

offering, among other things, to help him gather information
on the junta. He said that he might also be able to introduce him
to Greeks in Athens trying to fight the regime. Thornberry was
interested (there were already murmurings about torture) and
he returned to Greece in the autumn. Because of the prevailing
paranoia surrounding both the junta and the resistance, however, he decided to check Packard out with the British embassy –
unknown to Packard. He spoke to Thomas (later Lord) Bridges,
the head of chancery. At the mention of Packard's name, Bridges
became agitated and said a naval officer had no right to be
involving himself in Greek affairs. Such was the ferocity of his
denunciation, it convinced Thornberry that he probably could
trust Packard.

By the time the two men met in Athens, the draft constitution
had been obtained. A party was arranged in a house on Likavitos
as cover for a meeting between Thornberry, Filias and someone
referred to only as 'the judge', George Kouvelakis. When
Thornberry read the draft, it struck him as typical of much of
the gibberish spouted by the colonels. There was no adequate
protection for human rights or political freedom. He filed a
report to the *Guardian* and it too was picked up by the BBC
Greek Service. The following day in his hotel room, anonymous
telephone callers told him that people like him often met with
accidents.

As Thornberry left the country, Packard was summoned
to the embassy and berated for 'conduct prejudical to good
relations between London and Athens'. He was told that if
he wished to remain in Greece, he would have to keep away
from Greeks. Packard said this was hardly possible, as he
was attempting to polish his Greek and, in any event, his
in-laws were all Greek and if some happened to be opposed
to the junta, that was their business. All he had done was
introduce a journalist to some friends. According to Packard,
the embassy official pronounced that the Tsatsoulis family were
communists, a charge Packard knew to be both wrong and
ridiculous.

'Well,' said the official, 'they are anti-monarchists and that's
the same thing.' He said Packard would have to cut himself off.

'I don't care what you have to do. Go and live in a hut in Salonika if necessary.'

Packard ignored the warning and continued to work for Filias. In fact as their relationship and mutual trust grew, the resistance leader became increasingly dependent on the Englishman, the more so after the inevitable arrest of a number of leading activists. Among the first, once the wave of detentions that followed the coup had subsided, was Gerassimos Notaras, who was betrayed when a man whom the resistance believed it could trust turned out to be a police informer.

On 23 October 1967, Security Police bundled Notaras out of his office and away to the Athens Security Police headquarters, the notorious Bouboulinas Street building. For almost six years, he disappeared into a black hole of beatings, electric shock torture, mock executions and solitary confinement as he was moved from one jail to another. A military court sentenced him to eight years for anti-government activities, making propaganda and preparing bombs. Among Notaras' co-accused were fifteen naval petty officers, who had set up a Democratic Defence cell in the navy with his help, and 28 other Democratic Defence activists. The fifteen sailors were singled out for particular attention: all were tortured.

The arrests forced Filias to go underground. He had already arranged with Packard that if anything went badly wrong, a man would come to him with a special message. The man would utter a pre-arranged phrase and Packard was to respond with a pre-arranged answer. The day after Notaras' arrest, the man presented himself to Packard but was so nervous that he blurted out both question and answer. But the message had got through and Packard and his wife went to Filias immediately. He said a change of tactics was necessary, he would have to move out of his parents' home.

Packard and his wife took Filias initially to a new flat they had just moved into. It had the advantage of not having a doorman (who the Security Police could use as a spy), but it did have a front and rear entrance, as well as a roof terrace. It was clear, however, that something more permanent would have to be found and so Packard set about establishing a network of safe houses. He got three, two in the suburb of Klifada and one in the city centre. Under Greek law, landlords had to disclose to the police the identities of all tenants and so Packard used false ones. Filias posed as a visiting Jewish–American author, using the name Leftheris, while Packard posed as his driver, and adopted the name Hank.

One of the Klifada houses became Filias' office, the centre of his resistance activities. From there, he wrote pamphlets, getting friends to type them out and run them off the Gestetner. Some 5,000 were posted to military officers in an effort to undermine army support for the junta. Another 2,000 were sent to intellectuals and academics and about 3,000 to high ranking civil servants and people in key positions in society generally. Packard invented dozens of fake organisations alleged to be opposed to the junta. Whenever a conference took place in Athens, delegates from abroad would be deluged with letters from the mythical groups telling of the horrors of the regime and urging them to lobby their governments when they returned home. The scheme gave the impression that resistance to the junta was far more widespread than it actually was. And because it had the potential to damage the regime's image outside Greece, it particularly annoyed the junta.

In acting as Filias' messenger, Packard had several narrow escapes. On one occasion shortly after Filias went underground, he asked Packard to retrieve his gun, which he had been forced to leave with his brother for safekeeping, thus exposing him to possible arrest. Packard went to the hospital where the man worked as a doctor and met him in a medical examination room. As the gun was about to be handed over, a nurse warned that the police were conducting a search. The doctor told Packard to strip off and get onto an examination table. As he did so, the gun was tucked under his back. Seconds later, the police entered the room and Packard lay there, allegedly a patient but with a revolver sticking into his spine. Luckily, the police made only a rudimentary search.

On another occasion, Packard was dispatched to deliver a parcel of resistance propaganda to a former army general who had joined Democratic Defence. When he called to the man's home, Security Police agents were watching and approached him just as the man's wife opened the door. The woman had the presence of mind to greet Packard with exaggerated effusiveness, telling the police he was a family friend. They went away without examining the parcels.

Towards the end of 1967, Packard was reappointed to Malta after his six-month refresher course in Greek had ended. He was drafted into a NATO exercise about to take place off the island. Despite being formally back in the navy, however, he continued to work for Filias. While on Malta he recruited the first member of what was to become a loose band of helpers, a motley crew of adventurers who appear to have been drawn in by dint of Packard's personality and infectious enthusiasm, and the chance of some excitement.

Simon Morrisey had been in the navy with Packard in the 1950s and early 1960s. He left because, in his own words, he had grown to see his senior officers as 'bloody fools' and life in the navy as far too dull for his liking. Morrisey and his wife bought an old camper van and headed off to Greece where they got involved in the yachting business for a while. They sailed to Malta and, deciding on the spur of the moment that they liked the place, made plans to stay. He rented some property to open a bistro but turned it into an antique shop instead, buying goods in Britain and transporting them to Malta. When Packard was posted back to the island, the pair met and renewed their friendship.

Resistance to the junta in Athens was the only thing Packard could think about and eventually he broached the subject with Morrisey. Would he be willing to help? Sure, why not, said Morrisey, who was completely uninterested in politics. Although he knew there had been a coup in Athens, he had no idea that people were being jailed, beaten and tortured, and the thought never crossed his mind that there was anything that he could do about it. Packard soon changed that.

The London cell of Democratic Defence was trying to get an edition of their newspaper to Athens. Packard said he could help if they got it to him in Malta. In due course, several large parcels arrived, accompanied by a letter from

Asteris Stangos to Andreas Papandreou, who was still in jail in Athens.

A Royal Navy minesweeper based in Malta was about to make a courtesy call to Athens. Naval officers frequently used ships to transport personal belongings and so Packard loaded on board the minesweeper two sealed trunks containing the newspapers. He asked a colleague who was travelling independently to Athens to carry a letter to his wife, into which Packard inserted the letter to Papandreou, which he said would be picked up by a friend in Greece. Morrisey was dispatched to Athens carrying nothing that could draw his attention to the authorities. Everything was in place for a successful delivery.

For some reason which Packard never discovered, however, the officer carrying the letter for his wife gave it to an official from the British embassy. The official opened it and read it, along with the accompanying letter from Stangos to Papandreou. When the official realised what was going on, all hell broke loose among the diplomats. Meanwhile, Morrisey managed to retrieve the newspapers from the minesweeper and deliver them to Democratic Defence. The embassy demanded that Packard be disciplined for blatant involvement in Greek political affairs. Senior officers in Malta placed him under open arrest and arranged for him to be flown to London at the earliest opportunity, pending a possible court martial.

In due course, a three-man board of inquiry at the Admiralty called Packard to account. The presiding officer told him they knew everything he had been up to and asked for an explanation. Packard thought it highly unlikely that they had more than a cursory knowledge of the position. He replied that everything he had done was because he was the man the navy had made him. He said he was a strong believer in parliamentary democracy and that he had acted in response to what he believed to be the legitimate government of Greece. He had been guided by his conscience.

That was all very fine, said the presiding officer, but it was nothing to do with Her Majesty's navy. Either he had to stop what he was doing, now and for all time, or leave the navy. They offered him an easy way out: if he agreed to do nothing for a few months, by which time he would have clocked up sufficient years' service to get a small pension, he could retire quietly.

Packard agreed. As soon as he was out, he cashed in his pension and used the money to set up a clandestine resistance cell working in parallel with Stangos, Mercouris and Krimpas. This time, however, he was to start taking more direct action against the regime in Athens.

Chapter Twelve

Childish Ambitions

'I have decided to take command of the nation.'
King Constantine, 12 December 1967

The military airfield at Kavalla in Greece's northern province of Macedonia was blanketed in snow. A Gulfstream turbo-prop stood at one end of the runway, its propellers churning up the weather even more than the blizzard. In the cockpit, King Constantine looked down the unlit runway, or as much of it as could be seen. In the back of the plane sat a nervous and pregnant Anne-Marie along with her children. Also there was the king's mother, Queen Frederika, and the junta's puppet prime minister, Constantine Kollias. The king, who was co-pilot, urged the pilot to go. What if there is a log on the runway? asked the pilot, who was already worried about being overloaded and unable to achieve sufficient altitude to clear the mountains. We have to try, replied the king. In the event, the small plane made it, followed by a Dakota C47, equally overloaded with numerous suitcases of clothes, the queen's jewels and a retinue of the royal household staff, including Anne-Marie's obstetrician.

The vista that presented itself as the king looked down the runway in the early hours of 14 December 1967 was about as clear and promising as his own future. Soon after the plane was airborne, the pilot asked the king where he wanted to be taken. Constantine didn't know immediately. His mind was filled with thoughts about the botched opportunity he was leaving behind. His counter-coup against the colonels – his one unambiguous gesture towards the junta – had just taken less than 24 hours to collapse.

Constantine's blow against the dictatorship failed because of the appalling lack of organisation on the part of him and his supporters, because of a general distrust of the monarchy and because the one nation whose help would almost certainly have tipped the balance against the junta – the United States – chose instead to do nothing. In truth, the Americans had learnt to live with the colonels within a very few days of them coming to power.

In the immediate aftermath of the coup, the US ambassador, Phillips Talbot, cabled Washington with the suggestion that US policy towards the new government should be 'fairly starchy', according to still-classified State Department documents on the period. Both Washington and the Athens embassy believed, however, that relations should not be ruptured to too severe a degree, as illustrated by the reply to a suggestion from Talbot that embassy staff maintain 'only limited contacts with the government'.

'We agree with your approach up to now of remaining cool and aloof towards the Greek government and we recommend you continue it . . . at the same time keeping your lines of communication open,' the Department advised. In May, the Department, faced with a *fait accompli*, officially sanctioned the US arms embargo which Talbot imposed on 21 April on the spur of the moment. But Washington made clear to Talbot that it saw the embargo as a temporary measure.

'We plan to bring our influence to bear to get the government on the road to democratic processes and one means of leverage *vis-à-vis* the new government is our military assistance programme,' the Department cabled Talbot. 'We are delaying delivery of certain military items to the government of Greece.' The embargo was declared publicly on 16 May, and later that month, Washington's official approach to the junta crystalised further during an exchange with Talbot which showed that the US wanted it both ways.

'We agree that our approach to the new Greek government must be to walk a tightrope and that the problem is essentially how to show people that the US and the king are not attached to the new government while at the same time working with the government of Greece to get Greece back to the constitutional

road ... Our chief effort now must be to create a situation
in which the coup managers will feel compelled by their own
personal interests to give precise assurances and take concrete
actions towards restoration of constitutional government.'

But walking such a tightrope inevitably meant a relationship
of growing acceptance. Whatever Washington might say publicly about the desirability of a return to democracy, Greek
internal affairs were, as one US policy maker put it, 'about
number 32 on the list of Washington's priorities'. In July,
Talbot gave an off-the-record briefing for journalists in which
he attempted to put a gloss on what he insisted was an improving
situation. Normalcy had returned after the pre-coup upheavals
and the initial shock of the take-over, he insisted. No longer
were there riots, industrial stoppages and general chaos. Two
months later, the views of a former State Department official
emerged throwing more light on the real US position.

In a leaked report, Harry Schwartz, later to become a deputy
assistant secretary for international affairs at the Pentagon,
sought to deflect criticism of the US position on the junta
by saying it was purely an internal matter for the Greek
people and government. He equated Washington condemning
the junta with the junta giving advice to the US government on
how it should handle race riots. In an explanation of his views
following the leak, he said: 'We respect the efforts of individual
members of NATO to solve their domestic difficulties just as
they respect our efforts to solve our own internal problems.'

Heavy-handed US police and National Guard reactions to
civil rights protesters were thus placed on a par with the
system of institutionalised state torture in Greece which, by
the autumn of 1967, saw some 40,000 people arrested, brutalised
and detained without trial. What made the conduct of the junta
acceptable to Washington – or at least tolerable – was the crude
logic of the Cold War, the same logic that was applied in the
late 1940s and early 1950s when Britain and the US took sides
in the civil war and subsequently propped up persistently
repressive right-wing governments. In the mid-1960s, when
the anti-communist colonels were governing a NATO ally with
strategic importance for the West, the same logic applied.

The importance of Greece to the US was illustrated dramatically in June 1967 during the Six Day Arab-Israeli War. With Soviet naval vessels patrolling the eastern Mediterranean in a show of support for the Arab side, the US Sixth Fleet facilities in Crete were used to help the Israelis. From a US Air Force base on the island, Israeli bombers mounted raids as the Jewish state launched a series of pre-emptive strikes against Egypt, Jordan and Syria. American families trapped in the Middle East were airlifted to Greece, where they were given an especially warm reception by the junta.

According to John Owens, a State Department Greek desk veteran, the Six Day War changed everything. 'The Arab–Israeli conflict dramatized the importance of Greek land and sea space in the Mediterranean and the need for friendly relations with the Greek government,' Owens explained. 'Particularly with the build-up of Soviet forces in the Mediterranean, a co-operative Greece appeared extremely important to US interests in the area. Thus, while the "cool but correct" policy was to continue for many months, it was inevitably softened by the experience of the Six Day War.'

One tangible benefit for the colonels was an easing of the arms embargo on Greece. It was further relaxed following the Soviet-led invasion of Czechoslovakia in August 1968 and lifted completely in February 1969 as one of the first acts of the presidency of Richard Nixon and his Greek–American vice-president, Spiro Agnew.

Unfortunately for the Americans, while the colonels could be trusted to perform adequately to Washington's bidding on a bilateral basis, they had an uncanny knack of making a mess of US efforts to broker solutions to regional problems involving Athens.

As a consequence of the Six Day War, Washington resolved that the issue of Cyprus, a potential de-stabilising problem between no less than four NATO allies – the US, Britain, Greece and Turkey – should be resolved. At the behest of the Americans, the colonels agreed, in the autumn of 1967, to talks with Turkey, but their lack of diplomatic finesse was apparent when, ahead of the discussions, the junta suggested that its putative ally on the island, Greek–Cypriot president Archbishop Makarios, should resign. Their attitude to Makarios at this time was indicative of a loathing for him that would eventually precipitate their own downfall.

When the two sides eventually met on the Evros River frontier between Thrace and Turkey, Papadopoulos, accompanied by Kollias and Colonel Ladas, among others, offered the Turks a variation of the deal suggested – and rejected – several times in the past: Cypriot union with Greece and protection for the island's Turkish minority, guaranteed by the presence of a Turkish military base. The Turks argued for the idea of double *enosis*, which have also been previously rejected. This would effectively partition the two sides of the island, placing them under the control of their respective mother capitals. Ankara had the backing of the Soviet Union and the stalemate produced by the talks led to the resignation of the junta foreign minister. He was replaced soon afterwards by Panayiotis Pipinelis, the former interim prime minister, royalist and neo-fascist guru of the Greek Right.

On 15 November, General George Grivas, the impatient commander of the Cyprus National Guard, a force comprised largely of Greek mainland forces stationed on the island, launched an assault on Turkish Cypriots. To prevent an escalation into full-scale war, President Johnson dispatched his secretary of the army, Cyrus Vance, to Athens, Ankara and Nicosia, accompanied by the secretary-general of NATO and a representative of the UN secretary-general, U Thant. Faced with high pressure diplomatic arm-twisting and, in the cold light of day, the realisation of inevitable military defeat at the hands of a superior Turkish army that would certainly be drawn into any prolonged conflict, the colonels backed down. Grivas and his mainland forces were withdrawn and efforts to do something about the Cyprus problem went back into cold storage.

With friends like the colonels – useful for their bases and at providing welcoming parties for fleeing American families but dangerously out of control in a volatile region – it is something of a wonder that the Americans did not respond favourably to Constantine's plea for help as he mounted his ill-fated counter-coup.

The king had spent much of the summer of 1967 touring military bases trying to assess the potential level of support for him. But in deciding to move against the junta, Constantine failed to take sufficient account of events since the coup. Almost 700 officers, most of whom would have been loyal to him rather than the government, had been removed from key positions and pensioned off, with junta loyalists promoted in their place. Others who remained and who initially had little love for the junta, were dismayed by Constantine's early acquiescence with the dictatorship. In meeting members of the armed forces as he tried to rehabilitate himself, the king appears to have mistaken a degree of residual affection for him, predictably expressed in his presence, for latent commitment to die for his cause.

As he planned his move, Constantine was dangerously indiscreet. In the middle of October 1967, he telephoned his father-in-law, King Frederick of Denmark, and told him of his plans. He used a palace phone that was tapped by the junta. A few days later, Papadopoulos warned him against any notions of a coup. Constantine sniffily told an inquisitive general that 'the king does not conspire', but by early December, his plans were so well known in Athens that newspapers were reporting the efforts of Papadopoulos to dissuade him! He told Constantine that if he went to Salonika to rouse royalist officers there, he would be crushed. But that, almost exactly, is what Constantine tried to do.

On the evening of 12 December, Phillips Talbot was invited to dinner by a member of the king's staff. He was told that Constantine would be among the guests, his first opportunity to meet the king since the Cyrus Vance mission. When Constantine eventually arrived two hours late, Talbot sensed something was awry. For much of the evening, the king and his wife sat on a sofa holding hands, something he had never before seen them do in public. The king seemed to be tense, with Anne-Marie trying to comfort him. At the end of the evening, Talbot invited the couple back to his residence for drinks. Constantine refused but asked instead that Talbot call to the palace at Tatoi next day.

'Drop by at 8.15,' suggested the king. And then, thinking again, he said, 'No, make it 8.10', as though five minutes made a world of difference.

The following morning at the precisely appointed moment, Talbot's private car drew up outside Tatoi and the ambassador found himself greeted by Constantine dressed in his marshall's uniform. The king looked as though he had not slept all night.

'I have decided to take command of the nation,' he said.

He explained that in ten minutes he would fly north. The army generals were with him, he said. He asked Talbot for US support. He gave the ambassador a tape recorded message, which he wanted played by the Voice of America, and requested that the US Sixth Fleet exercise in a gesture of support. And with that, he was off.

The extent to which the king's plans were known (despite sending his junta-appointed minder off on a wild goose chase while he spoke to Talbot) was evident as soon as the ambassador arrived at the US embassy. Talbot was hardly inside his office when Papadopoulos was on the phone. He refused to take the call but the junta leader called back and demanded to be put through. Papadopoulos was on the offensive the second he got hold of Talbot. He insinuated that the ambassador was in cahoots with the king and demanded to know where Constantine was. Talbot said he didn't know. Papadopoulos then demanded that Talbot come around to his office. Talbot delayed a while but turned up eventually for his dressing down.

'He virtually accused me of conspiring with the king,' Talbot said afterwards. Talbot repeated his insistence that he had no idea where the king was but Papadopoulos didn't believe him and their talk ended on bad terms.

Despite the king's urgency with Talbot, he did not in fact fly north from Tatoi until about 10.15 a.m. Among the entourage apart from his immediate family, Kollias and the obstetrician, were Constantine Dovas, his military adviser, a nurse, two servants and a dog. In Athens, the luckless general given the task of delivering notice of the king's intentions to the chief of staff, General Odysseus Angelis, and who was ordered to take over his job, arrived at the Pentagon and was promptly arrested. Angelis was already well aware of the king's plans and had warned the commander of the army group at Larisa in northern Greece, whose job on behalf of the king was to cut telephone links between there and Athens, not to get involved. The commander cut the link anyway.

At about 11 a.m., the king's plane arrived at Kavalla where he received an encouraging reception from local people. While the royal family installed itself in the Astir hotel and Anne-Marie went shopping for a baby cot, the king went to the local army base to be greeted by the divisional commander who had been asked to join the counter-coup only moments before. By 11.30, Kavalla and Larissa radio stations were broadcasting the king's message but only on low-powered local transmitters. In seeking the backing of the people against the junta, Constantine employed the language of the dictators. He denounced the junta and asked members of the armed forces to rally to his side against 'the communists who are working for the destruction of the nation'.

Talbot, who by this stage was beginning to get reports of the counter-coup attempt, never gave serious consideration to having Constantine's message broadcast by the Voice of America. Events were moving too fast and, besides, he was not anxious for the US to get involved. There was no question at all of the Sixth Fleet doing anything to show support for the king. So Constantine's supposed rallying call went unheard in Athens, the most important place of all.

In Larissa and Kavalla, a number officers loyal to him tried to respond to his call by rallying support. But they were met with indifference or outright opposition and, in some instances, were arrested by subordinates loyal to the junta. The situation at the War Academy in Salonika was indicative of the shambolic level of organisation behind the counter-coup attempt. As soon as the general in charge of the academy heard of the king's arrival in Kavalla, he sent men attending a course out to local units in an effort to drum up support. Most ignored his call. Thus, in Greece's second city, the king's counter-coup was relying on virtual trainees.

The few units in Salonika that did swing behind the king were supposed to be bolstered by the arrival of members of the Third Army, whose headquarters had been moved from Salonika to Komotini in Thrace because of tension with Turkey. But when the brigadier in charge of the 20th Armoured Division, also stationed at Komotini, tried to take over the Third Army and move to support Salonika, he was arrested by junior officers. The army was taken over by Brigadier-General Dimitrios Patilis, the junta minister for northern Greece, with the result that the king's own base at Kavalla, barely an hour away, was under threat.

Swift action by junta loyalists also prevented the air force rallying to the king, despite the fact that the head of the air force was with Constantine from the outset. Junta commanders simply parked their tanks on runways. One plane did manage to take off but only to spill pro-Constantine leaflets on the people of Salonika. A number of naval ships began steaming up the Aegean but their gesture was irrelevant.

In Athens, meanwhile, troops, armoured personnel carriers and tanks loyal to the junta had surrounded the airport, radio station and other key installations in the city. The junta broadcast its determination to press ahead and finish what it called its 'revolution'.

'People of Greece!' said the broadcast, 'A few hours ago, a conspiracy against the state and against the public order was revealed. Common opportunists, motivated by childish ambitions and ignoring the interests of the nation, pressured and deceived the king and urged him to turn against the National Revolution, against the peace and quiet of the people, at this especially historic moment in Greek history.'

At bases all around the city, officers loyal to the king either surrendered at the slightest indication that the junta was prepared to resist or were arrested. Barely half a dozen shots were fired and just one man wounded. At nine o'clock in the evening, the junta announced that the counter-coup has failed and, within half an hour, appointed as regent general George Zoitakis, the defence minister and one of the original junta coup plotters. He took over Constantine's job 'in view of the unjustified absence of the king from the performance of his duties'.

It took Constantine another six hours to accept that the game was up but eventually he did. By 3 a.m., he and his entourage were sitting in their escape planes, the snow swirling about them.

'Which way?' asked the pilot as the mountains of northern Greece sank below them. 'I don't know,' said the king.

He thought for a while. To the east lay Turkey and the Black Sea. Clearly out of the question. To the north, Bulgaria and other Soviet satellites. Equally out of the question.

'Rome,' he said.

They landed with about five minutes' fuel left. Shortly after, Constantine told a visitor to his exile home that he had always tried to do whatever the Americans and the British asked of him. He felt betrayed, he said, that when he turned to them for help, it was not there.

Back in Athens, Papadopoulos took over as prime minister in place of Kollias and also assumed the role of defence minister. Pattakos became deputy prime minister and retained the ministry of the interior. The junta was stronger than ever.

Chapter Thirteen

Mad Dogs and Amateurs

'Mr Lambrou was very particular and kept giving orders
that my face not be touched. But when you are with a
pack of mad dogs, orders are not always efficient.'
Yannis Leloudas, torture victim, June 1969

The failure of King Constantine's counter-coup removed the last
vestige of hope that any of the established interests inside Greece
could unseat the junta. But it also had the effect of galvanising
those disparate individuals in Greece and abroad who had
committed themselves against the regime. Whatever they could
now do, they would do with bravery and determination, and
often in the face of international indifference, save for a few
notable and honourable exceptions.

In England, Martin Packard began to assemble his motley
crew of activists, most of whom remained unknown to the exile
Greek leaders of Democratic Defence. They were attracted by
the force of Packard's personality, his infectious enthusiasm and
the idealism of the age. They included a would-be photographer,
an aspiring journalist, a failed racing driver *cum* motor mechanic
and a host of friends, friends of friends, hangers-on and adventurers. Packard used anyone willing to help. His starting point
was Durham University.

While taking his course in Arabic for the Royal Navy, he had
met a young Anglo–Swede, Kit von Zweigbergk, a 21-year-old
geography student and squash player. Von Zweigbergk became
mesmerised by Packard, who was older and more worldly but
none the less receptive to the sort of ideas that did the rounds
on university campuses in the 1960s. Von Zweigbergk was
instinctively a liberal but had not developed political ideas of
his own. He and other students warmed to Packard who, despite

being senior in age, displayed little cynicism and conveyed a belief that anything could be changed.

In the summer of 1967, von Zweigbergk, Packard, his wife, Kiki, and a friend of theirs went to Greece. There, as the Packards met family friends and others involved in the embryonic resistance, von Zweigbergk listened to intense discussions about the junta and how it could be fought. It was clear from what people said and the atmosphere that pervaded Athens that the junta did not enjoy active popular support. The leaders of the regime reminded him of the sort of people his father had had to contend with when imprisoned in a German prisoner-of-war camp. As far as he was concerned, the situation in Greece was a simple case of right versus wrong. The people he met and liked were all on the side of right and, when he got back to England, von Zweigbergk offered to help Packard in any way he could. The danger of involvement excited him.

It was through von Zweigbergk that two other key activists, Roger Williams and Mike Hudson, were drawn into what fast became a resistance cell run by Packard. At the time, Williams was a 20-year-old south Londoner working for a mining industry magazine. He had been to school with von Zweigbergk and, like him, was essentially liberal in his outlook. When von Zweigbergk contacted him and floated the idea of helping people who were fighting the Greek junta, Williams had no hesitation in signing up. To Williams, the fight was a good liberal cause to which he could give some time, as he had yet to become totally caught up in his career.

Mike Hudson was Williams' flatmate. A former Formula Three racing car driver unable to make the top grade, Hudson had switched to being a car mechanic working occasionally with friends who ran a garage in Oxford. Recruited by Packard, Hudson and his friends began to scour the used car market for cheap vehicles that could make runs to Greece. Large cars, particularly old Humber Super Snipes, were favoured because their voluminous side panels and doors could be turned into secret compartments.

The Packards' home just outside Oxford – a detached house in a leafy suburban road called Arnold's Way – became the

centre for planning runs, communicating with Greece as much
as was possible, and faking all sorts of documents necessary
to move in and out of the country. Passport photographs were
removed and replaced with new ones, home-made fake rubber
stamps providing a hoped-for veneer of authenticity. Written
details did not have to be altered – almost impossible in any
event – because few Greek border guards could read English.
Passports were often obtained from willing friends who would
later inform the authorities that the missing document had been
lost. New ones were generally issued without much ado. Roger
Williams once found a New Zealand passport on a train which
was added to the collection.

    Williams and Kit von Zweigbergk both became couriers for
Packard. Williams' first run to Greece was via Bielefeld in
West Germany. There he collected from a former colleague
of Packard's a car and small printing press donated to the cause
by Karl Anders, a German Social Democratic Party associate of
Willy Brandt, the man who would shortly become Chancellor.
Williams stuffed the car with anti-junta propaganda (much of
it produced in the Oxford University rooms of Professor
George Forrest, a friend of Sir Maurice Bowra) and made
a successful three-day run to Greece where he delivered the
material to a Democratic Defence contact. The car was driven
back to England, fitted with false number plates, and re-used
several times.

    From late 1967 and throughout 1968, Williams made other
trips, usually in Hudson's specially adapted Humbers. He
smuggled into Greece several two-way radio sets, small portable
printing machines and, on one occasion, a gas cannister and
supply of balloons. In Athens, Democratic Defence activists
inflated them, attached anti-junta leaflets and sent balloons
floating off over the city. Like the exploding refrigerators,
they were part of a Democratic Defence resistance-can-be-fun
campaign. On another run, Williams and Packard smuggled
resistance propaganda from Italy. But the material was merely
put into a metal box and when Greek customs looked at it,
Packard said it contained medical literature. The officers didn't
bother to look inside. Hudson's secret compartments lessened

the chances of couriers being caught, the dire consequences of which were gradually becoming more apparent as word filtered out of Greece about what the regime was doing to its opponents.

One of the worst cases of abuse was that of Yannis Leloudas, a 30-year-old archaeologist who was connected to Mikis Theodorakis' Patriotic Front. Within months of the coup, Patriotic Front activists – some of whom also worked with Democratic Defence – had been able to explode bombs in Athens. The result was a determined effort on the part of the Security Police to catch the ringleaders, chief among them Theodorakis.

In the early evening of 21 August 1967, about fifteen policemen raided Leloudas' home in Athens, apparently under the impression that Theodorakis was there. When they realised he wasn't, they took Leloudas instead, hauling him off to a police station via a clearing in some woods just outside the city. In the woods, he was asked about Theodorakis and beaten for five hours. When he declined to co-operate, he was blindfolded and two policemen drew their guns, informing him that he was about to be executed. For several minutes fearing the worst, Leloudas stood in the blackened silence. But instead of blowing his brains out, the officers began beating him again.

'I started receiving blows on my hips, on the thighs, on the calves and generally on all the fleshy parts of my body. They did not hit anywhere where a bone might crack or any permanent damage be done,' Leloudas recalled afterwards.

The beating in the woods continued. The police thrashed his feet, first with his shoes off and then, after his feet had swollen and his shoes had been put back on, they pummeled him further. He was eventually taken to the police station and then to the Security Police headquarters in Bouboulinas Street, torture chamber of the infamous Inspector Basil Lambrou. Leloudas' ordeal – at times at the hands of Lambrou personally – continued without food, water, cigarettes and access to a toilet for one 48-hour period until 4 September, when he was transferred to Averoff Prison. Before that, however, he was subjected to persistent foot beating – *falanga* – and at one stage, pins were pushed under his fingernails. It made no difference that Leloudas' father was a retired navy admiral and that he was also the nephew of Queen Frederika's Master of Ceremonies. If anything, this only whetted the appetite of his torturers.

'In a revolutionary regime, people are killed,' noted one officer. 'We can very well kill you and forget you were here. Your body will be found in a month, two months, three months. Nobody will know who you are . . . You thought that because you are Leloudas' son you would escape this? You thought that because you are the admiral's son you would get off?'

Along with 30 others, Leloudas appeared before an Extraordinary Military Tribunal in Athens where he was convicted in November 1967. The following March, the junta announced a limited amnesty to appease its critics abroad and Leloudas was released.

Early in 1969, resistance activists in Athens decided to try to get Leloudas out of the country so that he could tell his story to a European Commission of Human Rights investigation into allegations that the junta was torturing its opponents. The problem was that Leloudas had been banned from leaving Greece and had neither passport nor driving licence.

Vassilis Filias asked Packard if he could help. By coincidence, Roger Williams was about to make another propaganda run to Athens and he agreed to try to take Leloudas back out with him. When Williams arrived in Athens with his Humber full of concealed leaflets and the latest London-printed edition of the Democratic Defence newspaper, he also had a doctored passport for Leloudas. Once Williams had delivered the propaganda to his contact, he took up residence in one of Packard's two Klifada apartments on the outskirts of the city.

Every evening for the next week, Williams went to a nearby café and waited. Occasionally a man would enter and signal to him. The man would then leave and Williams would follow after a few minutes. Down the road, secure in the knowledge that they had not been followed, the man would report the latest stage in the plans to smuggle Leloudas out of the country. Then, one night out of the blue, Leloudas turned up at the apartment. It was the first time Williams had seen him.

He decided they should leave immediately. There and then, they set off in the dark for the Yugoslav border. Leloudas spoke good English and they chatted at first about the journey and which route they would take. Williams asked Leloudas to tell him about himself. 'I can't,' said Leloudas. Williams said he didn't mean his real life. He didn't want to know about that anyway and was afraid to ask what he had been up to or what the police had done to him. He said he meant his cover story. Leloudas said he would tell anyone who asked that he was a student of Indian culture. He appeared to think of it on the spur of the moment.

Night passed as they headed up the main Athens to Salonika road. Leloudas fell silent, lost in thought. North of Salonika, they came to the main border crossing just beyond the village of Polikastron. At the frontier, the Greek border guards told them both to get out of the car. They examined Leloudas' false British passport and Williams' real one. They asked Leloudas to open his case. Williams was suddenly frightened: he hadn't asked what was inside when he loaded it into the car. But it was only clothes. The guards were slow and ponderous but after a fairly disinterested inspection, they waved them through. By dawn, they were in Skopje.

Williams drove back to England, suffering two punctures on the awful Yugoslav roads along the way. Leloudas stayed with him for part of the journey across Europe but eventually caught a train to Paris. His evidence to the Human Rights investigation was a devastating indictment of what was happening in Greece.

Meanwhile in Britain, the more public operations of Democratic Defence continued, run from Spiros Mercouris' Kilburn flat. From there, Mercouris, Asteris Stangos and George Krimpas produced anti-junta propaganda, either for distribution at demonstrations in London or for Packard and his associates to smuggle into Greece. They also lobbied MPs and others for support and money. Packard did what he could to help but never involved the Kilburn people directly in the clandestine activities he undertook on behalf of Filias and others back in Greece. He never joined in the organisation of protest rallies and fund-raising concerts, but he was instrumental in getting substantial financial support from Hugh Greene, the recently retired director-general of the BBC and brother of the novelist Graham Greene, and from Canon John Collins, the long-standing anti-apartheid activist who was funded largely from Scandinavia. Support came too from leading members of the Liberal Party, including its president, Lord Beaumont of Whitley, and from prominent figures in the entertainment world, including actors Vanessa Redgrave, David Hemmings and James Fox.

Sometime in 1969, Packard introduced Stangos to Dom Mintoff, the Maltese politician whose left-wing views and pro-independence politics had made him into a hate figure for the more Empire-minded elements of the British establishment and media. Mintoff had been prime minister in Malta from 1955 to 1958, when he announced that he was giving up office to lead the Maltese Liberation Movement, with the aim of winning full independence from Britain. In 1964, Britain granted Malta independence within the British Commonwealth, but still retained the Queen of Britain as head of state. It was a step towards full autonomy, but Mintoff wanted more. He achieved his ambitions in 1974 when, as prime minister once again, he saw Malta transformed into a fully independent republic. Packard got to know him while he was stationed there with the Royal Navy in the mid-1960s – attracted as ever to someone trying to buck the system. Packard's career in the navy did not bother Mintoff and they became very close friends.

When Packard became involved with Democratic Defence, Mintoff gave advice about how to go about organising propaganda and winning support. In 1969, when Mintoff came to London, Packard brought him to the Kilburn flat to meet Stangos. Late one night, Mintoff ran through a list of suggestions for running a resistance campaign, based on his own war of attrition with the British, which admittedly went not much further than politics. But Mintoff's contact with Democratic Defence had already produced some more practical help on his part.

Around March 1968, resistance activists inside Greece told Packard that they wanted to smuggle out George Mylonas, a lawyer and former key Centre Union minister in George Papandreou's government. Mylonas had spent time in the Greek foreign ministry and was present in San Francisco at the founding conference of the United Nations. Vassilis Filias saw him as an ideal figure-head leader for Democratic Defence activities in Europe. Mylonas was someone who could stand above the day to day strains of the campaign and who could visit foreign ministries and prime ministerial offices in his own right to make the case for ostracising the colonels from the international stage.

The junta had told Mylonas that he could not leave Greece, and Filias contacted Packard for help. At the time, Packard was on his way to Malta to see some navy friends. While there, he mentioned to Mintoff the problem of obtaining passports. Mintoff opened his desk, pulled out his own and said to Packard, 'Here, take this one, I won't be needing it for the time being.' In due course, Packard drove from London to Athens in a car with false number plates, carrying with him the passport of the leader of the Maltese Liberation Movement. Mintoff's photograph had been switched for one of Mylonas but the written description of the bearer, less easy to alter, had not been changed since 1958 and still maintained that his occupation was that of 'prime minister'.

The idea was to get Mylonas from Athens to a coastal village near the Albanian border and from there, by boat, to Italy. In the event, however, Mylonas' emotional attachment to Greece proved too much. His departure had been fully prepared and Packard himself was to bring him out but, at the last moment, Mylonas told his colleagues that he loved his country too much to leave, especially with so many of his friends in prison. It was a mistake, for within five months Mylonas was himself arrested and sent into internal exile on the small Aegean island of Amorgos. He was not able to escape for over a year and then only with the help of a relative.

In Britain, public opposition to the dictatorship was not left to Stangos and the others alone. Several parallel organisations also sprang up, frequently with overlapping memberships. There was the Greek Committee Against Dictatorship, chaired by

John Spraos, the professor from University College London, and comprised of exiled Greek academics and journalists. It specialised in lobbying the Foreign Office. Another was the North London Committee Against Dictatorship which included a mixture of British sympathisers and Greek exiles, many of whom lived in northern parts of the city dominated by Greek and Greek-Cypriot exiles. It was run by Peter Thompson, a journalist and would-be poet who had lived in Greece for five years in the early 1960s. While the Greek Committee lobbied behind the scenes, the North London Committee specialised in organising public demonstrations against the regime, including a massive rally in Trafalgar Square on the first anniversary of the coup.

Neither committee – nor indeed other individual lobbyists inside and outside parliament – had much success in changing British government policy on the issue of Greece. Even under Labour administrations, it remained a combination of public disdain for the colonels and private 'business as usual'. The Foreign Office apparently wished to do nothing to upset a NATO ally and adopted its well-worn public posture of wanting to keep lines of communication open, no matter how distasteful the regime.

In 1970, Spraos and Thompson came together to form, under the chairmanship of Hugh Greene, the European-Atlantic Action Committee for Greece. Greene had long opposed the junta – to the extent that the colonels were moved to brand him publicly as 'an ageing British communist'. Despite operating out of Thompson's less-than-prestigious offices (his flat above the Golden Girl strip club in Soho), the committee was able to use Greene and other well-known people, already committed to the cause of restoring Greek democracy, to tap into a European and North American network of established liberal voices.

Greene hosted dinners for influential figures like the British politicians Denis Healey, Douglas Jay and Monty Woodhouse. In America, he did the same for senators Ted Kennedy, Edmund Muskie, William Fulbright and Clayborn Pell. In Europe, such eminent figures as Willy Brandt of West Germany, Max van der Stoel of the Netherlands and almost the entire political establishment in Norway, Sweden and Denmark, lent their support.

But whereas Scandinavian governments were unequivocal in their condemnation of the dictatorship, similar support was not forthcoming from London. The British Conservative foreign secretary, Sir Alec Douglas-Home, once told Greene that he was unable to help. 'However much we may regret the abolition of the monarchy,' he wrote in a letter, 'its disappearance is likely to be popular in the army (far and away the most important of the services in Greece) where Republican feeling is strong.'

When the Labour Party came to power in March 1974, Roy Hattersley, a junior foreign officer minister in James Callaghan's government, also refused to commit Britain to supporting Canadian and Norwegian efforts, through NATO, to condemn the regime. However, Callaghan did cancel a four-day Royal Navy courtesy call to Greece by two warships. Callaghan said of his decision: 'There are nations whose internal repression of their citizens we deplore.' In July 1974 when the junta orchestrated a coup against President Makarios in Cyprus, Greene asked Hattersley to allow British troops help restore order on the island. The answer was negative. 'We can't because of Northern Ireland,' he said.

The activists produced several journals in an effort to keep the terror in Greece alive in the public mind. They included two monthly magazines, *Greek Report* and *The Greek Observer*. Both were backed by impressive lists of academics, exiled Greek politicians and sympathisers. The *Observer*, for instance, was edited by George Yannopoulos, of Reading University, and numbered on its editorial board several notable opponents of the junta, including Maurice Bowra of Oxford and Arthur Schlesinger, then Albert Schweitzer Professor of Humanities at the City University of New York and a former adviser to President John Kennedy.

The success of Yannis Leloudas' escape from Greece inspired Packard's team to attempt a bolder plan. Packard came up with the idea of having a yacht in Greece and two seventeen-foot Boston whaler launches that could ferry people out to it. The yacht could sail with impunity around the Aegean or off the

Peloponnese. Would-be escapees could be ferried out to it without arousing suspicion and without having to cross any frontiers on the way to Italy.

Packard's finances could not rise to a yacht but he was able to buy a small fishing vessel, a converted inshore patrol craft. It was called *Authoringa* and was a long, narrow vessel with two 100-horsepower engines which should have made it good for moving at about twenty knots. One of Packard's old colleagues from the navy sailed it to Poole in Dorset but it became apparent that its balance was awful, even in moderate sea conditions. Mike Hudson examined the engines which needed a lot of work. He also tried to make it more stable by putting in two ballast tanks. These, however, only served to make it more unstable and had to be pumped out.

Packard's friend eventually sailed it to the Mediterranean via the French canals and then to Greece. Meanwhile, Packard and Kit von Zweigbergk set off towing the first of the Boston whalers from England to Greece. Travelling through Belgium, it nearly slewed off its trailer into on coming traffic. But they got it to Athens in the end.

Von Zweigbergk rented an apartment in the city and for about six months carried messages between various resistance activists living underground. But the glamour of fighting the junta began to wear off when schemes and ideas for action failed to materialise. People didn't turn up for meetings, packages didn't arrive when they should and there were squabbling factions among the activists. There seemed to be lots of talk and little real action. He was looked after by one of Kiki Packard's friends but found himself spending increasingly lonely nights in tavernas. His involvement also caused him to fall out with his father who disapproved of Packard and his activities. It probably didn't help matters when Kit borrowed his father's car for a run and it was stolen from a back alley in Italy. He eventually accepted a scholarship at the University of the West Indies and left Packard's crew.

The second of the Boston whalers was towed to Greece by Packard and an old navy friend. Things didn't go quite according to plan this time, either. In southern Yugoslavia, not too far from the Greek border, the road was blocked. The only other adequate route was over 100 miles to the rear. However, the map showed a small unapproved road passing through what appeared to be a prohibited military zone. Packard and his friend decided to try it, but shortly found themselves on a collision course with a column of Yugoslav army tanks. With the launch behind them, they hid in thick woods until the army exercise was over, then continued on the short cut.

The Boston whalers survived but *Authoringa* had no such luck. First, she hit rocks at night while coming into Mesolonghi and lost both props. She was refurbished, but not long afterwards she sank in a heavy storm while moored in Kalamata harbour.

She lies there today, a momument to the amateur spirit and evidence of its limitations.

Chapter Fourteen

V8 Resistance

'You could become very paranoid.'

Roger Williams

Continuing repression in Greece showed that the junta was not prepared to tolerate even mild opposition to its rule. In the first two years of the dictatorship scores of opposition activists were rounded up, tortured and convicted after what amounted to show trials. The regime attempted to purge academia and the judiciary and stamp on society its spurious pseudo-ideology harking back to a corrupted vision of classical Greece. Many of those who became victims were people with a long history of political opposition to the sort of things the colonels believed in and practised. Others had merely engaged in the low level opposition carried out initially by organisations like Democratic Defence, helped by their friends abroad.

By 1968, the leaders of Democratic Defence decided it was time to upgrade their activities. Resistance newspapers, anti-junta leaflets and efforts to curry favour with liberal opinion outside Greece were adequate in their own way. But more was needed and, by the end of 1967, Vassilis Filias and others judged that some form of military action, however mild, should be used in an attempt to further unsettle the colonels. They had no illusions that they would be able to topple the regime by a campaign of guerrilla warfare. However, a modest bombing campaign – aimed at symbols of the regime rather than people – would be further evidence that not everyone was prepared to live forever under a dictatorship. Filias, who had been living underground since October 1967 when several key Democratic Defence colleagues were arrested and Martin

Packard had established a network of safe houses, turned again to the Englishman for help.

The graduation from propaganda to bombs posed a moral dilemma for Roger Williams and Mike Hudson. While they were happy to help smuggle literature into Greece and victims of the regime out, it was something else to take explosives across Europe, even in the days before the murderous activities of the IRA and other terror groups like the Red Army Faction sullied the cause of honourable resistance. The liberal conscience had little difficulty with the first phase of Democratic Defence's operations. Direct military action, however, raised commitment to a new level.

Filias assured the British activists that bombs would only be used as token gestures of defiance against government buildings and the property of those who supported the regime – US embassy cars, for example. Murdering people, even junta soldiers, was not the aim of the campaign. This assuaged the angst shared by Williams and Hudson. Ironically, one of the few people seriously hurt by a bomb was Professor Dionysius Karayiorgas, one of the founding members of Democratic Defence, who managed to blow himself up with a home-made bomb smuggled to Greece from Sweden. He barely survived, but, in the ensuing round up, 34 people were arrested, tried by military court and sentenced to lengthy jail terms, many of them after being tortured.

The cell of British activists obtained their first explosive from a part-reformed small time English crook who became known to them from their dealings with the motor trade. The explosives were packed into balsa wood containers (empty cigar boxes were a favourite), to minimise the possibility of shrapnel. The bombs were crude affairs: for detonators, they used gas cooker lighters or the miniature timer alarms motorists kept on their key rings to remind them when their parking meters had run out of money. Mike Hudson used the garage near Oxford to hide the bombs in cars he reconditioned for the journey to Athens. Explosives were hidden beneath the running boards, inside door panels (with the result that windows could not be opened), and in false compartments underneath the mudguards.

Despite satisfying himself about the morality of helping provide bombs to unsettle the junta, taking them down to Greece played on Roger Williams' mind. He wanted to carry the bombs for as little time as possible and so decided to drive non-stop from Calais until he was inside Greece. That meant staying awake for up to 36 hours. To help him, he took large quantities of pep pills. The consequent mixture of a false feeling of mental energy and alertness combined with physical exhaustion had its side effects, however. Once while in Italy, he became convinced that a load of explosives hidden in the spare wheel of his car were about to go off. Overcome by this feeling of paranoia, he stopped, got out of the car and frantically removed the spare, throwing it over the top of a cliff.

The first bombs Williams smuggled into Greece were used in an attempt to sabotage several Olympic Airways planes on the ground at Athens airport. The airline was felt to be a legitimate target because its owner at the time, the powerful shipping magnate Aristotle Onassis, had shown himself more than willing to do business with the junta. At best, Onassis was ambivalent about the regime; at worst, he was a junta supporter. The bombs were planted on the planes but they failed to go off and were discovered by the authorities.

Word of the failure got back to London and when Williams next took a load to Greece and met his handover contact outside Athens, he decided to test one of the bombs by the roadside. He set the timer on short delay and drove off at high speed. Seconds later through his rear view mirror, he saw a huge flame leap into the air accompanied by a great whoosh – more like a powerful incendiary than the sort of bang he expected from a bomb, but at least the devices worked. They were later used successfully in and around Athens by the resistance activists to whom they were ultimately delivered. Some were thrown at the entrances to military barracks, some at the American Express building in the centre of Athens and others still were used to blow up petrol stations owned by the Greek–American businessman Tom Pappas, the entrepreneur who boasted of his links with the CIA and who allowed the agency to use his Greek companies as employment cover for their agents.

The explosions caused little substantial damage but they succeeded in rattling the junta, provoking the colonels to shriek in ever more hysterical terms about communist insurgency. The lack of real impact, however, and the failure of the Olympic Airways bombs provoked the resistance to seek better devices.

Early in 1969, one of Filias' key associates in Democratic Defence, Nicos Constantopoulos, and Yannis Starakis, a colleague who straddled both Democratic Defence and Mikis Theodorakis' more left-wing Patriotic Front, approached a research chemist for help. Spiros Loukas, a 30-year-old member of the Patriotic Front and former member of the banned left-wing EDA party, was working at the time at the Greek Nuclear Research Centre and knew what was needed to create conventional bombs. Loukas had done his military service in the navy and specialised in underwater demolition.

Starakis showed him some of the Williams bombs. He dismantled one and tested the powder – it just fizzed. 'The timing mechanism was very amateurish and the powder hopelessly inadequate. They worked in theory but the materials were not good enough,' he said later. Loukas gave Starakis a shopping list of materials needed if Democratic Defence wanted to create real bombs. It included potassium nitrate, sodium nitrate and magnesium. Starakis took the list to London and gave it to Asteris Stangos who set about finding a supplier so that Packard could take new and better bombs back to Athens.

Among the Greek exiles living in London were Raphael Papadopoulos and Ion Siotis, both nuclear physics researchers at Imperial College and both active on the Greek Committee Against Dictatorship through which they knew Stangos, Spiros Mercouris, George Krimpas and John Spraos. At Stangos' request, they agreed to help make bombs – providing both the materials and the know-how. Both also attempted to obtain support for the resistance from regimes favourable to the cause of guerrilla opposition to oppressive right-wing governments. The idea was to get a sympathetic regime to supply arms and have them shipped to Crete. From there, a major assault would be mounted against the junta.

One such effort by Siotis and Papadopoulos resulted in

a bizarre escapade into the Algerian desert. At Siotis' suggestion, he and Papadopoulos flew to Algeria where Siotis
made contact with a man he had known years earlier as a
student in Switzerland. The man was now part of the ruling
elite in newly-independent and pro-revolutionary Algeria and
told Siotis he would try to arrange what help he could. When
Siotis and Papadopoulos arrived at Algiers airport, an official
delegation whisked them off to a city hotel where they waited
two days before being contacted by a senior representative of
the government. He was Suleyman Hoffman, whose unusual
name was the result of an Algerian mother and German father.
Hoffman was attached to President Boumédienne's office and
was responsible for the government's programme of bankrolling
foreign revolutionary organisations and supplying them with the
hardware of guerrilla warfare.

Siotis and Papadopoulos were ushered into Hoffman's office,
its walls covered with pictures of revolutionary heroes, Che
Guevara chief among them. They told Hoffman what they
needed – the wherewithal to mount and sustain a guerrilla
campaign against the Athens junta. Hoffman listened and told
them he would send them to a Saharan military base where their
needs would be met. Two days later, they were flown to the base
and ended up in a nearby military camp where they spent ten
days in the company of Russians, Czechs and others from the
Communist Bloc who seemed to regard the place as some sort
of holiday resort, passing their time lounging beside a swimming
pool and sunbathing.

Despite repeated requests for information and meetings with
relevant people, Siotis and Papadopoulos were apparently
ignored by local commanders. Eventually, they decided to
leave – escape as they saw it at the time. They walked out of
the camp and caught a desert taxi-bus to Oran and then a train
to Algiers. Siotis' friend in the government apologised, saying
there had been a breakdown in communications. They should
have been met at the camp and helped. It would be sorted out.
But it never was and Siotis and Papadopoulos left the country
soon after, having achieved nothing. Other overtures to foreign
governments for serious military support to fight the junta also

came to nothing. Through their own efforts in London, however, Siotis and Papadopoulos men did have an impact. Their bombs were ferried to Greece directly by Williams or others to whom they were given en route, in Paris, Bonn or Rome.

The activities of Martin Packard's cell in Britain and their associates in France, Germany and Italy were complemented by the efforts of others in the United States. In the year after the coup, about seventeen anti-junta propaganda committees were formed across the US. Their members included US academics, drawn to the cause by their friendship with Andreas Papandreou, and Greek exiles either resident in the US at the time of the take-over or who fled there after the coup. The various groups were co-ordinated in a federation. In 1968, Julius Iosifides, a member of the federation's executive committee was sent to Stockholm to see members of Democratic Defence. There, he met Lena Doukidou, Vassilis Filias' helper from Athens, and soon after became involved in assisting direct military action against the junta.

Iosifides was a Greek-born pathologist in his 30s, a medical graduate of Salonika University who had done post-graduate study in America. He had been thinking of returning to live in Greece and, on the day the colonels took over, found himself in Athens job hunting. Any thought of staying in the country vanished with the military coup and he left almost immediately for the US where he had been on the staff of Jefferson Medical College in Philadelphia. Through Doukidou, he met the leaders of the London cell of Democratic Defence and, through them, Martin Packard.

When Iosifides returned to Philadelphia, he immediately began using what few contacts he had to collect, manufacture and send to Europe explosives and bombs for use against the junta. A women friend had a relationship with a policeman and, through them, Iosifides was able to obtain two cases of riot control tear gas grenades. Inside the garage of another friend, he prised open the bottoms of large cans of V8 vegetable juice. Wrapping the grenades in plastic, he put one inside each can, topping the cans up with juice and re-sealing them with a tool designed for home canning. The cans were then re-cased and

sent to Europe with friends and sympathisers who left them
by arrangement in places like the Milan airport or the Gare
du Nord railway station in Paris. The largest single shipment
of 24 V8 grenade cans was taken to Paris by an American friend
moving to France. The man was so nervous lest the oddity of
carrying a large quantity of V8 juice on a voyage to Europe
arouse the attention of customs officers that throughout the
journey he and his family constantly drank V8 to show how
much they liked it.

Most of the grenades got to Greece (though there was some
anger amongst resistance activists when they realised they were
not bombs as such) but some had to be dumped when handover
contacts failed to show. In one case, a batch was flung into the
Seine when the person to whom they were supposed to be given
didn't appear.

Iosifides' career as supplier to the resistance ended when an
associate, a chemist who worked in plastics, was trying to
concoct a more powerful mixture that could be sent to Greece.
The man demolished his garage in an unscheduled explosion and
only barely succeeded in convincing the authorities that the blast
was the result of legitimate scientific research gone wrong. At the
time, Iosifides had ten V8 grenade cans in his house ready for
shipment. Fearing the authorities were about to raid him after his
colleague's misadventure, he took the cans to the Delaware River
and threw them in. Thereafter, Iosifides confined his activities to
lobbying and anti-junta propagandising on Capitol Hill, though
he did manage to deliver some James Bond-style fountain pen
guns to a resistance contact in Switzerland and, in 1973, his wife
smuggled two-way radios into Greece.

One result of the bombing campaign against the junta was that
Vassilis Filias officially became public enemy No 1 in the eyes of
the Security Police. By mid-1968, police documents described
him as the most dangerous person opposing the revolution and
his photograph was issued to all police patrol cars in and around
Athens. For some seven months, there were sustained efforts
to capture him. Activists unlucky enough to be arrested were
usually tortured in the hope that they would collaborate and
betray him. Few talked and only then after the normal human

capacity to resist had been bludgeoned out of them. In the end, Filias was captured not because of betrayal but through routine police work.

It began with the breaking of the Salonika cell in May 1968 when Stellios Nestor was arrested and tortured. From papers found in Salonika, the police discovered the involvement of Lena Doukidou, the Athens–Salonika courier. Instead of arresting her, the Security Police decided to follow her in the hope of trapping others. In June 1968, she unwittingly led them to Filias.

After Nestor's arrest, Filias was anxious to re-establish operations in Salonika as soon as possible. He asked Costas Kalligas, his minder in the absence of Packard, to arrange a meeting with Doukidou to discuss what could be done. Doukidou had earlier asked to be allowed leave for Italy because she feared her involvement had been compromised. Her fears were brushed aside, however, and on the night of 26 June, the three met in Barba Costas taverna in Piraeus, a favourite haunt for activists. After an initial discussion, they left in one car to meet other senior activists, including George Kouvelakis, the judge who would shortly assume a commanding role in the resistance.

They hadn't got far when three police patrol cars stopped them, two swerving in front, one blocking their rear escape. Filias showed his false French passport and said that he was a painter. But the police just laughed – his identity was too well known. All three were hauled into the Security Police Bouboulinas Street headquarters.

As she sat inside the building waiting her turn with the much feared Inspector Lambrou, Doukidou was in a near panic. In the bag of groceries she was carrying was a message she had been about to send to Democratic Defence in London. But when she was left alone briefly, she took the message, shredded it into tiny pieces and stuffed it into a half-full waste paper basket. When the police returned to interrogate her, Doukidou denied being in the resistance and said only that she was friends with Kalligas and Filias. The police already knew this to be a lie and she was questioned for some fifteen days but not tortured. Other women taken in by the Security Police were not so lucky. Kalligas was similarly uncooperative and was eventually released – after three months in custody – because of lack of evidence.

The Security Police concentrated their efforts on Filias but he was neither tortured nor ill-treated. Possibly his status as public enemy No 1 was a restraining influence. Perhaps the police also held residual esteem for a former member of the elite Hellenic Raiding Force commando unit. In any event, within days of his arrest, the authorities were aware that they were holding a hot potato. In London and other European capitals, Packard and other resistance activists launched an immediate lobbying campaign to get Filias released. Sir Maurice Bowra had him elected a member of Wadham College's common room and was thus able to lobby the British government to pressurise the junta to free a senior member of British academia. The result of all the pressure was that the colonels knew that, at the very least, if anything happened to Filias, there were likely to be serious international reprecussions.

Filias was held in Bouboulinas Street for a total of three months. During initial interrogation, he feigned a mixture of nonchalance and arrogance by telling them not to bother with isolation techniques, as he had been trained in the army to withstand such pressure. They adopted the usual police good guy/bad guy approach which Filias initially resisted. However, after spending about twenty hours in solitary confinement and being deprived of proper food, Filias said to them, 'All right, you've won. I'll tell you everything.'

The problem was what to tell them. The police congratulated each other on having broken the leader of the resistance and complimented Filias on his good sense. Over the following twelve days, Filias dictated a 75-page statement that was a clever mixture of fact and irrelevant information. He was able to concoct a plausible statement because he had been in the unique position that, as de-briefer of several resistance activists questioned by the police and then released, he knew what the police knew . . . and a lot more, which he kept to himself. As he dictated his statement, the police expressed delight, reacting to each piece of information with nodding of heads and smiles of recognition.

He gave them the address of the 'clean' house in Klifada, believing that there was nothing incriminating there for them to find. He learnt later that his housekeeper had guessed that he was not a visiting Jewish–American professor, as he had told her, and had hidden from the police the only incriminating item she found after his arrest – a book containing the names of activists and sympathisers willing to help and whose identities were not known to the authorities. The only thing she did say to the police was that Filias had had a visit from a foreigner, probably an Englishman, who was accompanied by a dark-haired woman, although she did not know their names. When the police told this to Filias, he said that he had been visited by an Australian professor and his Maltese wife. He said that they were abroad doing work for Democratic Defence. The police brought hundreds of pictures of academics to see if he could identify the man but he said he was unable to.

The police never did identify Martin and Kiki Packard but in due course when Filias and over 30 others were tried, among the accused but absent from court was a certain Hank, Packard's *nom de guerre* as Filias' driver. Hank, like the others, was convicted. Filias sowed further confusion among his interrogators by telling them that one of his contacts with anti-junta youth activists was a student at the industrial high school in Piraeus. This was not true but it prompted the police to dig out some 3,000 photographs of students in the hope that he might be able to identify his alleged contact.

After telling the police about one of the Klifada houses, Filias smuggled a message to his brother, Thanos, from inside Bouboulinas Street. A note hidden inside a tube of toothpaste (a present which Filias returned saying he did not like the particular brand) asked Thanos to contact some Democratic Defence associates and get them to clear the second Klifada house of incriminating items and information. The note contained the address of the house (only Packard in London and Filias knew its precise location), and a few days later activists removed two printing machines, explosives sent about ten days before Filias' arrest by two Italy-based academics, and a file of anti-junta propaganda. However, they missed a photocopy machine, bought by Packard in London and hidden in a sofa bed, and some paper with Filias' handwriting.

Despite Filias' efforts, the police found the second Klifada house after the landlord reported what appeared to be a break-in. The police found the photocopy machine. Notes in his handwriting and some clothes which were the same size as Filias'. When the Security Police heard of this, they knew the house must have been used by Filias and questioned him. The discovery of the house as a base for resistance activity presented Filias with a problem: its existence was clear evidence that he had held back important information. He got around it by saying that he had been having an affair with an English woman and had used the house as a secret love nest, unknown to his wife.

The Security Police appeared to accept this explanation but, shortly afterwards, two military police came to Bouboulinas Street to examine Filias' statement. They read it and ridiculed their colleagues, saying that Filias had pulled the wool over their eyes. However, the police had little option but to defend the fruits of their own work: to accept what the MPs were saying would have been to admit that they were fools. Their own pride forced them to stick with Filias' version of the truth.

Despite Filias' lengthy period in the Security Police building and his voluminous statement, not a single person was arrested as a result of his interrogation. Clearly, however, his removal from the scene had serious implications for Democratic Defence.

Chapter Fifteen

Smuggling

'You can always tell the Security Police. They're the ones in khaki socks.'

Takis

A few days after the Security Police arrested Vassilis Filias, George Kouvelakis received a visitor in his office inside the parliament building overlooking Constitution Square. Kouvelakis' double existence – as a senior member of Greece's legal establishment and a resistance activist – was completely unknown to all but a few in the building. Certainly the junta ministers and their minions who worked in adjoining offices in the parliament were unaware of what he was up to, and what he was about to become.

The visitor brought with him a message from Filias' wife. It was addressed to Koumbaros, meaning Godfather, a code name adopted for Kouvelakis because he was godparent to Filias' son. The message gave details of the various Democratic Defence groups and individuals that Filias had been co-ordinating up to the time of his capture. It asked that Kouvelakis assume his mantle as leader of the resistance. Filias proposed setting up new executive committees in Athens and Salonika. In due course, Kouvelakis brought together a group that included himself, Dionysius Karayiorgas, the economics professor at Athens University, and Nicos Constantopoulos, the former student leader. For the next year, until Kouvelakis was forced to leave Greece for Switzerland fearing he was about to be arrested, this group waged an active campaign against the junta.

Shortly after the group was established, Filias got another message to Kouvelakis. It was written on toilet paper and his wife had managed to smuggle it out of his prison cell wrapped in dirty linen. The new message said that Kouvelakis should get in touch with an Englishman called Martin Packard who was living in Britain. The message said that Packard was the only one who knew the location of a number of safe houses and apartments in and around Athens – bolt holes separate to the two in Klifada raided by the Security Police. Packard could be useful and Kouvelakis should use him, said the message. Asteris Stangos and the others in London would know how to contact him.

In the autumn of 1968, when Packard went to Athens for his first rendezvous with the new leader, a man he knew only as 'the judge' met him in the Athens yacht club and looked nothing like a resistance activist. Kouvelakis whom Packard did not remember from their earlier brief encounter with Cedric Thornberry was in his early 30s and had the sort of relaxed, playful and jovial manner that lent itself neither to the popular conception of an eminent jurist nor that of an urban guerrilla leader. But then Packard was hardly the typical former Royal Navy officer. The two got on famously.

Packard had brought with him an edition of the resistance newspaper and about seventeen bombs ferried across Europe and south into Greece through Yugoslavia in a convoy of Mike Hudson's specially adapted cars. The consignment was handed over at a follow-up meeting in a secret Athens flat. In the following months, Kouvelakis and his team used the bombs in an effort to cause mayhem for the junta.

Several were left in litter bins in Esso–Pappas petrol stations, others under cars used by US embassy officials. One was put inside the American Library – with the help of an American-born activist. When those who set the bombs returned to the scene of their activity to inspect the damage, it was clear that not all were entirely successful. Some had clearly gone off and the library suffered an amount of fire damage. But inspections (necessarily casual and brief) of other targets showed no apparent damage. This gave rise to recriminations within the organisation, directed not least at Packard whom some of the more hot-headed activists began to suspect was a traitor in their midst. However at

subsequent trials, it emerged from witnesses that the devices
had in fact gone off. They were simply not powerful enough to
make any significant impact. Spiros Loukas was able to tamper
with the remaining bombs, adding a chemical ingredient to make
them more effective. Kouvelakis planted one such device outside
the Greek national tourist office in Constitution Square timed
to go off at 8 p.m. when it had closed and, he thought, few
people would be around. Having set the bomb, he realised that
the office would in fact still be open at eight. He gave himself
the chilling task of returning, removing the primed device from
a litter bin outside the entrance and disarming it.

Another batch of bombs, this time from Scandinavia, was
used to wreak havoc on a single night in the city. Kouvelakis
and Loukas led a party that targeted three prominent buildings
in Constitution Square – two Greek banks and the American
Express building. After planting several bombs and incendiaries,
the team scattered. Kouvelakis retreated to his Council of State
office on an upper floor of the parliament building. He flung
open the windows for a panoramic view of the square and
watched as the bombs went off one after another at 9 p.m.
One was so powerful that it shook the parliament. Had the
police looked up at that moment, they would have witnessed the
extraordinary sight of an excited and cheering judge surveying
the chaos and damage below him in the square. Amazingly,
no one was killed but when the rush of excitement abated,
Kouvelakis had uncomfortable thoughts about where resistance
ended and terrorism began.

The smashing of the Salonika cell of Democratic Defence
and Filias' subsequent arrest gave rise to fears that Nicos
Leventakis' days of freedom were numbered. Takis, as he was
known to everyone, came from Crete but had been a student at
Salonika polytechnic before the 1967 coup. He was active in the
Centre Union's student organisation and, through it, knew Nicos
Constantopoulos. Immediately after the coup, he returned to
Crete, travelling on a false identity for fear of arrest, and lay low
there for several months. Before the year was out, however, he
was back in Salonika, organising opposition and working with
Stellios Nestor and others in the local Democratic Defence cell.

Takis became sufficiently well known in anti-junta circles to be contacted by some army officers loyal to King Constantine on the eve of the king's counter-coup fiasco and asked to help create diversionary support. On the morning of the king's move, Takis and his associates were able to muster 2,000 to 3,000 anti-junta protesters in Salonika for a demonstration in the square in front of the college. Riot police stood by and took no action but when the counter-coup failed, police searches for Takis intensified and, within days, he moved to Athens. He lived underground in the capital and, through Constantopoulos, played a role in distributing anti-junta propaganda and lobbying foreign journalists.

By late 1968, Kouvelakis feared that it was only a matter of time before Takis was arrested. It was impossible for someone to take such a leading role in two of the country's major cities and not eventually get caught. While Takis never achieved the Public Enemy No 1 status of Filias, the machinery of the police state was sure to get him sooner rather than later. Kouvelakis was advised that he could be useful in western Europe because of his links with international students' organisations and his command of English. He might also be able to help the anti-junta forces abroad trying to collect evidence of torture in Greece for the European Commission of Human Rights. Kouvelakis got word to Packard – now back in London – that someone needed to be smuggled out. Packard agreed to do it.

At the time, Packard had been assembling another run to Greece – this time to bring in more propaganda and a number of bombs and detonators. He had already asked Berit Thornberry, wife of Cedric, if she wanted to come with him. Roger Williams was coming too but only as far as Frankfurt, Germany. There, he would take a train to Italy to pick up a car and take it to Greece separately.

Packard and Williams met Berit Thornberry in London and on the way to Dover called at the home of two sympathisers, a painter and a school teacher, who lent their passports. The original photographs were replaced and the forgery made to look genuine with the help of a fake, homemade passport office rubber stamp.

The journey across western Europe went smoothly, though each time Thornberry began to wind down a window, Packard would shout at her to stop. When she asked why, Packard told her it was better she did not know exactly what was in the car. In fact, explosives had been hidden in the door panels and under the wheel arches.

In Yugoslavia, the bitter winter cold caused the car brakes to freeze near the Croatian city of Zagreb and Packard had to leave the car in a garage for repairs. In order to prevent an unsuspecting mechanic finding some of the bombs, Packard unpacked those near the brakes. The repairs carried out and the journey hastily resumed, disaster almost struck south of Skopje in Macedonia, the last major city before the Greek-Yugoslav border. Packard stopped the car to put the explosives back into their hiding place so they would have a better than even chance of crossing the frontier if border guards searched them. It was pitch dark and a blizzard was blowing. Packard was upside down and half under the back seat replacing detonators when another motorist, assuming him to have mechanical trouble, stopped to offer assistance. Packard scrambled out of his car but lost his shoes as he went. He walked in stocking feet through the snow to the other car to assure the driver that everything was all right. Bemused at a barefoot Englishman standing nonchalantly in the snow in the middle of Yugoslavia, the driver departed in haste leaving Packard scurrying back to his car to complete the task of hiding the bombs.

The border crossing went without a hitch and, two days after arriving in Athens and checking into a hotel as a tourist, Packard delivered his car and its illicit cargo to a resistance contact. He informed Kouvelakis where the other safe houses were and was told where he would meet Takis – at a coffee shop in the city. Packard said that Takis would recognise him because he would carry a particular newspaper. Thornberry laughed at the cliché made real, but Packard chided her. Over twenty people had been arrested in Security Police sweeps looking for Takis and thirteen of them had been tortured, he said.

The next day Thornberry rented a holiday apartment and, at the agreed time, went with Packard to the coffee shop to collect

Takis. He looked like a wild mountain man and had apparently been living rough for some days. He was wearing thick clothes and rugged boots. On the way back to the apartment, their car was stopped three times by police and Thornberry had to nudge Takis to answer yes when they asked if he was English. He certainly didn't look it but the police let them go.

Once safely installed in the flat, new clothes were bought for Takis and for the next week he was schooled in his new identity – a British student returning home from a holiday in Greece. Packard, Roger Williams, who had arrived safely with the escape car from Italy, and Simon Morrisey who came with him, doctored a British passport for Takis. Greek entry stamps had to be inserted in case border guards looked to see when he had entered the country. Chopped-up English language rubber stamps were assembled into a Greek one. The English letter M turned on its side doubled as a Greek sigma. When everything was ready, they set off, Takis saying a last goodbye to a friend bundled out of the car in Omonia Square.

Packard's initial plan was to leave the country on a ferry bound for Italy from Igoumenitsa, a west coast port near the Greek–Albanian border. Customs and passport clearance went without a hitch and they drove onto the ferry. But once on board, an unexpected and heart stopping announcement ordered them to return to their car. Their papers were not in order, an official said. The car was not the one in which they had entered Greece. Packard thought as fast as he could. Yes it was true, he said, their own car had broken down and they had borrowed one from a friend. The official said they would have to obtain the necessary exit papers for the car from Athens.

They drove off the ferry fearing they had aroused suspicion, a fear made worse when Takis said as they disembarked that the Security Police were watching them with more than casual interest. He thought he recognised one, an officer he had known in Salonika and who he was sure knew him. Packard sped off down the road to Ioannina and turned up a side road into the mountains. They stopped at a monastery where one lone monk kept the faith. He obliged them with beds for the night, not knowing, and not asking, whether they were a couple of junta thugs with a woman in tow, resistance activists or lost tourists. Packard and the others said they were tourists. As the sun set, the three of them sat on a terrace in the monastary, drinking local wine and homemade liquor as, far in the distance below them, police cars canvassed the country roads.

Back in Athens the following day, the trio decided not to draw further attention to themselves by trying to sort out the bureaucracy over the car. The car in which Packard had entered the country was now with Williams, having been relieved of its bombs and detonators. They swopped back and Packard, Thornberry and Takis set off again, this time for Patras, a large port in the Peloponnese and one where they were less likely to be noticed.

On the approach to the port, Thornberry powdered Takis' face to lighten his complexion so that he looked more like an Englishman. As they waited in the queue of cars to board the ferry, Takis tried to calm his nerves with brandy. 'You can always tell the Security Police,' he said apropos nothing in particular. 'They always wear khaki socks.' Thornberry noticed it was true as one of the policemen broke away from a group lounging at the entrance to the ferry and followed them on board. Officials examined their papers and passports – Takis', it seemed, with particular care – but no objections were made and the ship sailed for Brindisi in Italy. Throughout the journey, they remained inside a cabin, worrying about the man who had followed them on board.

When the ship docked in Brindisi and they disembarked, the man sidled over to their car and propped himself against it. Looking straight at them and with exaggerated purpose of movement, he took a cigarette, put it in his mouth and lit it, never averting his gaze. Thornberry leant over to him, raised her hand and, with a flick of her wrist, signalled that he had placed the wrong end on his mouth. The man spat it out and stomped back to the ship, his exercise in intimidation deflated.

Chapter Sixteen

The Colonels Brought to Book

'Man's life is a struggle. We must struggle. The struggle
becomes a sacred one when it concerns the presentation
of truth.'

George Papadopoulos, November 1967

Jens Evensen was sitting in his hotel room in Strasbourg working
on papers for the case he would be presenting next morning
to the judges of the European Court of Human Rights. As he
toiled through the night, his concentration was interrupted by
a rustle coming from the direction of the door. He paused to
listen and then turned around to see a slip of paper being poked
under the door.

If you want to know about torture in Greece, said the note,
go to such and such hotel in London and wait. Curious,
Evensen followed his instinct and made the journey on the
date mentioned in the note. In the ensuing months and years
there unfolded before him a catalogue of evidence that the regime
in Athens was run by a bunch of bullying, torturing thugs.

Evensen was an unlikely hero of the international campaign
against the Greek colonels. Born in 1917, he had had a career
in the law that made him quintessentially a member of Norway
and Europe's legal establishment. But he was also outraged when
he learnt of the systematic abuses being inflicted on the people
of Greece by their government, a government which long after
the colonels seized power continued to sit in international
forums alongside law abiding democracies like his own and
the all-powerful but virtually mute United States. Like some
others who dedicated themselves to the cause of restoring Greek
democracy and respect for human rights, Evensen's personal

experience drew him to the conclusion that the colonels were little short of being latter day Nazis.

As a young man in his 20s, Evensen had been involved in the Norwegian resistance to the German occupation. During the war years, he was a junior in an Oslo law firm. The firm also happened to act as a distribution centre for explosives used by the resistance in the greater Oslo area. Evensen's job was to catch the Oslo-to-Lillestrom train once a week, carrying with him a suitcase full of explosives for use in the town, just north of the capital. His instructions were to place the case on the overhead rack of one carriage and to sit in another. That way, if the train was searched and the case discovered, Evensen could plausibly claim that it was nothing to do with him. Each case was delivered in Lillestrom to a contact, usually at the pre-arranged meeting in one of the town's shops. Evensen came through the war without being caught but he was not unaware of the horrors of the Nazi occupation. At the end of the war when the Germans withdrew from Norway, one of his tasks was to release prisoners who had been held in and around Oslo. For the rest of his life, Evensen retained a vivid memory of the conditions in which he found some of his countrymen. One was discovered sitting in a corner, squat like a monkey, with his arm broken and shattered bones sticking through punctured skin. Thumb screws had been applied to the man's testicles.

After the war, Evensen continued his legal career and, by the early 1960s, had risen to be director-general of the Norwegian foreign ministry's legal department. In that position, he was the senior legal adviser to the minister, who in the mid-1960s was John Lyng, a member of the right-of-centre Conservative Party. When Evensen returned from his visit to London, Lyng, who had himself been ill-treated during the Nazi occupation, had no hesitation in authorising him to mount a human rights case against the Greek government on behalf of the Norwegian government.

In their case against the colonels, the Norwegians were joined by the governments of Sweden, Denmark and the Netherlands – the only governments among the western democracies and Greece's international partners to take such action. All were

members of the Council of Europe, all had signed the European
Convention on Human Rights and all, save Sweden, were
members of NATO. The determination of the Scandinavians
and Dutch that Greece should be pursued and made to adhere to
its obligations was not always welcomed by others in the western
alliance. The United States in particular lobbied hard behind
the scenes whenever Norway, Denmark and the Netherlands
sought to have NATO condemn the junta. The American view
remained, despite mounting evidence of repression in Greece,
that Athens was an important ally in the Cold War against
communism. The US perspective gave little comfort to the
victims of torture in Greece.

While in London, Evensen had met Lady Amelia Fleming, one
of the best known of the international campaigners against the
junta. Through Lady Fleming and other key players among the
Greek exile community (many of them members of Democratic
Defence), Evensen had instant access to allegations against the
junta. As he collected stories from Greeks living in France,
Germany, Scandinavia, Britain and Switzerland, the tales of
abuse grew into an impressive volume of evidence which
the colonels were anxious should not be given credibility by
international institutions such as the European Court of Human
Rights, which ruled on breaches of the Convention following
investigation by a Commission of Human Rights. Reports
were sent to the Council of Europe, a pan-European assembly
increasingly over-shadowed by the European Community but
which retained considerable moral authority.

When the four governments made their approach to the
Commission in September 1967, alleging that Greece was in
breach of the Convention by suspending articles of the constitution concerning civil liberties, the Commission decided almost
immediately that the case was admissible and set up a special
committee to investigate. By March 1968, Norway, Sweden and
Denmark laid further charges against the junta – that it was
indulging in systematic torture of political prisoners. The junta
tried to wriggle out of its obligations by submitting a derogation
to the effect that, because of an alleged 'public emergency' in
Greece, it did not have to adhere to the Convention.

In 1968, not long after Evensen began his investigation in earnest, he was warned by the Norwegian police that agents of the junta were making threats against his life, against the life of his wife and of his assistant, Ulf Underland, and his wife. For over two years, until Greece withdrew from the Council of Europe in the face of certain expulsion, Evensen, Underland and their families were given 24-hour police protection. Because he conducted much of his research and analysis of evidence in Paris and Strasbourg, Evensen was also warned by the French police not to stand near windows nor to move about his living quarters at night with the lights on, lest he provide a well illuminated target for an assassin. The French police said their concern about his safety grew from the fact that two high powered, long range rifles with sophisticated sights had been brought into France in Greek diplomatic bags. Evensen asked them to go public, but they declined saying they did not want to create a diplomatic incident.

The threats did not stop Evensen, however, nor his Dutch colleague, Max van der Stoel, who concluded in May 1968 after an initial investigation that the Greek regime was 'still a dictatorship in which the state of siege is continued, the majority of human rights and fundamental freedoms suspended, and considerable restrictions imposed by the government'. Athens accused him and Evensen of being communist stooges.

Key evidence against the junta was provided by George Mangakis, the lawyer who had acted for Gerassimos Notaras, the first senior Democratic Defence activist to be arrested and one of the first Greeks to experience first-hand the Security Police's predilection for torture. Perhaps not surprisingly, as a military court had sentenced him to eight years in prison, the junta refused to allow Notaras give evidence to the Commission's inquiry. As a second best, the Commission summoned Mangakis, but two weeks before he was due to leave Greece for Strasbourg, he was arrested and sent into internal exile in a village in northern Greece.

None the less, Notaras' own claims at his trial – that he was beaten and subjected to electric torture while on board the prison ship *Elli* – caused the Greek military authorities to hold an internal inquiry when his allegations were reported across the world. That inquiry concluded, not surprisingly, that his claims were untrue. But transcripts of the questions put to him and his replies, plus what he said at his trial, were available to the Commission. His assertions were supported by other witnesses who appeared in person, notably the former prime minister, Panayiotis Kanellopoulos, and one of his former ministerial colleagues, Constantine Mitsotakis. The Commission decided that what Notaras claimed was corroborated to some degree and amounted to a prima-facie case against the junta.

The case of Stellios Nestor, serving sixteen and a half years after being beaten senseless by KYP agents and members of the Security Police in Salonika, also stood against the junta. Nestor and George Sipitanos, his Democratic Defence colleague arrested at the same time as him, were able to get a written submission smuggled to the Commission detailing their treatment. Junta lawyers were unable to produce witnesses to counter their allegations and the Commission concluded there were 'strong indications that the statements made by Nestor [and] Sipitanos . . . as to [their] ill-treatment are substantially true'.

Pericles Korovessis, the actor arrested in October 1967 and subsequently subjected to severe beatings, electric shock torture, a mock execution and who was made to lick up his own vomit after a urine soaked rag was stuffed into his mouth, was able to tell the Commission his story in person. In March 1968, Korovessis was one of a number of people freed under an amnesty, after being held for five months without being convicted of anything – even by a military court. He managed to have a statement smuggled out of Greece to the inquiry and, in June 1969, gave evidence in person.

Various junta officials, including Inspector Basil Lambrou who had personally taken part in Korovessis' torture, denied any ill-treatment. Indeed Lambrou said he couldn't even remember interrogating the actor at Bouboulinas Street – a reflection, perhaps, not so much on his memory as on the sheer number of people who had passed through his hands. But other people who saw Korovessis immediately before and after his time spent with Inspector Lambrou and his colleagues testified to his condition. The Commission concluded that Korovessis' allegations were true.

Further strong evidence against the junta was provided by Yannis Leloudas, the man smuggled out of Greece by Roger Williams. The Commission was discreet as to how Leloudas came to give evidence in person in June 1969. 'Although living after his release without a passport or even driving licence, he succeeded in leaving Greece in early 1969,' it said without further explanation in its final report. Williams worked with Evensen in putting Leloudas' case together and the Norwegian was particularly impressed with his wife, Theodora Leloudas, who was able to give a graphic account of hearing her husband's screams. She told him that on one occasion while in custody she tried to kill herself by slashing her wrists, such was her fear that she might say something, anything, that could make his predicament worse.

Evensen had to work hard to coax some witnesses who were understandably worried about the consequences of giving public testimony against their tormentors. One was a young actress, Kitty Arseni, whom Evensen first met in France in the summer of 1968. She had been tortured but feared for her mother and brother, still living in Greece, if she told her story to the Commission. By November, she had changed her mind, however, and at the end of the month appeared in person before the inquiry.

Her story was familiar enough: she was taken by Lambrou and others to a spot outside Athens and beaten. Later in Bouboulinas Street, her feet were beaten, her head was bashed on a bench, lighted matches were placed so close to her eyes that it hurt and officers stood on her stomach. What made her case noteworthy, however, was the flippency of the response to her allegations by Lambrou and one of his officers.

Lambrou declared to the Commission that Arseni was using her professional skills to indulge in fantasy. 'Perhaps this child saw this in the cinema because she is an actress,' he said. Lambrou's colleague, an officer called Evangelos Mallios, quoted the professor of criminology at Athens University whom he claimed had classified her 'in the category of the mentally retarded'.

The Commission thought otherwise. 'Given the consistency of Miss Arseni's evidence, [we] do not consider that her account has been invented or exaggerated and consequently accept her version of the ill-treatment,' it said.

As Evensen continued to amass witnesses and evidence against the junta, more and more people began to come foward. One of the most poignant tales came from Anastasia Tsirka, the 26-year-old wife of an Athens law student, who presented herself to Evensen at his Strasbourg hotel one day in the early summer of 1969. When Evensen saw her, she seemed like a frightened, wounded animal. How could such a person be a threat to any state? he wondered. But to the Athens Security Police, Tsirka was a dangerous subversive.

She was arrested in September 1967 after a police raid on her and her husband's home during which they found a number of anti-junta pamphlets. They also seized a translation of the German philosopher Nietzsche's *Morgenrote*. The title in Greek was *Avghi* – the same as the newspaper of the much hated and banned left-wing EDA Party. The police thought that Nietzsche was an underground activist.

When she arrived at Evensen's hotel, her hair dyed and travelling on a fake British passport, he decided to whisk her immediately to Norway for fear that the French authorities would expel her as an illegal alien. He enlisted the help of a sympathetic French security agent, one of the team guarding him. Evensen feared there would be problems leaving France if border guards examined her passport too closely.

The agent told him to cross the frontier with Germany at a particular point and at a particular time. He said there would be a queue of cars. He advised Evensen to pull out of the queue and speed towards the checkpoint. Because Evensen's car had *corps diplomatique* plates, the border guards were sure to let him through without so much as even a cursory check. The plan worked and once they were across the frontier into Germany, Tsirka began to laugh hysterically with relief. They had similar success leaving Germany for Denmark and once inside the Nordic common travel zone, Evensen drove straight to his home outside Oslo. There, Tsirka told him her story.

She said that after her arrest, she and her husband were taken to Bouboulinas Street. 'Just be truthful,' said her interrogators. 'Tell us your friend's names. We know all about you.'

When Tsirka said she had no idea what they were talking about, one of the officers hit her. Immediately, she took a doctor's certificate from her handbag showing that she was two and a half months pregnant. The officer took her to see Inspector Lambrou who showed her a file of pictures of her taking part in anti-war protest marches. He then began to pull her hair and bang her head on a wall. Shortly afterwards, she was frog marched onto the roof terrrace, the place where Lambrou and his associates conducted the worst of their beatings.

'I am going to have a baby,' she pleaded.

'Who cares about that. It will be another person like you. It is better not to have it,' said one of the men.

'Be careful, please,' she cried.

But it didn't help. The men began beating her feet and when she screamed with pain, they stuffed a rag into her mouth to muffle the sound. After this, she was taken to a washroom where beating continued, peppered with questions about where the pamphlets had come from.

'Tell me a person,' said one of the men. 'Tell me how he looks, tell me his face. Tell me names, names, names, names. Just one name.'

When she still refused to co-operate, they said they would take her back to the roof and throw her off. In fact, she was brought to a lower cell and placed in isolation where she began to haemorrhage. She fell into a groggy sleep and woke in the small hours to find her legs, stomach and face covered in blood.

'I was very, very afraid,' she recalled later, speaking in broken English. 'I thought, I am going to lose my baby. One of them bring me to Alexandras Hospital. As soon as I was in a doctor, I say, "My name is Anastasis Tsirka and I lost my baby and I have been tortured in Bouboulinas." They say, "You take it easy, you are safe now, we are doctors, we are not belonging to Bouboulinas, we take care of you. Do not worry and you may not have lost your baby." They were very kind to me, very.'

But after four days in the hospital – with guards never leaving her – the doctors said the baby was dead and they would have to remove it. Three days later, she was returned to Bouboulinas Street and subjected to more foot-beating. She began bleeding again and did so on and off for a further 40 days. In the middle of November 1967 – two and a half months after her arrest – she was transferred to prison. At her trial in December, the prosecutor described her as a dangerous person and made the remarkable observation that she lost her baby because 'such people should not have babies'. He demanded eight years imprisonment but, in a rare display of pity, the court gave her four. She was freed in April 1968 under an amnesty. As a result of her beatings and profuse bleeding, Anastasia Tsirka suffered so much internal damage that she was unable to have children again.

When Tsirka told her story to the Commission in July 1969, junta lawyers argued that because the Security Police were aware of her and her husband's activities and views, 'there was no practical interest in exercising a psychological or physical pressure on them in order to obtain a confession'. They said nothing in response to her allegations about losing her baby, and the junta's own internal inquiry into her claims did not even question the hospital doctors. The junta's inquiry concluded that her claims were 'vague, evasive [and] without any concrete element'. Given the 'absence of a clear and objectively defined border-line between psychological and physical coercion' her story was nothing but the impression of every detainee that acts of the police aim at such coercion. The Commission thought otherwise. It accepted her account of her treatment and the loss of her baby as 'substantially true'.

After collaborating with Evensen and telling her story to the Commission, Anastasia Tsirka went to live in Sweden. Once the account of her treatment at the hands of the junta had been made public, the notoriety it generated acted as a sort of guarantee for her safety. Before she left Norway, she made embroideries for Evensen and his wife, thanking them for all they had done for her.

Evensen, Max van der Stoel and their colleagues unearthed scores of torture victims, dozens of whom told their stories to the Commission of Human Rights. Two hundred and thirteen cases of torture and ill-treatment were catalogued and 33 torturers named. By far the most allegations were made against Inspector Lambrou and a handful of his immediate associates. The Commission found evidence that five people had died in custody. As the hearings and investigation continued during 1968 and 1969, the junta banned van der Stoel from entering Greece to gather evidence, apparently because he had the temerity to criticise the colonels during an address to the Dutch parliament.

The mounting evidence seemed to matter little to the junta's biggest overseas protector, the US, and other members of the western alliance. In February 1969, President Nixon, then just one month in office, resumed heavy arms shipments, suspended immediately after the coup by Ambassador Phillips Talbot as a mark of US – or rather his personal – displeasure. The grounds for resuming supplies were given by a State Department spokesman, Robert McCloskey. He said there was a need to strengthen NATO following the August 1968 Warsaw Pact invasion of Czechoslovakia. In reality, however, the embargo had been a sham: in the financial year 1967/68, US military supplies to Greece in the immediate aftermath of the coup amounted to some $65 million. De-classified US papers revealed that American officials told a NATO meeting in June 1969 that the US intended 'to resume shipments [to Greece] when there is evidence of satisfactory progress towards a return to constitutional processes in Greece'.

According to a senior US military officer in Greece, selling arms to the junta was 'the best way of making friends'. Notwithstanding the Nixon administration's decision, the US sought to convince its NATO allies that American military dealings with the junta depended on a return to democracy. At the June 1969 NATO meeting, the US told Greece to take further steps to release the estimated 5,000 political prisoners, many of them held in Aegean island detention camps, and to restore basic freedoms of free speech and proper judicial procedures. But the Greek representative attending knew that American arms were already flowing to the junta. There was no need to do anything.

America's view of its relationship with Greece was well explained in 1971 by David Packard, the US deputy defence secretary, when he gave evidence to Congressional hearings on the International Security Assistance Bill. 'I think we have to recognise that Greece is a very important country in the eastern Mediterranean,' he said. 'It is one of the keystones in the southern flank of NATO. And it is a country that has the manpower and has the will to provide for defence in that area ... I am not supporting the attitude of the government but I am simply saying that our military considerations are overriding. Furthermore, I think we have a better chance to influence the government to change if we continue to work with them than if we turn our back on them.'

Thus the Cold War calculation that enemies of the Soviet Union were friends of America – irrespective of whether they adhered to the principles of democracy and freedom the US claimed to be defending – held true under the junta.

In April 1969, two months after the American 'resumption' of heavy arms supplies to the junta, Britain's Labour government under Harold Wilson sold ships, planes and other military equipment to the regime. In May, the UK Atomic Energy Authority announced that a £30 million nuclear reactor it had designed was to be built in Greece under an agreement that gave Britain a long-term contract for supplying spare parts, fuel and training. The US and Britain were not alone in their business-as-usual attitude towards the colonels. A month before America resumed its arms sales, France voted against a Council of Europe resolution declaring that Greece's human rights abuses put it in violation of the conditions for membership.

Despite the American, British and French unwillingness to ostracise the junta, the Council pressed its case. In May, it told the colonels to clean up their act or face expulsion. In the ensuing months, some 450 more people were arrested in Greece and detained on political charges. Over the same period, over 300 anti-junta bombs were set off. KYP agents reported that the resistance campaign of 'terroristic activities conducted by anti-nationalistic organisations are causing an increasing amount of concern. The number of acts of violence, especially bomb detonations, is increasing.'

Towards the end of the year, the official west European response to the Scandinavian and Dutch government's charges against Greece gathered pace. A lengthy report to the Council of Europe by Max van der Stoel accused the regime of continuing to be 'undemocratic, illiberal, authoritarian and repressive'. He called for a final decision on Greece by the end of the year. 'If by then the Greek Government has not voluntarily withdrawn from the Council,' he wrote, 'the decision of the Committee of Ministers could logically only be to suspend Greece's right of representation within the Council until such a date as a democratic parliamentary regime is again functioning in that country.'

In December after the Commission of Human Rights presented its 1,200-page report to the Committee of Ministers, the junta's minister for economic co-ordination, Colonel Nicholas Makarezos, summoned the ambassadors of seven Council members to his office in Athens to tell them of the dire economic consequences for Greece if the rest of Europe isolated the country. But the evidence was too overwhelming. Even Harold Wilson, though prepared to sell arms to the junta, said he was not willing to abstain or vote against Greece's expulsion from the Council.

On 12 December 1969, Greece withdrew from the Council in the face of certain expulsion. Four months later, the Committee of Ministers accepted the report from the Commission of Human Rights. They didn't bother passing it to the Court of Human Rights for judgement: the case against Greece stood. On the same day, the US Senate gave in to pressure from President Nixon and rejected efforts to have restrictions placed on arms sales and other forms of US aid to Greece.

With the advent of the Nixon administration, America's real

relationship with the junta came more into the open. Vice-president Spiro Agnew was the most senior Greek–American to hold elected office in the US and he made little effort to hide his affection for the regime in Athens. He made an early visit to Greece and was fêted by Papadopoulos and other junta ministers.

There have been allegations that Nixon's dealings with the junta may have been exceptionally close. Indeed, according to Elias Demetracopoulos, a Greek journalist and anti-junta lobbyist living in Washington, the Greek intelligence agency, KYP, donated money to the Nixon–Agnew election campaign. Given that KYP was heavily funded by the CIA, such a donation raised the extraordinary possibility that US taxpayers' money was effectively laundered through domestic and foreign intelligence agencies to influence a presidential election.

Demetracopoulos identified the link man as Tom Pappas, the Boston-based Greek–American businessman, friend of the colonels and provider of cover for CIA agents in Greece. Pappas was a long-standing friend of the Republican Party. He had been one of President Eisenhower's senior and most successful fundraisers and his relationship with Nixon went back to the late 1940s. Pappas has been credited in some quarters with having persuaded the Nixon camp to bring Agnew onto the presidential ticket.

Demetracopoulos alleged that between July and October 1968 three separate payments totalling $549,000 were made to the Nixon–Agnew campaign in one-thousand-dollar-bill transfers from a Pappas account in the National Bank of Greece. The payments drew their reward for the junta in September 1968 when Agnew made one of the strongest speeches by any US politician in support of the colonels. He endorsed their regime and characterised those against it as communist fellow travellers.

Demetracopoulos believed that his efforts to interest the Democratic Party in these completely illegal contributions to the Nixon election campaign were what prompted the Watergate break-in that eventually led to Nixon's downfall in August 1974. Agnew was lost to the colonels in October 1973 when he was forced to resign while facing bribery charges. In a plea bargaining deal, he admitted evading tax while governor of Maryland and was fined $10,000 and sentenced to three years' probation.

This Watergate theory originated in a visit Demetracopoulos made in October 1968 to Larry O'Brien, chairman of the Democratic Party. He told O'Brien about the Pappas money and urged the Democrats to use the information against Nixon. It was O'Brien's office in the Watergate building in Washington that Nixon's burglars raided in June 1972 during his re-election campaign, and Demetracopoulos believed they were looking to remove evidence of his allegations, as well as any available dirt Nixon could use against the Democrats.

Pappas emerged in the subsequent Watergate cover-up. He was asked to help fund defence costs and is known to have given Nixon's attorney general, John Mitchell, $50,000. The Watergate tapes disclosed the White House conspirators referring to Pappas at the time as 'the Greek bearing gifts'. Demetracopoulos, a flamboyant and effective lobbyist, paid a high price for his anti-junta activities. The US government tapped his telephone, he was followed regularly, KYP agents tried to kidnap him and, on one occasion, a Nixon official threatened to have him deported.

It was Pappas' relationship with Nixon that prompted Phillips Talbot to resign his post as ambassador to Greece immediately after Nixon came into office in January 1969, rather than wait re-appointment or hand over to his successor. One of Talbot's last gestures of his personal distaste for the junta was to attend George Papandreou's funeral in Athens in November 1968. The old man of Greek social democratic politics had died peacefully after being released from house arrest one year earlier. The junta offered a state funeral but his family declined. Their private burial was attended by some 300,000 people who staged what amounted to the largest anti-junta demonstration ever seen in the capital. Talbot made sure he was there, in the embassy Cadillac with two stars and stripes flags flying ostentatiously on the front of the car. He could easily have stayed away.

The man who took over from Talbot was Henry Tasca, a grocer's son from Brooklyn who, in secret testimony to

the House of Representatives intelligence committee in 1976,
allegedly confirmed Pappas' illegal $549,000 donation to the
Nixon–Agnew campaign. Talbot loathed Pappas and felt that
his boasting – about how he made Agnew vice-president and
of his close ties with the White House – would have made
his job of ambassador impossible. Tasca, on the other hand,
reserved a special venom for Demetracopoulos. He called him
a 'a dangerous and mysterious enemy' and a 'subsidised agent'
– a view shared to this day, but without any evidence, by some
retired CIA agents who claim Demetracopoulos worked for
Yugoslav intelligence. Tasca's gung-ho attitude towards the
junta was illustrated by his advice to Washington regarding
the resumption of military aid. He said simply that it had to be
restored. 'As far as the rest is concerned,' he said referring to the
regime's frightful human rights record and lack of democratic
legitimacy, 'make it look as good as you can.'

With Nixon and Agnew in the White House and Tasca in the
Athens embassy, the resultant sea change in US–junta relations
was mirrored in the CIA. In 1968, Jack Maury was transferred
and his job as station chief in Athens went to James Potts, deputy
head of station from 1960 to 1964. Potts revelled in his role and
took delight in provoking public rows with opponents of the
regime. At social functions, he would verbally abuse those who
questioned the regime. An unfortunate physical disability – his
legs were withered – contributed to his sinister image. He used
two pairs of crutches but was able to move about with great
speed, his lifeless legs flailing as he went. With his crippled
body, he projected a particularly menacing impression as he
hobnobbed with members of the junta.

Although Tasca's regime inside the embassy had more time
for the CIA than did his predecessor's, agents retained their
traditional distaste for the diplomatic corps and its trappings.
They did little to hide their dislike of Tasca's Italian-born wife,
who thought a great deal of herself and harboured pretentions
to nobility. Mrs Tasca's father had been a life-long friend of
Mussolini and after the Duce's Fascist Party came to power in
1924, he rewarded his friends with lucrative utility contracts.
Mrs Tasca's father got the garbage contract for Rome. In

recognition of her background, CIA agents in Greece used to refer to her as the Contessa del Garbagio. Tasca's Greek detractors took delight in his name which, when pronounced with force, sounded remarkably like the local word for human excrement.

The resistance did the best it could under the circumstances of the new, openly cosy relationship between the junta and the Nixon administration and the consequent boost of confidence for the colonels. Andreas Papandreou, who was released under an amnesty on Christmas Eve 1967 and went into exile, inevitably became a figure-head leader for much of the opposition outside the country. He went to Paris and London and eventually settled for a time in Stockholm. While in exile, however, the worst of his character flaws emerged, much to the detriment of others opposed to the junta.

Papandreou was a strong-willed man with a magnetic personality. However, he could only flourish ultimately by surrounding himself with sycophants. In June 1968, he founded his own resistance organisation, PAK – the Pan-Hellenic Liberation Movement – and set about assiduously undermining other anti-junta groups. His favoured tactic was to enter alliances but then work to discredit his supposed colleagues so that anti-junta opposition became synonymous with him personally.

After Democratic Defence made a co-operation agreement with the Patriotic Front in February 1968, efforts were made to establish a similar one with PAK. Lena Doukidou went to Paris with proposals drawn by Vassilis Filias before his arrest. Doukidou, fearing that she was being followed by junta agents, gave the proposals to Julius Iosifides, who happened to be in the city at the time. When Iosifides gave them to Papandreou, the PAK leader said yes, co-operation was not only possible but a good thing. Next morning, however, *Le Monde* reported that Democratic Defence had approached PAK with a view to a merger. True to form, Papandreou had tipped off the newspaper and was trying to ensure that he alone emerged in any alliance as the undisputed leader. The result was that negotiations were broken off and a potentially powerful joining of forces – with Democratic Defence strong inside Greece and

Papandreou, inevitably because of his earlier political career, strong abroad – failed to come into being.

In America, Papandreou took his revenge on Iosifides by undermining the anti-junta federation there to such an extent that it ceased to be effective. In Europe, he attacked Democratic Defence saying that it was a front for foreign intelligence agencies. At one stage, he offered Martin Packard the job of leading a PAK military campaign against the junta. When Packard declined, he accused him of being a spy for British intelligence – a damaging and groundless allegation that dogged Packard for years.

Chapter Seventeen

Likeable, Well Meaning Eccentrics

'You couldn't have people trundling bombs across Europe.'
British Special Branch officer

Roger Williams was in his west London apartment watching television when he heard a rattle at his front door. It was followed by a snap and the soft thud of something flopping onto the floor. He got up, went out of the living room and picked up the small envelope which had neither name nor address on it. Inside were the keys and registration papers of a sports car. Williams opened the front door and peered down the quiet, leafy street lined on either side by prim red brick Victorian houses.

The Porsche was there all right but there was no sign of life. The messenger had vanished. He went out and examined the car to check that all was in order. To his horror he found that the licence plates stood out for a mile: they were a distinctive type, issued only to military personnel serving with the British Army of the Rhine. They showed white numbers on a black background and, like all plates on cars registered to members of Britain's 57,000-strong force in West Germany, they ended with the letter B. The car belonged to Danae Brook, a journalist and former society model, who bought it for £500 several weeks earlier from her brother, a major in the Rhine army recently transferred to the Middle East. Brook had not yet re-registered it in her own name but was persuaded by Martin Packard, whom she had met by chance some years earlier, to lend it to Democratic Defence. The consequences were to prove deeply embarrassing for Brook and her brother.

They came from an Anglo–Irish background steeped in

British military history. Brook's great–grandfather, Admiral
Sir Francis Alton, fought in the Boxer Rebellion in China in
1900. Her grandfather had been a captain and surgeon in the
Royal Navy and her father was in the British army. Her uncle,
Commander Paul Murray-Jones, was the first man to cross the
Atlantic in a submarine. It was as a sort of honour to him that
his niece was given her unusual christian name. On the day she
was born in February 1941, Murray-Jones was aboard the HMS
Danae, a Royal Navy light cruiser named after the mythical
mother of Perseus.

When Brook's career as a model came to an end, she launched
herself as a freelance journalist doing articles for some of
London's fringe magazines as well as the more conventional
Daily Express. In 1967 her name was spotted by the navy's public
relations department who were trying to drum up publicity
for the completion of their latest frigate, a new HMS *Danae*
(Commander Murray-Jones' ship having been sold for scrap in
1948). In September 1967 the new ship was due to set sail amid
a flurry of naval pageantry and Brook, fresh from a summer on
the Greek island of Mykonos, was invited to Plymouth to meet
the crew and write a piece for *Navy News*.

Martin Packard happened to be the officer assigned to show
her around and they soon fell into conversation about Greece.
Brook had developed strong views about the junta as a result
of her sojourn in the Aegean and the two became friends. She
subsequently wrote a number of articles highlighting how the
colonels were surpressing artists, including Mikis Theodorakis
and Melina Mercouri, and told Packard she would like to write
a piece about the people trying to topple the regime.

It was natural therefore that when Packard came to her in
June 1969 and asked if he could borrow her car, Brook did not
hesitate. There was only one condition: Packard had to get one
of his motor mechanic friends to re-spray it purple, the colour
in vogue at the time. Packard agreed. When all the necessary
arrangements had been made, he telephoned her and told her to
leave the car outside her Carlyle Square home, with the driver's
door unlocked and the keys under the seat. The following morning, she looked out her window and the Porsche was gone.

By dawn it was inside Mike Hudson's garage near Oxford. Hudson had been due to use it himself for a run to Greece but was injured in a car crash in Devon. Although he discharged himself from hospital, he was unfit to make the gruelling journey but was able to help by servicing the car and finding space in it to hide six time-bombs and a number of detonators. He removed the carpets and cut a panel out of the heating duct beneath the running board on the driver's side. There was just enough room to slide the explosives, packed into wooden boxes, into the duct. Once done, Hudson delicately spot welded the compartment closed and replaced the carpet. Finally, he turned off the heating system, lest the hot air cause an unfortunate accident *en route* to Greece.

The run to Greece was also to be used to convey to the leadership there various new codes covering military targets. In addition, Williams carried a personal address book which held the contact details of many UK supporters and activists. The Porsche was due to be handed over in Athens but, before that, Williams had to deposit it in an underground car park in Paris where another member of Democratic Defence would pick it up and drive it on to Greece, leaving Williams free to return to London. A bogus advertisment in the *Daily Telegraph* set up a precisely timed rendevous in Athens.

Now, as Williams looked at the car outside his London flat and with everything supposed to be in place, the military plates bothered him. He may have been an amateur but he had enough common sense to know that when smuggling anything, it was best to attract as little attention as possible. British Rhine army plates singled you out as different at the precise moment when all you wanted was to look like everybody else.

At 5 a.m. just before he was due to leave to catch an early morning ferry from Dover to Calais, he phoned Packard seeking a mixture of advice and reassurance. Packard apologised for the cockup. He told him that the false British plates were in the boot and suggested Williams wait until France to do the switch – any further delays and he would miss the ferry. Williams also asked where the explosives had been hidden.

❊   ❊   ❊

In the back garden of his modest south London home, Detective
Chief Inspector Harry Nicholls was enjoying a balmy Saturday
afternoon, when the telephone rang, breaking his tranquillity.
It was the duty man at Scotland Yard.

Arrest in Dover. Some young chap with a pile of explosives.
Serious implications and nobody knows what the hell is going
on. Documents named people all over the place. Boss wants you
to take charge.

Nicholls drove to his office immediately and began making
phone calls. In Dover, Roger Williams had taken up residence
in a cell of the local police station.

It didn't take Nicholls long to find out what had happened.
Williams, like everyone else trying to board the ferry, had driven
up to the passport control barrier. All appeared to be in order, as
far as the immigration officer was concerned. It was the young
Special Branch detective constable and a customs officer who
became suspicious. A combination of the car's military plates
and Williams' unkempt appearance intrigued the policeman:
surely this bloke wasn't a squaddy? Williams' scruffy clothes
and beard were not the hallmarks of a young soldier. The
detective began questioning him: Where was he going? Owner
of the car? Purpose of the trip?

Williams explained that the car had been borrowed from a
friend, Brook, but actually belonged officially to her brother,
a soldier. He said that he was making a short trip to Paris but
when the detective examined his ticket, he found that only the
passenger half was booked for a return journey. The car, it
seemed, was not coming back to England. What was to become
of the vehicle? asked the detective. Besides, said the customs
officer, imported British army cars can be used only by the
person importing them for the first year after they have been
brought into the country.

Williams became flustered, and clammed up. The policeman
told him to pull over to one side and began a detailed examination. He opened a package left in the car by Packard and
intended for his Democratic Defence colleagues in Athens.
Williams had not had time to conceal it and to his horror he saw
that it contained not just coded communications – they at least

would be unintelligible to an outsider – but references to military installations around Greece, various bits of military hardware available in the United States and some names. Williams' limp explanation – that he was merely delivering the case for a friend – was as unconvincing as it was desperate.

The detective summoned his superior who ordered that the car be driven onto a ramp and examined thoroughly, top to bottom. Nothing was found until a customs officer scraped mud off the right-hand side running board and saw fresh weld marks. Resigned, Williams said they had better not use an oxyacetylene torch to open the panel.

There was a morsel of consolation for Harry Nicholls. If his weekend had to be spoilt, at least he didn't have to trudge down to Dover. The bombs had been made safe and Williams locked up in a cell. It was the documents that were most interesting. They identified Takis and made reference to rifles, pistols, underwater charges, dynamite, as well as a host of military and security installations around Greece. Among the officers detailed to question Williams was Inspector Peter Imbert, later to become one of Britain's foremost police experts on terrorism and Commissioner of the Metropolitan Police. Despite Imbert's best efforts, Williams told him little more than what was already apparent from the documents. He never revealed Packard's role and tried to limit the damage by claiming to have packed and loaded the explosives into the car himself.

The documents were taken to London. For Harry Nicholls, they disclosed details of an organisation whose very existence was unknown to the Special Branch man. And the people named – activists and sympathisers – surprised him. They included prominent political figures, senior academics, actors and some moderately well known media figures. Nicholls did the only thing he could: follow the few leads he had.

Nicos Leventakis spent his Saturday sorting out the trip he was about to make to Germany to see Democratic Defence colleagues in Bonn. He went to the travel agency where another activist exile, Andreas Christodoulides, worked, and borrowed his passport before dropping in on Spiros Mercouris and Asteris Stangos in their office. Stangos was planning to make the German trip with him. Takis had everything arranged by late afternoon – including the fake rubber stamp to alter Christodoulides' passport – and so headed out to west London and his bed for the night.

As soon as he opened the door to Roger Williams' flat, he sensed that something was not quite right. You Takis? asked one of the officers who emerged from a room, his search disturbed. Takis was promptly arrested under the Aliens Act and taken to Scotland Yard.

Several more police were pursuing the Danae Brook lead. Around midnight her husband Michael opened their door to the knock of several eager Special Branch men. They rushed past him and dispersed into every room, including the bedroom where his wife, in an advanced stage of pregnancy, was resting. The couple were placed in separate rooms for questioning. The police divulged scant explanation for the raid and it seemed to matter little that Michael was a solicitor, a detail he was not slow in disclosing. The detectives asked them about the car: who owned it and where was it? The couple answered as best they could but were unable to say anything about it from the time it had been taken by Packard. It was not until they saw Monday morning's headlines that they appreciated the full significance of the police visit. 'Detectives Swoop on Car at Port', said the *Daily Mail* front page splash. Brook felt let down. Despite all their talk about the awfulness of the regime in Athens, Packard had not trusted her enough to tell her why he needed the car. She felt used.

By Sunday afternoon, Packard had his own problems. A bunch of policemen were digging up the back garden of his Oxford home. Harry Nicholls, curious to meet the man who appeared to be behind the whole escapade, decided this was one raid in which he would participate personally. As Special Branch officers tore the house apart, Nicholls sat in the living room nursing a whisky while Packard, with characteristic enthusiasm, tried to convince him of the justness of the anti-junta cause. Nicholls concluded that Packard was a likeable, well meaning eccentric. The police found no explosives buried in the garden, nor did they discover anything about how the resistance was organised or went about its more serious business. But they did find several two-way radios which Packard intended to send to Greece plus a large amount of anti-junta propaganda and details of Democratic Defence fund-raising efforts. All the papers were removed by the police but there was no evidence to arrest Packard, who had hidden anything that might have incriminated him.

The homes of several other Greek exiles were raided that weekend and over the following days, sending shock waves through the anti-junta community. Among those questioned were George Krimpas and Spiros Mercouris, neither of whom was intimately familiar with Packard's role, though they knew in general about the various schemes to get explosives to Athens. Nicholls and a colleague called at the Belsize Park home of Krimpas and showed him some of the papers found in the Porsche. His first reaction was that it had been the work of amateurs to have the names of activists in the car alongside brochures about military hardware. Krimpas was taken to Scotland Yard and questioned for a few hours but his lack of information meant he was of little use to the police.

Takis continued to be held in Rochester Row police station where it took Harry Nicholls and his colleagues some days to establish that he was not Andreas Christodoulides. Their prisoner stuck to his *nom de guerre*, Takis Sofianos, and resolved to help his interrogators as little as possible. In fact, he refused to say anything except in the early hours of the mornings. When all was quiet in the police station, he would start banging on his cell door and shouting through the peep-hole that he wanted to co-operate. In would troop questioner and note-taker only to hear Takis launch into a lecture about the exploits of Alexander the Great or some other figure from classical Greek history.

Nicholls regarded Takis as 'a very intriguing little man'; his colleagues on the early shift didn't agree. But however little the Special Branch knew about Takis, it didn't take long to realise that he had friends in high places. Within 24 hours of his arrest, Nicholls was getting telephone calls from prominent Labour Party MPs demanding access to the prisoner and informing him that they were taking the matter up with their political boss, Home Secretary James Callaghan. Packard's network of influential people was proving itself useful. Despite the pressure, it cut little ice with Harry Nicholls, however. Do what you like, he told the callers. I'm just doing my job.

Takis was questioned on and off for over a week before being taken to Pentonville Prison while the government decided what to do with him. Labour MPs Ray Dobson and Peter Archer, plus the Liberal Party president, Lord Beaumont of Whitley, lobbied furiously on his behalf, urging Callaghan not to deport him to Greece. Dobson had just returned from Athens where he had been refused entry to the trial of Vassilis Filias. He wrote to Callaghan saying that if Takis was sent to Athens, he would face immediate arrest, torture and indefinite imprisonment by the junta. 'As you know,' he told the Home Secretary, 'the political situation in Greece is not one that an active socialist can ignore.'

The political lobbying worked. The authorities adopted a sympathetic approach to the jailed student. Takis agreed to leave the country and was released from jail on condition that he stayed with Packard and reported to his local police station every day. Takis spent much of his time in Oxford with Packard and the two would often go fishing on the lake at Blenheim Palace while discussing future strategy. In early August, the Norwegian government granted him permission to enter the country and he flew out of London with an official form giving his false name but little else: spaces for age, religion and nationality were left blank. At the bottom of the form there was a section headed: 'Evidence to support the above.' A single word had been inserted: 'None', it said.

A month after his arrest, Roger Williams stood in the dock at Lewes court in Sussex and pleaded guilty to attempting to export explosives without a licence. In mitigation, he told the court that he was a member of a resistance organisation fighting a military dictatorship in Greece. He had helped people flee the country, he said. He apologised for breaking the law and promised never to do it again. Cedric Thornberry corroborated his story and gave evidence of his good character. He said that Williams, under conditions of considerable danger, had collected evidence of human rights abuses by the colonels. The evidence was being used by lawyers acting for the governments of Norway and the Netherlands which were taking a case against Greece before the European Court of Human Rights. Williams had acted for no financial gain to himself, said Thornberry.

The judge was impressed. He admonished Williams for being willing to drive car laden with explosives onto a passenger ferry. It could have led to the most appalling disaster, he pointed out. But he let him off with a fine of £50. Williams had prepared himself for five years behind bars.

He wasn't the only one surprised by the sentence. Harry Nicholls and his colleagues were incensed. They thought a fine of £50 was ludicrous, an invitation to others to do the same thing. They thought Packard, Williams, Takis and their friends were 'a bunch of ideological dreamers', as one put it. 'It was all very well for them to want to overthrow the colonels but you couldn't have people trundling bombs across Europe. We couldn't give a fuck what they did in Greece. It was how they got the stuff there that bothered us.'

The views of the disappointed Special Branch men were shared by others. Back in June when Williams was caught, the authorities did two things once the implications of the Dover find sank in. First, what little information the Special Branch had was shared with MI5, Britain's internal security service. This was done as a matter of course through the Branch's permanent liaison officer with the service. Secondly, Nicholls sounded out his police colleagues in Europe to find what they knew about Democratic Defence. There was a speedy exchange of information, speedy because there wasn't a great deal to tell: it was apparent that no one knew very much at all. The result of Nicholls' querying was a decision that police in Britain, France, Germany, the Low Countries and Scandinavia would make enquiries to gauge the size of Democratic Defence and what the organisation was up to in their respective countries.

The picture that emerged was fairly accurate. Police across Europe concluded that Democratic Defence had sympathisers and activists all over western Europe, dedicated to propaganda against the Greek colonels and smuggling explosives to Athens.

As one of those involved in the investigation put it: 'There was a growing realisation after Dover of the extent of Democratic Defence. We were surprised. The decision was taken to do all possible to stop their activities in the arms and bombs area outside Greece. Special Branch concluded that at no time did the organisation pose a deliberate threat to the United Kingdom or anyone in it, or any other European countries, except Greece. What they did there was their business. All of us – police and intelligence services – agreed that they had to be stopped moving guns and explosives through our countries.'

This pan-European determination eventually paid dividends and allowed the German police to achieve a second blow against Democratic Defence. Within two years of the Dover incident, several police forces, notably those in Britain, West Germany and Sweden, had amassed a mountain of intelligence about the activities of the organisation and its leading activists. Knowledge was acquired through direct surveillance of individuals and telephone tapping. Andreas Christodoulides was the most senior activist caught and, through the simultaneous arrest of a colleague on the German-Danish border, the police seized a consignment of pistols, ammunition and electronic detonators purchased on the Swedish black market, which the colleague was delivering to Bonn for on-passing to Athens.

Christodoulides was struck during his interrogation at the amount of information the German police already had. As they questioned him, they ruffled through thousands of papers. 'It was clear that there had been a long surveillance operation. They had details of our telephone conversations and knew a lot about the organisation. Despite that, they asked us both a lot of questions and wanted to know more about Andreas Papandreou.'

Christodoulides and his colleague were held for nine months before being tried and were not so fortunate as Roger Williams. A Cologne judge sentenced them to one year's imprisonment but they were released almost immediately because of the length of time they had already spent in custody. Christodoulides was deported and banned from returning to West Germany for - several years.

For his part, Roger Williams kept the promise he made to the Lewes judge and stayed on the right side of the law . . . more or less. About a year after his conviction, he and a few other Democratic Defence propagandists staged a mock bomb run for the benefit of BBC television cameras. Harry Nicholls was on their path once again but there were no charges this time: there were no bombs.

For Packard, the Dover fiasco had serious implications. First, his cover as a Democratic Defence activist had been blown to the police. Second, it renewed MI5 interest in him. The service was already partly aware of his views and interests following his brushes with the British embassy in Athens, incidents which did not escape the notice of MI5's overseas sister organisation, MI6. He had also to face an embarrassing reunion with Danae Brook.

In trying to get to the bottom of the affair, Harry Nicholls followed every line he could think of. There was always the possibility that the registered owner of the Porsche, Major Patrick Brook, might have been the source of the explosives, courtesy of Her Majesty's Armed Forces. Major Brook, recently appointed arms procurement adviser to the Sultan of Oman, was not amused when a military policeman arrived in the Middle East to grill him at length. It was some time before he convinced them that he had nothing to do with Martin Packard, Roger Williams or Democratic Defence.

Such incidents could damage a military career and Major Brook was not at all pleased with his sister. Packard tried to mollify her with £200 for the car (it was sequestered by the authorities and never seen again) and asked to be allowed try and patch things up with her brother. Some months later, Danae telephoned Packard and her brother and arranged for them to meet in a west London pub, The Bunch of Grapes, on Brompton Road. Packard entered the bar and sipped a drink for a few minutes before a man approached.

For about ten minutes they spoke about the resistance, its various activities and what happened at Dover. But Packard sensed something was wrong and cut the conversation short. Apologising for the loss of the car, he left. When he arrived home in Oxford, there was a message from Danae on his answering machine. Sorry, it said, Patrick was unable to keep the appointment. Some other time perhaps?

Someone was keeping an eye on Packard.

Chapter Eighteen

A Home from Home

'There is no place like Greece to offer the facilities that
we have got.'
           US ambassador to Greece, Henry Tasca, January 1972

When Takis arrived in Oslo following his deportation from
Britain in August 1969 he was met by Jens Evensen, the
human rights lawyer, and Arne Treholt, a Norwegian anti-junta
activist. The Norwegian immigration authorities were no wiser
than their British counterparts as to Takis' actual identity. The
papers issued to him by the Norwegian embassy in London
named him as Takis Sophianos, just as the British Home Office
deportation papers did. The Norwegian authorities didn't mind,
partly because Takis had the weight of Evensen behind him. He
chose to go to Norway after Evensen advised him privately how
to go about seeking political refugee status from the Norwegian
government. As soon as he passed through the airport checks,
Takis was taken to Treholt's apartment in Oslo where he lived
for several months.

Treholt, a tall man with typical Norwegian steely blue
eyes, was a 27-year-old reporter with the a newspaper called
Arbietbladat (Labour News). To those anti-junta activists and
members of Democratic Defence who knew him, Treholt
appeared like many of their number: a liberal idealist with
a taste for a bit of adventure in pursuit of a good cause. In fact,
Treholt was a naive romantic whose gullibility would one day
land him in extremely deep trouble. By the time Takis went
to live in his Oslo apartment, Treholt was already well known
to Norwegian intelligence agents who had begun tapping his
home telephone the year before.

Treholt first became interested in Greek affairs when he interviewed Andreas Papandreou in 1966. At that time, Papandreou was the firebrand ex-minister in the government of his father brought down by King Constantine in 1965. After a visit to Athens, Treholt wrote a series of reports about the turmoil in Greece and Andreas Papandreou's predictions that it would all end in a coup. When the coup came, Treholt was one of the few people in Norway who knew anything about contemporary Greek politics. His background articles brought him to the attention of resident exiles who formed, as in so many other west European countries, a committee to co-ordinate anti-junta propaganda. Treholt became committee secretary and the Oslo activists quickly established close contacts with the Swedish committee which sought to give voice to the 20,000 or so Greek migrant workers living in the Stockholm area.

Treholt's first encounter with resistance activists (as opposed to anti-junta propagandists) was in early 1969 when some exiles asked if he could help two activists coming to Norway – Martin Packard and Takis. He said he would and when Packard and Takis arrived, they stayed in his apartment. Treholt helped with introductions to politicians and trade unionists. He used his position as a journalist to arrange meetings with people like the chairman of the Liberal Party, Hans Hammond Rosbach, who was active on the Norwegian committee, Jacob Aano, a MP for the Christian People's Party and Jacob Ona, director of the Labour Party press office. Packard and Takis sought political and financial support and were usually successful. In Scandinavia, unlike most other western countries, establishment politicians, of both Left and Right persuasion, and trade unionists were openly committed to the anti-junta cause.

Packard and Takis were the first people Treholt met who were involved in direct action against the junta and, when they explained to him what Democratic Defence was about, he asked if he could join. 'I was very curious to look a little more into their activities, especially in Greece,' he recalled in an interview some years later.

Before Packard left Oslo, he told Treholt that he would see if he could join one of the delivery runs to Greece. Packard told him that something might happen in the summer and he would get a call from London if it was all right for him to come along.

In June 1969 the call came and Treholt flew to England with his wife, Britt, and stayed at Packard's Oxford home. Packard told him that bombs were being assembled in Paris and that a car from Britain would be used to deliver them to Greece. He told Treholt to go to Calais where he would meet a Democratic Defence courier. The courier would take one of Mike Hudson's bomb laden Humbers across Europe to Athens. The idea excited Treholt. 'It was crazy but I was very young.'

Treholt did as instructed and the trio set off through Germany and down into Yugoslavia. Treholt made his way separately from Skopje to Salonika by train, leaving his wife and the driver to cross the Yugoslav–Greek frontier posing as husband and wife. He was afraid that his profile as an anti-junta propagandist in Norway might have been known to the guards and compromise the mission. It hardly mattered because, although everyone got to Athens, the delivery failed when their contact, a young student, did not know to whom he was supposed to give the bombs. The problem was resolved when the three drove to a remote spot on the Athens to Corinth road, dug a hole and buried the devices, leaving the student to worry about getting them eventually to the rightful recipients.

By the time Takis took up residence in Treholt's Oslo apartment in late 1969, the Norwegian appeared to have established his credentials as far as the resistance was concerned. But living with Treholt was quite another thing and Takis quickly became worried about him.

There was a constant stream of Soviet embassy officials visiting the apartment and Treholt seemed to lead a life beyond the means of a not very prominent journalist on a Labour newspaper. During long evening discussions when Takis was present, the embassy officials sought Treholt's opinion on this and that world situation and what he thought the Norwegian government's position was. At times, they seemed to pander to Treholt's ego by asking him to write papers detailing his thoughts. Takis felt deeply uneasy about the Soviet interest in Treholt and, quite apart from that, began to think that the Norwegian was decidedly odd. As an instance of his peculiar behaviour, one evening he sat on the floor, cutting his toenails and eating the clippings. At other times he would speak obsessively about his father who had apparently been a harsh disciplinarian and left his mark on Treholt.

Takis remained in Norway for about three months until he obtained Norwegian identity and travel documents. Once he had these, he was able to move freely around Europe, contacting other activists and arranging supplies for the resistance. He was able to act as liaison between activists in Britain, France, Luxembourg, Italy, Germany and Scandinavia and helped set up supply routes into Greece. In Sweden, where a Democratic Defence cell had been making bombs for some time, he became involved with Pierre Schori, a leading light in the Social Democratic Party and adviser to Olof Palme, the Swedish prime minister. On one occasion, Takis and Schori, who later became head of the Swedish foreign ministry, tested a device in some woods outside Stockholm.

In Czechoslovakia, guns were readily available on the open market and Takis bought several. He smuggled pistols into Greece during three clandestine trips there after his expulsion from Britain, trips made at enormous personal risk. In Italy, he bought a number of rifles which were placed in store until such time as they could be smuggled across the Adriatic to Greece. But the guns added little to the capacity of Democratic Defence to wage an effective military resistance campaign against the junta. In the absence of a strong overall command or a self-sustaining strategy for local action, the weapons were simply kept by individual activists, most holding onto them for personal protection.

In any event, there was a considerable division among activists about the targets and the scope for armed action in Greece. Democratic Defence never launched an action that aimed to result in death nor did it harbour realistic expectations of overthrowing by force the regime in Athens. Its major weapons were petards rather than anti-personnel devices. Explosives were designed to demonstrate the existence of resistance, to extend a voice of clandestine opposition and to cause a succession of pinpricks. The real objectives of Democratic Defence were to keep the junta under pressure, isolated at home and abroad, and to preserve some national integrity for the new generation of Greek leadership. In this it resembled the pattern of Danish wartime resistance to German occupation, rather than that of the French.

In these limited aims Democratic Defence may be judged to have been a relative success. Even the Dover fiasco, despite its knock-on effects for activists elsewhere in Europe and the temporary freezing of lines of weapons delivery, gave notice to European governments – some of which had already come out against the junta but some of which were ambivalent at best, collaborationist at worst – that a resistance network did exist. If there had still existed a strong clandestine leadership in Greece with an effective representation abroad it would have been possible to exploit the propaganda effects of incidents like Dover. But most of the original hardcore leaders of Democratic Defence were already in jail and, abroad, Andreas Papandreou had destroyed the possibility of a unified opposition, seeking instead to secure his personal position at the expense of other resistance groups which he saw as a threat to his political future. Thus, by the early 1970s, the resistance had lost much of its momentum.

Vassilis Filias and several other members of the organisation, notably Spiros Plaskovitis, the Council of State colleague of George Kouvelakis, were convicted *en masse* by a military court in May 1969. Filias, who was the principle defendant, got eighteen years' imprisonment but not before he delivered a spirited defence of his actions.

'We who struggle against the present government do not consider ourselves illegal,' he told the army officers sitting in judgement. 'It is the government which is illegal and it is we who have the legitimate right to resist . . . The Greek people will never come to terms with a fate of slavery but will fight to overthrow the dictatorship with all possible means that are necessary.'

Immediately after his conviction, Filias was taken to Averoff
jail in Athens where he was held under heavy guard. The junta
regarded him as particularly dangerous. Pattakos informed a
representative of the International Red Cross that, in the view
of the regime, Filias was one of the most dangerous prisoners
held anywhere in Greece – 'dangerous enough to kill,' he told
the Red Cross man excitedly. Filias tried to do what he could
to irritate the regime, which was necessarily limited.

From the beginning in Averoff, he organised as many of the
political prisoners as he could into a group which they named
the National Liberation Front, or EAM, after the World War II
resistance group so hated by Papadopoulos and his associates.
Filias organised group protest actions and wrote a stream of
statements smuggled out of Averoff, and out of Koredalos
prison near Piraeus where he was transferred. Many of the
statements found their way to Britain and Germany and were
broadcast back to Greece via the BBC World Service and
Deutsche Welle, the German foreign broadcasting system. The
declamations infuriated the regime which couldn't fathom how
Filias managed to get them out of jail. If he wasn't in solitary
confinement, he was watched all the time during exercise with
other prisoners or with visitors. Filias did it by kissing his
visitors when they were leaving and passing carefully folded
notes, mouth to mouth. Other times, books lent by his family
were returned with messages hidden in the spines or pasted
inside the covers.

Within a year, Filias incarcerated had become almost as
serious a problem for the junta as Filias free and running
Democratic Defence. His conviction had already drawn protests down upon the heads of Greek ambassadors in several
European capitals and now, from inside prison, his activities
were proving to be a continuing disruption.

In June 1970, the junta tried to silence him by transferring
him to Kalami jail in western Crete, an old Turkish fortress that
had been turned into a high security prison. In Kalami, he was
classified as extremely dangerous and his guard doubled. The
day he arrived, he was placed in solitary confinement which
prompted him to declare an immediate hunger strike. Amid

growing problems for the prison authorities, he was brought to the governor's office and told that if he didn't come into line, he would face severe consequences. Filias adopted an aggressive, arrogant posture and shouted at the governor that if he ever threatened him again, he would kill him. It was a tactic he used several times and his jailers, more familiar with ordinary criminals who for the most part took their punishment stoically, did not know how to react. On one occasion when he was caught trying to have a note smuggled out, he was summoned to the director's office and confronted by a military captain. Filias again adopted his bullying pose and demanded why the captain wanted to speak to him. After the officer asked about the note, Filias hectored him: 'Captain, for me you do not exist so I won't discuss anything with you. Furthermore, if I had remained in the army, I would be your superior and I don't talk to junior men.' The captain left, dazed.

From Kalami, Filias contacted Martin Packard, who was now permanently resident in Athens, passing messages in the spines of books each time his mother visited him. He told Packard to make all necessary preparations for an escape. Packard assembled the means and the people for just such a venture but Filias was moved to another jail before the plan could be put into action.

When the administration of Kalami jail was handed over to the navy, the army transfered Filias to Halikarnasis prison near Heraklion. A further transfer saw him serve out the remainder of his sentence on the island of Corfu, from where he was released under an amnesty in July 1973. Until the collapse of the dictatorship a year later, he was kept under 24-hour surveillance but he nevertheless renewed the partnership with Packard who prepared new safe-houses in Athens and generated a new network of contacts.

One of the prisoners locked up with Filias on Crete was Professor Dionysius Karayiorgas who was captured after a bomb went off accidentally in his home in July 1969. The explosion badly damaged his hand and he also sustained head injuries. Despite this, he was tortured while in custody and later given an eighteen-year prison sentence. At his trial, a

total of 54 people were dealt with *en masse*. Thirty-four were
present, the twenty others were outside the country or living
underground in Greece. In addition to Karayiorgas, there were
several eminent members of the pre-coup Greek establishment,
including General George Iordanidis, a 69-year-old retired
Greek representative to NATO who was described by the
junta as the leader of Democratic Defence and the moral
instigator of the bombing campaign, and a leading lawyer,
Professor Alexander Mangakis. The absent twenty included
Jules Dassin, the French film maker, his wife, the actress
Melina Mercouri, and 'Hank'.

Karayiorgas' capture and what followed were yet another
serious blow to the resistance, already down to second- and
third-level leaders following the arrest of the original hard
core. It could not be long before they learnt of the role of
George Kouvelakis and arrested him too.

In the aftermath of the Karayiorgas incident and wave of
arrests that flowed from it, Kouvelakis decided to leave the
country. First, however, he had to dispose of a number of
bombs he had been planning to use and it was a measure of
the disorganisation that now surrounded Democratic Defence
that he was unable to hand them over to an activist remaining
in the country. Instead, he hid them inside files in Council of
State offices in parliament. They remained there until after the
collapse of the junta when, in the absence of a clear recollection
by Kouvelakis as to where he had left them, it took an army
bomb disposal squad one week to find and neutralise the
explosives.

Kouvelakis left Athens on 3 August 1969, using his own
passport, on a flight to Paris. He went on to London where he
met Martin Packard and the anti-junta propagandists but moved
on to Switzerland after an offer of an appointment to the International Labour Organisation. But the Greek representative to
the ILO vetoed him and he had to settle for a scholarship in
Geneva to study international law. Later, France's Conseil
d'Etat provided for him after French lawyers learned of his
plight, and he was able to tour European countries drumming
up support for the anti-junta cause. During his exile, Kouvelakis

was haunted by a sense of guilt, knowing that many of those he left behind were arrested and tortured. He found it harder to live abroad than underground in Athens and the strain eventually broke his marriage.

Despite all the international opprobrium attached to it, the junta showed little inclination for liberalisation. It marked the new year in 1970 by instituting a law governing the conduct of the press. Under the new law, the courts could suspend the publication of a newspaper if, within a five year period, it had twice committed certain offences. These included publishing articles offensive to the king and royal family, even though they remained in exile, or to the Greek orthodox church. Suspension would also follow the disclosure of military information, incitement to sedition, propagation of the views of outlawed parties, defamation and libel. The decision as to what constituted military information, incitement or sedition was, naturally, left to the junta and could be taken to mean anything the colonels decided challenged their power. Publishers, editors and journalists were to be held collectively responsible for the accuracy of what appeared in their newspapers, and punishment ranged from heavy fines to life imprisonment.

Later in the year, the junta decided that all journalists working in Greece, including foreign correspondents, would be subject to heavy prison sentences and fines for disseminating what were euphemistically referred to as 'false reports'. The following year, the government announced a 'code of ethics' for all journalists working in the country. They would have to work in a manner 'serving the interests of the people and the nation, being inspired in this by the Hellenic-Christian traditions'. Under the new measures, several journalists were jailed for writing anti-junta tracts, a poet was imprisoned for publishing what were termed insults to the army, and the Directorate of National Security took it upon itself to ban the works of several internationally renowned writers, among them Chekhov, Brecht and Gorky.

The junta was constantly trying to offset the bad publicity generated by its more repressive measures by announcing ostensible reforms. In April 1970, for instance, several articles of the revised constitution were brought into force. Article 10 stipulated that no one could be arrested or imprisoned without a warrant issued by a judge and unless the culprit was caught in the act of committing an offence – an anodyne restraint on authority in any state which respected human rights but one which the colonels could point to as evidence of their alleged liberal credentials. However, the reality was quite different.

Four months after the announcement, the regime admitted that it still held at least 500 political prisoners in what was termed preventative detention. At the end of the year, over 100 of the regime's opponents – including two former Centre Union members of parliament, leading judges and retired military officers – were arrested because they were 'incriminated in subversive activities directed against the country's security'. Some were freed shortly after, but about 100, including the Centre Union politicians, continued to be detained incommunicado. The government announced that the prison camp on Leros would be closed in April 1971, but instead of setting the inmates free, at least 450 of them were simply transferred to prison cells or house arrest in remote villages in the interior of mainland Greece.

In the month that the Leros closure was announced, Greece was visited by President Nixon's secretary of commerce, Maurice Stans. In a speech to the Hellenic–American chamber of commerce, Stans lauded the junta, and Papadopoulos in particular, and said he wished to express Nixon's 'warm regard for the people of Greece, for the wonderful way in which Greece has kept its commitments to NATO and for the way in which the two countries are working together'. Turning to Makarezos, the junta's deputy prime minister and minister for economic co-ordination, he praised 'the wonderfully close relations that exist today between our two countries'.

'You have provided an economic miracle up to now and I'm sure that miracle will continue to grow,' said Stans. 'We in the United States government, particularly in American business, greatly appreciate Greece's attitude toward American investment, and we appreciate the welcome that is given here to American companies and the sense of security that the government of Greece is imparting to them ... It is my own feeling that, given the continued economic stability and continued political stability, there is no limit to the growth that can take place in Greece.'

Within a year, Greek inflation was the highest in Europe and, by 1973, it stood at a full 30 per cent a year. For the ordinary people of the country, there was precious little economic stability from the colonels and certainly no economic miracle.

Under President Nixon, the military relationship between the junta and Washington grew even stronger. In 1971, negotiations began to give the US Navy Sixth Fleet what was known as homeport facilities in the Athens–Piraeus area. This meant that the US navy, under a contract agreed with the junta, would have all the docking, service and staff accommodation facilities in Greece necessary to sustain the operations of the fleet. At the time, US navy ships patrolling the eastern Mediterranean were based in ports on the east coast of America and had to ply back and forth across the Atlantic at six monthly intervals to carry out their work.

The idea of homeporting in Greece was the brainchild by Admiral Elmo Zumwalt, Chief of Naval Operations, according to a US Navy senior officer who was involved in the ensuing negotiations with the junta. Far from being embarrassed by further enhancing an already close relationship with a dictatorship, Zumwalt regarded the junta in Athens as an opportunity for closer ties between Greece and the US, rather than as a stumbling block.

'Once the junta took over, from a military point of view we were more secure in Greece,' the officer recalled afterwards. 'In the 1970s, we didn't think about [the morality of doing business with the junta] at all. [President] Carter was ahead of his time. To look back in hindsight and say "Gosh, isn't this terrible", OK, but we weren't ready to spill that much blood for human rights. The first responsibility of the nation state is to protest its own interests and, as far as we were concerned, they were best served by the junta. It was a shame but there was not much inclination [at that time] to undo this. We were not willing to take the long-term perspective and see that the junta could endanger Greece's role as a democracy and in NATO.'

Washington's perspective on homeporting was apparently confined to the view that what was good for the US military and US defence spending was good for America as a whole. The financial incentives were considerable indeed. In testimony to House of Representatives hearings on the proposal, Admiral Zumwalt calculated savings of around $29.4 million against an initial outlay of just over $13 million. Annual running costs would be about $13.4 million, most of which expenditure would have to be met wherever the fleet was based. He said that homeporting in Greece would involve relocating some 10,000 US naval personnel and their dependents, and the construction of full docking facilities for a carrier, a carrier task group and air wing, and a squadron of six destroyers. Contemporary reports describe the resultant facility as 'the American Navy's largest home port in Europe'. Zumwalt said that fifteen alternative ports in the Mediterranean had been examined and all were found wanting. Athens, he said 'stood out loud and clear as the only one that really satisfied a substantial number of criteria'.

All suggestions that homeporting implied approval of the junta were rejected. One Nixon appointee, Assistant Secretary of Defence Warren Nutter, said the logic of that position would lead to the conclusion that if the US improved its relations with a communist regime, the US was endorsing such a regime. 'In fact the basis of such a policy is quite different,' he said. 'The basis is essentially pursuit of our national interests.'

Despite eloquent testimony against the proposal by several Greek exiles, who detailed the appalling nature of the regime with which Nixon wanted to have such close ties, and the conclusion of the House committee examining the proposal that it was 'a serious mistake', the president pushed it through. A five year deal with the junta was signed in January 1973.

What the Greek navy thought of the actions of their American colleagues may be gauged by what was going on behind the scenes as Washington and Athens negotiated the agreement. The Greek navy had always been less than enthusiastic about the junta of army colonels, as was clear from the way Gerassimos Notaras had been able to establish a cell of navy petty officers for Democratic Defence not long after the military seized power. Despite the brutal crushing of that cell, the same fertile seedbed of opposition was still there six years later. In May 1973, when naval officers struck again against the dictatorship, they failed, but their action fatally undermined Papadopoulos.

The essence of the plan, devised by Admiral Konofaos, was that Commander Nicos Pappas, one of the navy's most respected senior officers and captain of the Greek destroyer *Velos*, was to take control of the Aegean island of Syros and at the same time blockade Athens and Salonika under cover of a NATO exercise. From Syros, messages broadcast to the junta would demand that it resign or face the consequences. They included the possible shelling of oil installations near Piraeus and cutting roads in and out of the capital.

Martin Packard was one of the very few non-Greeks aware of the naval officers' plans. He moved back to Greece in early 1970 but only after he obtained an assurance from the British authorities that details of his resistance activities, known to MI5 as a result of the Dover incident, would not be shared with Greek intelligence. Packard got the assurance through using political contacts established while lobbying against the junta and old Royal Navy intelligence contacts from his time on Malta. An approach was made to Home Secretary James Callaghan. The problem was that, by 1970, Packard's MI5 file contained a wealth of information which would almost certainly have resulted in his arrest if it became known to the Greek Security Police. Once arrested, it would not have taken the police long to establish that Packard was the Hank convicted in the trial of the 54 Democratic Defence activists. The file detailed much of what Special Branch inspector Harry Nicholls had found out after arresting Roger Williams, as well as Packard's supposed attitudes from his earlier period in Greece, which had been collated by Britain's overseas intelligence service, MI6, as a result of his enounters with the British embassy in Athens.

Some years after the collapse of the dictatorship, MI5 was still running a bulky file on him, with information apparently culled from British and American sources. It included the following assertions dating from the early years of the resistance:

- that Packard had a history of involvement in Greek Politics through his wife's [Kiki's] family, the Tsatoulis's;
- that the family were known anti-monarchist and liberal, as well as anti-American and anti-CIA;
- that the family and Packard were associated with Democratic Defence which was 'known' to be anti-American, anti-CIA and anti-Karamanlis;
- that while in Athens, Packard was associated with a British journalist who had links with the Soviet embassy there;
- that Packard had been apprehended using a fellow officer, without his permission, to pass resistance information to people inside Greece, and that, as a result, he had offered the choice of accepting the consequences of his actions or leaving the Royal Navy and continuing his activities. 'He chose the latter course,' said the summary.

Rarely do intelligence files of this nature come into the public domain – and with good reason. As with so many such files, the information held on Packard was a mixture of unsubstantiated libel and a number of rather cock-eyed views held by intelligence agents. The Tsatsoulis family were, like most Greeks, against the continuance of a failed and discredited monarchy in Greece. That was a far cry from being anti-monarchist in general, and being opposed to the CIA did not necessarily mean that someone was opposed to America *per se*. Democratic Defence was neither anti-American nor anti-Karamanlis. But its members reflected the widespread view among Greeks that foreign interference in Greece's internal affairs, especially interference by foreign intelligence agencies, was a bad thing.

Packard believed that any information released by MI5 to the CIA was likely to find its way to KYP, the Greek intelligence outfit, which would lead in turn to his arrest and lengthy imprisonment if he returned to Greece. After the approach to

Callaghan, word was relayed back to Packard via Ray Dobson, the Bristol Labour Party MP, that the information held on him by British intelligence and the police Special Branch would not be passed on to any foreign country.*

With this assurance, Packard and his wife returned to Athens in 1970, calculating that, even if he were arrested, the consequent publicity about his case would prove a powerful blow against the junta and fireproof him against its worst excesses. Once back in the city, he renewed and maintained his links with George Kouvelakis and Nicos Levantakis. Soon after his return, he received word from Filias in prison and from then on the pair remained in near constant contact. In messages written on toilet paper and hidden in the spines of books, Filias asked Packard to re-establish links with key activists and to prepare a plan for Filias to escape.

Preparations by naval officers for a strike against the junta were well advanced by the time Packard was approached. Admiral Konofaos was a close friend of the Tsatsoulis family, as was another key figure, Captain Dennis Troupakis. Troupakis told Packard the general outline of the plan, which was that the Greek fleet should sail under cover of a NATO exercise, seize the island of Syros, blockade Piraeus and declare an insurrection. Packard was asked to help by setting up an escape route for some officers who would remain in hiding in Athens, should the plan fail. He thought initially of renting a yacht large enough to ferry the officers to safety if necessary but then became intrigued by the possibilities thrown up by a courtesy visit to Piraeus by the Royal Navy.

He suggested to Troupakis that he could get one of his former colleagues who was on board the British vessel to organise a

* The assurance was almost certainly broken at some future date. CIA records in the United States contain references to Packard but the agency refused a Freedom of Information Act request to release the relevant files to the author. Long after democracy was restored in Greece, Packard and his wife found themselves embroiled in conflicts with business associates and rivals. He believed that a large and powerful American company with which he had had dealings obtained CIA data on him which it threatened to use against him. A Greek associate once received a phone call from abroad with the message: 'Tell your friend [Packard] that we have had access to his files.'

cocktail party and invite would-be defectors. Packard reckoned there would be more political and propaganda mileage if, rather than escaping clandestinely, Greek officers used the occasion of the party to defect. The colleague need not be told that his guests might defect between martinis and canapés – with who knows what diplomatic consequences for Anglo–Greek relations. But Packard's plan never happened because the naval plot against the junta was strangled at birth.

Exactly when the junta became aware of the plot remains unclear. It was due to be launched in the early hours of 23 May 1973 but it was apparent that the junta knew something was afoot long before that because of the arrest of at least one of the ringleaders. If they didn't know everything, the junta almost certainly gained full knowledge of the plans on the eve of their execution when the plotters, including Konofaos and other senior figures, held one of their final meetings in the waiting room of an Athens hospital where Dennis Troupakis' wife lay dying from cancer.

One of the people visiting Mrs Troupakis at the time happened to be Colonel Joseph Lepczyk, King Constantine's squash playing friend and CIA spy in the now defunct palace. Although Lepczyk retired from the US army in July 1969, he and his wife remained living in Greece where his pension was paid to him via the US embassy. Lepczyk in retirement maintained close links with members of the social circle he established while working in Athens – which included palace insiders, members of the military establishment and the Greek intelligence service, KYP – as well as with his former employees in the US military, diplomatic and spying apparatus in Greece. It was because Lepczyk kept up his social and professional connections while in retirement that he went to visit Mrs Troupakis . . . just at the time when the naval plotters were openly discussing their plans.

Packard asked Troupakis if he was aware of Lepczyk's background and was told the leadership felt that American support was critical to their plans. Lepczyk, whose first loyalty was to a country whose agencies were deeply supportive of the junta, thus became aware in detail of a plot to destroy it. Within days, almost all the plotters were rounded up by the junta. Pre-emptive action was taken to block access to Scaramanga naval base on the morning the fleet should have sailed. Only Commander Pappas and the *Velos*, already at sea, were able to declare for the insurrection. Within 24 hours of the planned start of the blow against the regime, the junta was able to broadcast that a 'comic opera' plot against the government had been discovered and seen off. Commander Pappas sailed the *Velos* immediately to Italy where he and six officers plus 24 crew were offered political asylum.

Papadopoulos said that the plot had been hatched with the help of Greek exiles, chief among them, in his view, the former prime minister, Constantine Karamanlis, in Paris and the exile King Constantine in Rome. There can be little doubt but that had proper secrecy been maintained and the plans of Admiral Konofaos executed effectively, a profound blow would have been struck against the junta. But as it was, the attempted insurrection showed at least that after six years of dictatorship and suppression of all countervailing opinion, the junta had failed even to unite the armed forces behind it. It also gave the lie to the US government contention that the neo-fascist regime brought stability to Greece and strength to NATO's southern flank.

Dennis Troupakis was one of those who escaped immediate arrest. His wife died on the day of the failed insurrection, he in hiding unable to be by her side. Packard and his wife attended her funeral. The church and graveyard were crawling with Security Police and KYP agents waiting for the rebellious officer to show. Burdened by the stress of events and the loss of his wife, Troupakis surrendered to the authorities a few days later and spent several humiliating months in jail before being freed in an amnesty.

Although the naval plot was even less of a pin prick than Constantine's abortive counter-coup of 1967, it provoked Papadopoulos to consolidate his power. At the same time, he tried a further exercise in liberalisation, in the hope of placating critics at home and abroad.

On 1 June, he announced the abolition of the monarchy

and with it the office of Regent established after Constantine's flight into exile. In place of the monarchy, Greece was to be a republic with Papadopoulos proposing himself as president for an eight-year term. The king and Karamanlis condemned the action, with Constantine proclaiming himself from Rome as the sole continuing source of legitimate constitutional authority in Greece. Papadopoulos sought to give his new status a fig leaf of respectability by announcing the return of civilian government. But the presidency would retain absolute authority in matters of public order, defence and foreign affairs, the ministers of which Papadopoulos would appoint himself, and in other matters of government, his writ would run superior to that of the prime minister.

The legal basis for the changes was a referendum, held on 29 July, in which voters were presented coloured ballot papers, white for Yes and grey for No, under the watchful eyes of junta officials who were present in large numbers in and around most polling stations. Not surprisingly, 72 per cent of people who voted said Yes. Twenty-one per cent voted No, and of those eligible to vote (participation was supposed to be compulsory), over 25 per cent abstained. On 19 August, Papadopoulos was sworn in as president, promising an end to martial law, the abolition of military courts and the freeing of political prisoners.

With the emasculation of the resistance, the enhanced relationship with the US military, the cosy friendship of the Nixon White House and Papadopoulos installed as president of Greece, the junta strongman thought his future was secure.

Chapter Nineteen

Democracy Restored

'The CIA ... was unable to contain its enthusiasm for
Ioannides.'

Tom Boyatt, State Department
Cyprus desk officer, August 1974

The Americans couldn't save Papadopoulos, even if they tried.
The resistance had helped keep him isolated internationally but
it could not topple him either. When the end came, it was
brought about by a combination of divisions within the junta
and a foreign adventure that had catastrophic consequences
for Cyprus, Greece's number-one foreign policy concern. The
vulnerability of the junta stemmed from its near total lack of
popular support. The catalyst was a student revolt.

Confrontation between the students and the colonels had
been brewing for some time. In the early years of the regime,
the junta dismantled virtually all representative bodies elected
at university and polytechnic level by the students themselves.
In their place, the colonels appointed committees of stooges to
control student unions. Mass student opposition to the regime
was neither strong nor consistent but, throughout 1972 and
much of 1973, there were sporadic spats between students,
college administrators and the government resulting in occu-
pations and arrests as activists pressed to be allowed to run
their own affairs. The regime feared that if students were
permitted a measure of political independence – or if the
typically youthful excesses of student politics were tolerated
– the universities would become a focus for more widespread
opposition and an example to others.

With the advent of a quasi-civilian government following

the failed naval coup of August 1973, and with the promise
of elections in early 1974, student activists brought renewed
pressure on the authorities. Papadopoulos found himself in a
position familiar to all tyrants who seek to mollify opposition
to their rule by introducing mild reforms. Those whom such
regimes seek to appease develop an insatiable appetite for real
freedom – freedom that can only be won at the expense of the
dictatorship.

In early November 1973, the fifth anniversary of the death
of George Papandreou was the occasion for yet another display
of popular support for the tradition of Greek democracy which
the life of the former Centre Union leader represented. In
violent clashes with police, nearly 40 students were arrested
and seventeen of them were speedily put on trial. Twelve were
acquitted but five got suspended sentences. In the immediate
aftermath of the trial on 13 November, students gathered in
Athens polytechnic to discuss the outcome. What started as
a loose assembly quickly developed into an occupation of
the campus. Within 24 hours, the students were demanding
the right to elect their own representatives by 4 December
and unfurling banners across the front of the main building
denouncing the junta.

Over the next two days, a curiously chaotic state of affairs
developed. A hotel opposite the polytechnic became a sort of
safe haven for both sides: the police set up a command post
there and, when sporadic clashes broke out between police
and students in the road between the hotel and campus,
the wounded (almost all of them students) fled inside for
protection. As the students held press conferences in the
polytechnic and sought to round up supporters, the police
in the hotel engaged in furious phone conversations with their
masters in the Ministry of Public Order building a quarter of
a mile away.

The students managed to set up a radio station inside the
polytechnic, partly with the help of Gerassimos Notaras of
Democratic Defence. After his release from prison, Notaras
had devised a way of monitoring police radio traffic with the
aid of some naval communication equipment from the days

when he had helped organise the Democratic Defence cell of naval petty officers. When the student revolt began, Notaras went to the polytechnic and helped them listen to what the police were saying to each other on their radios. But the students' action was not organised by Democratic Defence, nor indeed by any of the other established resistance groups like the Patriotic Front or Rigas Feraios, a student resistance group whose name was associated with sporadic youth opposition to the dictatorship. What the Athens students got up to in November 1973 was far too disorganised to have been pre-planned, though a hastily chosen 'organising committee' was set up.

By Thursday 15 November the occupation had grown to several thousand strong and similar action was breaking out in colleges in Patras and Salonika. Twice the following day, Friday 16 November, a number of the students in Athens and some of those who had joined them (some of whom were almost certainly junta agents provocateur) attacked the Ministry of Public Order building. On both occasions, the police opened fire on the unarmed rioters but soon realised that they could not maintain control. Shortly before midnight, the police formally requested army support. Papadopoulos agreed immediately, as the students learnt from their radio when his decision was relayed between the military and police.

Prior to the army moving in on the polytechnic, some 40 students had been wounded in clashes with the police but major casualties had been avoided. All that changed when the army, supported by tanks, came in on the side of the police.

There were hundreds of students in the forecourt of the polytechnic in the early hours of Saturday 17 November, when the tanks drew up outside. One turned its gun on the building, its commander standing upright in the turret surveying the protesters. A powerful searchlight scanned the roof and windows for snipers. There were none. The commander directed his tank to make a rush at the gates and the machine burst through, crushing one of the students. As thousands of students streamed out of the campus, they were met by a hail of skull bashing truncheons, kicking boots and worse. In the mêlée that ensued as the unarmed students rushed into territory controlled by the security forces, 24,000 bullets were discharged by the police. The number of students who died has never been established accurately but seems to have been astonishingly low. The official death toll was at least 23 and up to 200 others were wounded. About 1,000 students were arrested. The police suffered less than a dozen injuries, none of which was due to gunshot wounds.

By 3.30 a.m. the last of the students had left the polytechnic, their revolt decisively crushed despite initial dithering by the forces of the state. None the less, over the next three days, anti-junta demonstrations erupted in Athens, Patras, Salonika and Ioannina. The army responded with bullets and over 50 people died. As with the storming of the Athens Polytechnic, the final death toll was never known. Papadopoulos declared martial law about eight hours after the tank burst through the polytechnic gate and, as the ensuing clampdown seemed to squash resistance, thought his regime's position was secure once again. By 24 November, martial law was being relaxed and control of universities and colleges throughout the country was returned to their governing bodies.

Inside the junta, however, the polytechnic rising and the army's crushing of it provided Papadopoulos' critics with the excuse to overthrow him. In the early hours of 25 November 1973, army units took over key installations in the centre of Athens in almost exactly the same way they had done on 21 April 1967. As the city slept, tanks rolled through the streets. The telecommunications building was taken and phone lines cut. The police headquarters and other key centres of power and control fell without resistance. Around 4 a.m., Papadopoulos was woken by army officers and handed a statement saying that he and his government had resigned 'at the request of the armed forces'. He would be allowed to follow further developments on television.

The man who took over, Brigadier Dimitrios Ioannides, had been one of Papadopoulos' original 1967 coup plotters and was head of National Military Security. Ioannides had in fact been planning a move against Papadopoulos for some time, angry at the way he and others from the 1967 cabal had been sidelined by Papadopoulos' assumption of the presidency and by apparent moves towards the restoration of civilian government.

Ioannides was also one of the Central Intelligence Agency's most prized assets in Greece. According to one still classified State Department analysis of the 1974 Cyprus crisis, 'the CIA station [in Athens] . . . was unable to contain its enthusiasm for Ioannides'. The agency maintained particularly close links with him throughout the life of the Papadopoulos junta. Stacy Hulse, the station chief who took over from James Potts in 1972, was in very regular contact with him when he headed military security, a relationship that gave the agency unique access to the centre of power after he overthrew Papadopoulos. (When Potts left Athens, he was given a send off party attended by virtually every member of the junta, such was their liking for him.) In fact, such was Ioannides' closeness to the CIA and distaste for diplomats – despite Washington's cordial relations with the junta under the Nixon administration – that ambassador Henry Tasca was bypassed by Ioannides when he wanted to deal with the Americans. Instead of using diplomatic channels, Ioannides dealt direct with the CIA.

Ioannides had several lines of communication into the agency. There was the former station chief, Jack Maury, who although back in Washington maintained regular contact with the junta, whether led by Papadopoulos or Ioannides. Maury's successor, Hulse, had an equally close liaison with him as did several individual agents, notably Peter Koromilas, a Greek–American also known as Peter Korom whose links with the CIA dated back to the days of that other Greek–American, Tom Karamessines, who had done so much to establish the agency in Greece.

According to a US lawyer who investigated the link between Ioannides and the CIA on behalf of Congress, the new strong-man in Athens 'had no use for the ambassador and in some quarters Tasca was regarded as a dangerous liberal . . . Tasca was taken out as a messenger, removed from the pipeline. There was a falling out between Henry Tasca and the junta, and between Henry Tasca and Secretary of State Henry Kissinger.'

Ioannides' career and appalling views did him little damage

in the eyes of the CIA. In 1964 while serving as an intelligence
officer with the Greek National Guard in Cyprus, he opined to
the Cypriot president, Archbishop Makarios, that the island's
entire Turkish–Cypriot population should be liquidated to
'resolve' once and for all the communal rivalry between it
and Greek–Cypriots.

As head of military security under Papadopoulos, he was
largely responsible for the terror that swept Greece after
1967. Apart from the general clampdown and torture that
followed the coup, Papadopoulos turned to him at times
of particular need. One such occasion followed the August
1968 attempted assassination of Papadopoulos by Alexander
Panagoulis, a young army deserter and Centre Union activist.
Shortly after a bomb failed to demolish Papadopoulos' car, with
the dictator inside it, police arrested Panagoulis hiding nearby.
When they were unable to extract any useful information from
the would-be assassin, Papadopoulos ordered him handed over
to Ioannides and his henchmen. A wave of arrests followed.

The men who seized power with Ioannides in late 1973 were,
for the most part, disgruntled army majors and colonels. An
exception was General Phaidon Gizikis, commander of the First
Army at Larissa, whom Ioannides installed as president, retain-
ing for himself the position of head of military security. The
new prime minister was Adamantios Androutsopoulos, finance
minister in the deposed Papadopoulos regime. Androutsopoulos
wielded no more actual power under Ioannides than he had
as one of Papadopoulos' ministers. His appointment as prime
minister was merely a fig leaf for Ioannides who, while not
giving himself a title in the new regime, remained none the
less its boss. Relative to Ioannides, Androutsopoulos had little
actual power or authority but, according to Philip Deane, King
Constantine's former aide and critic, the new prime minister was
an ex-employee of the CIA in the 1950s – another potentially
useful window on the new regime for the agency.

Any prospect of a return to full civilian government in early
1974 vanished with Ioannides' take-over. Martial law was back
in force and holding centres and jails for opponents of the
new regime began to fill again. And while repression was back

firmly on the agenda in Greece, the new junta began to turn its attention to Cyprus, long an obsession of Ioannides who had developed a deep loathing for President Makarios. Ioannides' distaste for Makarios was mirrored in Washington by Kissinger who regarded the archbishop as, at best, a pest and, at worst, a potentially dangerous leftist whose pro-Arab leanings were an unnecessarily complicating factor in Israeli–Arab relations. The Americans were wont to see Makarios as a sort of Castro of the eastern Mediterranean.

Ioannides did not like Makarios' independent streak and the way in which he tried to maintain control over the island's security, as opposed to leaving it in the hands of the locally-based Greek National Guard. Makarios was also at odds with General George Grivas, the champion of *enosis* (union with Greece), who had returned to the island secretly with the help of the junta and in defiance of an agreement that he would remain on mainland Greece. Whereas Makarios was willing to compromise to reach a lasting accommodation with Turkish–Cypriots, any such suggestion was anathema to Grivas, not to mention his patron in Athens.

Grivas had been invited back to Cyprus by the Makarios government in 1964 in an effort to restore control in outlying areas but then forced to leave that same year under the threat of Turkish invasion. His second return followed an attempt to kill Makarios in March 1970 – an attempt sponsored by the Papadopoulos junta which, when it failed, resulted in the killing of the would-be assassin. Back now on Cyprus with the blessing of Ioannides, Grivas founded a new terrorist organisation, EOKA-B, whose target, apart from *enosis* was Makarios and his left-wing supporters. Not long after Ioannides took over, one of Grivas' most loyal lieutenants, Nicos Sampson, went to Athens and discussed the situation on the island with a former head of the CIA station there.

In January 1974, Grivas died and Ioannides was robbed of his most trusted agent on Cyprus. Around the same time, tensions between Athens and Ankara rose because of a dispute over oil prospecting rights in the Aegean. Meanwhile in Cyprus, talks between political leaders of the Greek and Turkish communities broke down. By April 1974, Makarios was claiming publicly that the Greek government was behind a renewed outbreak of violence by EOKA-B and demanding full control over senior appointments in the National Guard, whose primary loyalty was to Ioannides and not Makarios. Faced with this crisis, Ioannides decided to remove the archbishop by mounting a coup against him at 8 a.m. on 15 July. In the event, Makarios escaped and was airlifted by the British to London via Malta. After four nominees refused to be installed in place of Makarios, Ioannides turned to the notorious Nicos Sampson and set him up as puppet president the following day.

On 20 July, five days after the anti-Makarios coup, Turkish forces responded by invading Cyprus from the north. The junta made a pathetic attempt to fight back. Fifteen planes were dispatched from Greece to take Nicosia airport. Four were shot down and the other eleven returned without being able to land. Both Britain and the US concentrated on evacuating their own nationals to safety. In August, by which time the junta in Athens had collapsed in disgrace, there was a second Turkish invasion and Cyprus was formally divided. Turkish forces seized about a third of the island, including part of the capital, and tens of thousands of people lost everything they owned. Families of Turkish Cypriots living in the southern part of the island abandoned their homes and fled north to Turkish held territory. Greek Cypriots in the north fled south. In an orgy of communal violence, thousands of people were killed. To this day, almost 2,000 Greek Cypriots remain unaccounted for; most if not all must be assumed to be dead. On 19 August, Roger Davies, the US ambassador on Cyprus who had begged Washington to warn Ioannides of the likely consequences of toppling Makarios, was assassinated.

The key questions in this whole affair were whether the US administration, specifically Henry Kissinger, knew what was afoot, and whether the CIA was involved. The evidence is at best conflicting but sufficient to bolster claims that the answer to both questions may be yes.

According to one of the most senior State Department officials dealing with Cyprus in July 1974, Kissinger had a particularly cynical attitude towards the island's travails, insofar as he took any interest in the place at all. 'Kissinger was prepared to let the situation evolve violently. In his Machiavellian way he thought, "these boys are going to sort it out, I'll just sit back and see what happens." But a lot of people got killed and it all could have been avoided,' the official maintained.

The official did not believe that Kissinger specifically authorised a move against Makarios by indicating the US would not balk at such action. Others however, did not share this view. The Congressional investigating lawyer suspected that Kissinger's role was far more than that of the passive bystander: 'I believe that Kissinger tipped off Ioannides that a move against Makarios would not incur US wrath. The CIA was used to convey the message. We [the investigation team] believe that Jack Maury went to Athens just before the move [against Makarios] was made. It was the agency. No question. There was a long pattern from before the coup [against Makarios] of very, very close contact and a very, very short leash.'

There can be no doubt that the CIA was deeply involved in the run-up to the coup against Makarios and that Kissinger, via diplomats acting under his orders, used the agency to communicate with Ioannides, the man who ordered the coup. It is not possible to prove whether Kissinger led Ioannides to believe that the US government would not object to a move against Makarios. What is clear, however, is that Kissinger lied about the crisis as soon as it blew up and questions were asked about his prior knowledge of the impending disaster. As Turkish troops invaded the island in response to the junta toppling of Makarios, Kissinger sought to give the impression that he and the State Department had been taken by surprise. He said the entire affair was a failure of intelligence and that information which might have led him to act other than he did was not 'lying around in the streets'. In fact, it was lying all over his own department.

Much of the role of the CIA and Kissinger was recorded in detail in an eleven-page secret memorandum, entitled Criticism of US Policy in the Cyprus Crisis. Written on 7 August 1974 by

Tom Boyatt, head of the Cyprus desk in the State Department. The document was addressed to Henry Kissinger and, to this day, remains classified. Every page has the word SECRET stamped on it twice, at the top and at the bottom.

Boyatt's criticism disclosed that, by mid-May 1974, Greek and Cyprus experts in the State Department were sufficiently worried about Ioannides' intentions to direct Ambassador Tasca to warn him off. Tasca was told to tell Ioannides that 'if the [Greek] National Guard and EOKA-B succeed in getting rid of Makarios and installing a leadership responsive to Athens, a direct confrontation between Greece and Turkey would become inevitable'. What worried the officials in Washington was what Ioannides was telling the CIA through his personal contact Jack Maury and the station chief in Athens Stacy Hulse. The mid-May warning had little apparent effect as, at the end of the month, Ioannides was telling the CIA that he had not yet decided what to do about Makarios. But all that soon changed.

'In late June or early July [Ioannides] told his CIA contact that he was planning an anti-Makarios coup,' according to Boyatt's criticism. The contact on this occasion was allegedly CIA agent Peter Koromilas. But on 15 July, 90 minutes after junta planes began bombing Makarios' presidential palace in Nicosia, the CIA station in Athens reported that Ioannides had decided not to intervene on Cyprus. As Boyatt noted, 'it is clear that Ioannides deliberately misled the United States government through his CIA contact.'

Ioannides' intentions may have prompted conflicting assessments as to what he might actually do, but they could hardly be dismissed, as Kissinger did, as amounting to no warning that something was about to happen. Indeed, Boyatt and other area specialists in the State Department clearly tried hard to get Kissinger and the Athens embassy to act firmly in the run up to the crisis.

When Tasca was told on 17 May to warn off Ioannides, he argued against such a move, according to Boyatt. 'Among other things he maintained that, as a staunch anti-communist who viewed Makarios as too relaxed toward communist activities on the island, Ioannides would react negatively . . . Although he was personally unsympathetic to Ioannides and his regime, Ambassador Tasca feared that Ioannides would find a *démarche* over Cyprus offensive and that it would thus jeopardize US security interests in Greece . . .

'On 8 June, after vigorous representations of working level personnel, the State Department again directed the Ambassador to convey an expression of concern to the Greek government, but left the details of this representation to the discretion of the Embassy.'

But Tasca failed to carry out the order until 17 June, a considerable delay bearing in mind the urgency of the situation and the substance of the message. When the message was eventually delivered it went not to Ioannides as directed (Tasca refused to deal with him as he had no official position in the regime) but to the Cyprus desk officer at the foreign ministry in Athens – 'A level,' Boyatt noted, 'which almost guaranteed that it would not be taken seriously by Ioannides . . . Only after our embassy in Nicosia intervened with Washington to urge continuing efforts to warn Athens did the decision makers of the State Department perceive the need to get the word more directly to Ioannides that the United States government would strongly oppose the removal of Makarios by force.'

An order to warn Ioannides was made on 3 July but it was not until 10 July, a full week later, that Tasca confirmed it had been delivered 'through CIA channels'. But the message was not necessarily an accurate reflection of views of Washington for, as Boyatt noted, 'both the Ambassador and the [CIA] station chief were apparently very reluctant to tell Ioannides what he did not wish to hear, ie, the US government was opposed to a Greek coup on Cyprus'.

The 3 July order was the last pre-coup contact between the Nixon administration and Ioannides recorded by the Boyatt criticism. Whether there was another, unofficial, contact through former station chief Jack Maury (as at least one of the Congressional investigators believed), a contact that effectively gave Ioannides the go-ahead to topple Makarios, cannot be proven. If Maury was involved, the action against Makarios would have caused him few qualms. In 1982, he told an interviewer that he found 'nothing morally wrong with assassination'.

'The problem', he said, 'is that you're never sure that the person who succeeds is going to be an improvement on the one who's gone.' In the case of Cyprus, Nicos Sampson was an acknowledged murderer who, during EOKA's 1950s campaign against British rule, used to celebrate his birthday by personally assassinating unarmed British dependents.

Kissinger's alleged warning to Ioannides may have been sufficiently ambiguous or tame for him to have thought he had Washington's approval, or at least acquiescence in his plans. 'It is reasonable to ask whether this US action was perceived in Athens as a reflection of the depth of Washington's concern about Ioannides' scheme to oust Makarios,' wrote Boyatt. 'Clearly General Ioannides had much ground to believe that, in light of the direct contact he enjoyed with the CIA station, he would have received a stronger, more categoric warning if the US were genuinely exercised about protecting Makarios, whom he regarded as a Communist sympathizer . . . All this leads to one basic conclusion: I believe that strong representations to Ioannides would have prevented the crisis.

'In his reluctance to intervene forcefully and decisively with Ioannides, Ambassador Tasca was reflecting a frame of mind consistent with the non-interventionist policy laid down by the top levels of the Department of State regarding the Ioannides regime. This policy of tolerating authoritarian government in Athens (indeed, of cooperating with it) has poisoned the atmosphere for the USG [United States Government] in Greece and has contributed to our continuing difficulties there. At the same time, the general US stance before 15 July must bear a large share of the responsibility for conditioning our representatives in Athens against perceiving the dangers of not intervening decisively against Ioannides to stop the move against Makarios.'

As the crisis was building up in the days after Makarios' removal, the CIA's blind devotion to Ioannides was illustrated in an extraordinarily ill-judged cable dispatched to Washington, with Ambassador Tasca's concurrence, on 18 July. 'The Greek military are now solidly behind strongman Brigadier General Ioannides,' said cable number TDFIR-314/04650–74. 'What Ioannides has achieved for Greece [on Cyprus] is parity with the Turks . . . any Turkish invasion of the island would unite all of the Greek nationals behind Ioannides.'

As Tom Boyatt wrote in his criticism directed at Henry Kissinger: 'It would be hard to imagine judgements more divorced from reality than these. As events were to show, the facts of the matter were just the opposite.'

Epilogue

Few people were more excited about the collapse of the junta than King Constantine and the former prime minister, Constantine Karamanlis, in exile in London and Paris respectively. As news of the fiasco of the anti-Makarios coup ricocheted around the world, the exile Greek community suspected rightly that the junta had now gone too far and would surely collapse.

The king had been watching events in Greece with more than a passing interest. Despite his ignominious flight to Rome after his failed counter-coup in late 1967 and the junta's subsequent declaration of a republic, the king harboured ambitions of returning to Greece as head of state. In conversation with other exiles, he liked to cast himself as a hero of the resistance, if not *the* hero, though he did give some credit to Alexander Panagoulis, Papadopoulos' would-be assassin. Those who risked their lives fighting the junta and who in many cases paid a frightful price found it hard to pin down exactly what it was that the king had been doing for the cause while in exile, apart from issuing the occasional statement against the regime. But his main aim had always been to manoeuvre himself into such a position that, if the junta collapsed, Greeks would rally around him as a focal point of national re-birth. Various attempts by resistance groups, including Democratic Defence, to involve the king against the junta came to nothing, partly due to the deeply mixed views activists held for the deposed monarch.

Karamanlis had, for the most part, also maintained a dignified silence while watching events from France. He kept in touch with eminent exiles, played the occasional round of golf with Laughlin Campbell, the former Athens CIA station chief lately transferred to Paris, and was consulted from time to time by

European prime ministers and former prime ministers who had worked with him as head of pre-coup Greek goverments. Like the king, he issued occasional statements deploring the junta and calling for a return to democracy.

In November 1973 when events in Greece began to look as though the junta was finally going to implode, the king and Karamanlis established regular contact. As the Athens students were squaring up to Papadopoulos' tanks, the telephone lines between London and Paris were buzzing as the two men debated what they should do. According to sources close to the king, Constantine wanted them to issue statements simultaneously but Karamanlis demurred. In the event, the polytechnic rising was crushed and Ioannides ousted Papadopoulos.

In the aftermath, the king was bitter about Karamanlis. A few weeks after Ioannides took over, one of the king's contacts close to Karamanlis told him that when the former prime minister was urging caution, he had his own bags packed ready for a swift return to Athens. Constantine believed that, just before the Ioannides coup, Karamanlis had been approached by other disaffected members of the Papadopoulos regime who were plotting their own take-over and hoping the former prime minister would back them but no such plan was ever put into action.

In June as tensions were rising over Cyprus, the king met Karamanlis in Paris. Constantine told him it was imperative for both of them to do something: the king said that his job was to help, to facilitate Karamanlis, because Karamanlis was the politician. After about two hours, Karamanlis agreed that they should work together. The anti-Makarios coup and subsequent Turkish invasion terrified both of them. Karamanlis said it would surely lead to war. The king suddenly found the courage of the exile. 'So be it,' he replied. 'We are all Greeks and we will fight together.'

But events in Athens moved too fast for any royal clarion call to resistance to be meaningful. On 23 July, eight days after the move against Makarios and three days after the Turkish invasion of Cyprus, Ioannides threw in the towel. The Greek armed forces were unable to mobilise effectively against a threatened Turkish invasion of Thrace, let alone do anything about the actual invasion of Cyprus. In some cases reserve forces found that their weapon stores had been pillaged during the dictatorship and that ammunition boxes were filled with stones. President Gizikis and the heads of the army, navy and air force announced that in view of the national emergency leading politicians were being summoned to form a civilian government. Ioannides was effectively sidelined by senior military colleagues who now saw the threat of a general war with Turkey as the sole imperative.

During hectic discussions in Gizikis' office on 24 July, it was agreed that an interim government of national unity should be established. George Mavros, leader of the Centre Union, would be deputy prime minister. But who would be prime minister? Gizikis tried to veto Karamanlis because he had been abroad for so long. He proposed Panayiotis Kanellopoulos, his successor as leader of ERE, the right-wing National Radical Union. But there were doubts as to whether Kanellopoulos would be a strong enough personality to lead a government under the circumstances. Mavros asked for time to think and left Gizikis to ponder.

Meanwhile in London, the king had got wind of the discussions and telephoned Karamanlis with the news. According to aides to the king, the former prime minister laughed and said: 'Let me tell you, they sure don't want me and they sure don't want you.' The king retired to Claridges, London's exclusive hotel favoured by royals and ex-royals and a virtual home away from home for Constantine. While resting in his room, the phone rang. 'The president of Paris is on the line,' said a confused switchboard operator. Constantine slammed the phone down thinking it was yet another ruse by one of the legion of newspaper reporters pursuing him. Anne-Marie intervened saying that it must have been Karamanlis. Constantine hastily picked up the phone again. It was.

What Constantine didn't know at this stage was that after Kanellopoulos and Mavros left Gizikis, the president called Karamanlis and offered him the premiership. Karamanlis was initially reluctant but was told there was no time for delay. He agreed to return. Gizikis offered to send a plane. Karamanlis said there was no need: the French president, Giscard d'Estaing, had already placed one at his disposal.

When Karamanlis spoke to Constantine, the former prime minister was reportedly 'hysterical . . . out of control'. According to sources close to the king, Constantine tried to calm Karamanlis down, but he said that Gizikis was pulling the country to war. The king said that Karamanlis should go back and offered to charter a plane. He said that he wanted to return to Athens with Karamanlis, but the former prime minister was non-committal. According to the sources, Karamanlis said he wanted the king back but had not broached the question with Gizikis.

'He wanted the king back so that he and the new government could swear allegiance to the legal head of state,' say the sources. 'Karamanlis said that he would call him. He never did.'

The king put out a statement recording his deep satisfaction at the collapse of the dictatorship and said he looked forward to returning home shortly. In the meantime, he decided to sit back and wait for the call to return. But it was Karamanlis who made the triumphant return to Athens on his own, receiving exactly the sort of reception of which Constantine dreamed and felt was his due. In the early hours of 25 July, Karamanlis' plane touched down at Athens airport, greeted by what seemed like the entire population of the city.

Over the succeeding days and weeks, Constantine remained in London, an irrelevance to the hectic political developments in Greece. By the end of the year, Karamanlis was elected prime minister and George Mavros was leader of the opposition in the new parliament. In December, a referendum on the monarchy turned down Constantine's ambition to be restored to the throne by a margin of over two to one. Greeks had finally given their true verdict on the monarchy which Churchill had foisted on them after the war.

Constantine refused to accept the decision, complaining that he was not allowed to return and campaign for his reinstatement. To this day, he continues to style himself His Royal Highness King Constantine of the Hellenes, spending much of his time keeping in touch with Greek affairs while flitting between social gatherings of Europe's past and present royals. Surrounded by a band of die-hard loyalists, he operates from a small office near Claridges. The walls are covered with large detailed maps of Greece as if those who look witstfully at them each day have some grand scheme for their return. Short-wave radios are tuned constantly to Greek stations and the news from Athens is followed avidly. The former king and his ever faithful aide, Major Arnaoutis (now promoted brigadier by a would-be king who is no longer commander-in-chief of an army), wait for the call.

Queen Frederika became increasingly out of touch with the real world. In exile, she wandered from place to place and flitted from interest to interest. Her only constants were philosophy and spiritualism. She went to India in search of truth and spent time in ashrams listening to gurus. She gave talks to students at Madras University. She died in 1981.

Philip Deane, Constantine's erstwhile former secretary general, had an extraordinary life after he left the service of the Greek government. He spent the dying years of the junta working in Washington, before moving to Canada to join the Canadian Broadcasting Corporation. Later, he studied for a doctorate in classics and became head of the Arts and Science Faculty at Lethbridge University in Alberta. He was spotted there by a senior civil servant attending a seminar who convinced him to come and work for the government.

Joining Canada's public service commission, Deane became a Senior Executive Officer in charge of the government's language training programme. A successful career as a high flying adviser seemed assured. But eighteen months before the junta collapsed, Deane was suspended without explanation, although he was left on full pay. For over three years he was given menial tasks only and all efforts by him to establish a reason for the sudden and catastrophic blight on his career proved fruitless.

In 1977 after being reinstated, again without explanation, he was plucked from relative obscurity by the Canadian prime minister, Pierre Trudeau, and appointed his special adviser. Deane created a computer programme which gave Trudeau exceptionally speedy access to vast amounts of information, allowing the prime minister to stun the opposition with his seeming omnipotent grasp of the facts.

At the end of 1980, a grateful Trudeau rewarded Deane with a seat in the Canadian senate, the rough equivalent to Britain's House of Lords. It was only then that Deane, with access to his own intelligence file, was able to find out what had provoked the hitch in his public service career.

It turned out to have been caused by KYP, the Greek intelligence agency, and a gullible 22-year-old Royal Canadian Mounted Police officer just out of sergeant's college. KYP had fed Canadian intelligence samples of Deane's anti-junta writings and their claim that he was a Soviet agent, just like George Blake, his co-captive in Korea who betrayed British intelligence by working for the Russians. Reading his file, Deane discovered that the RCMP officer had taken the KYP information to Deane's boss, John Carson, who apparently accepted it verbatim and shunted the hapless Deane into obscurity. It was only when Carson's successor, Edgar Gallant, examined the file in 1976 and ordered the RCMP to seek corroborative information that a thorough search was made. Contact with intelligence services in no less than 59 countries failed to elicit any proof. Even the CIA said that Deane was clean.

In the years immediately following the coup, most of the senior US government diplomats and CIA agents retired. Laughlin Campbell continued to play golf in Paris before moving back to Washington to live out his final years. Harris Greene likewise retired. James Potts left the agency and, availing of his expert knowledge as a former senior CIA man, established himself as a consultant for US corporations seeking to do business in the world's trouble spots. Joseph Lepczyk, Stacy Hulse and Jack Maury retired and are now dead, as is Charley Lagoudakis of the State Department. Kay Bracken, Phillips Talbot and OK Marshall also retired. Tom Boyatt's criticism of US policy in the dying days of the junta went unanswered but his career did not end there. Before retiring from the diplomatic service, he served as US ambassador to Upper Volta and Chile.

Martin Packard was not able to leave his past behind him

with similar ease. As the junta tottered towards disintegration, Packard discovered that Papadopoulos and his three senior colleagues were deeply involved in corruption. A business associate, unaware of Packard's earlier involvement with the resistance, asked him if he could use his contacts in Greece to obtain a casino licence for central Athens for a British-based gaming group. Packard passed the request to a business colleague who had good relations with the junta. The contact in turn used a friend in the finance ministry to approach Makarezos.

Word came back that a similar approach had just been made by an American who was believed to be fronting for the Mafia. The junta was apparently worried that a substantial Mafia presence in Athens might in time threaten its own position. So, even though the Mafia contact was the higher bidder, the junta was willing to negotiate with the British concern. The price, however, would be high, as they would have to break an exclusive contract under which a Greek–Cypriot, Frixos Dimitriou, was authorised to operate a casino at Mont Parnes, about twenty kilometers from Athens. Packard's business colleague was told that in order to get his licence, Dimitriou had paid an initial bribe of $5 million cash, and thereafter 50 per cent of the casino proceeds, amounting to as much as $100,000 a day, into a secret account.

The British would have to do better, it seemed. In order to get a foothold in Athens, the British group would have to build a $75 million hotel complex in the city centre (development which the junta would use as propaganda to counter evidence that Greece was internationally isolated and the economy on its knees) and pay $25 million into four separate bank accounts in Switzerland, to be opened in the names of the wives of the four leading junta members, Papadopoulos and Makarezos included. In addition, there would be ongoing payments from the proceeds of the casino and hotel.

Packard and Vassilis Filias prepared to put the information to good use against the junta. Rumours of corruption had been rife for some time, most of them featuring the name of the Greek–American, Tom Pappas, but international publication of the hard details of the Dimitriou deal might have helped provoke more liberal minded military officers to remove Papadopoulos and wind up the whole dictatorship. Should a deal go through involving the British group, Packard was to receive a large finder's fee which he was going to give to Democratic Defence.

But in the event, Ioannides seized power just before Papadopoulos was to have initialled a contract for the new casino. There were rumours at the time that the coup against Papadopoulos may have been prompted by the discovery of the extent of his corruption as much as by disagreements over policy matters. Packard and his wife were in Germany on a mission for Filias when news came of the collapse of the junta and the restoration of democracy. Frixos Dimitriou was killed shortly afterwards, reportedly run down by a Greek army truck.

When Constantine Karamanlis set about re-building democracy, a number of the members of Democratic Defence were approached to see if they were willing to serve in the new government. One of them was Filias who declined the offer but was approached subsequently by a Karamanlis minister seeking his help.

It was 1975 and Lebanon was sliding further into civil war. The minister told Filias that the CIA wanted to move its substantial Lebanon headquarters to Greece and that it had approached Karamanlis for Greek government help – including several thousand blank Greek passports for its agents and for anyone else to whom it wished to give a new identity. The minister said that Karamanlis was adamantly opposed to the agency's proposal. Although he knew it was necessary to have good relations with Washington, he felt that Greece had suffered enough from the activities of the CIA and its associates.

The suggestion of increased CIA involvement in Greece (if only by way of using the country as a base for activities elsewhere) indicated just how out of touch the agency was with popular sentiment in the country at the time. The US was widely reviled for its support of the dictatorship and seen to have been deeply involved in the Cyprus debacle. As an indication of the emotions aroused, in December 1975, the new CIA station chief in Athens, Richard Welch, was shot dead outside his home. The assassination was carried out by elements of 17 NOVEMBER,

a recently appeared anti-American terrorist organisation named
in commemoration of the crushing of the polytechnic students'
revolt. In his criticism of US policy over Cyprus, Tom Boyatt
had warned of the consequences for American interests in the
region. His observations went unanswered. His critique was
forwarded to the State Department's Policy Planning Department and, contrary to proper procedure, he never received a
substantive reply. Immediately after putting his views down
on paper, he was transferred from the Cyprus desk and into
a department called 'Senior Seminar', a move that was 'better
than being shot', as a colleague noted.

Some people in Washington were clearly oblivious to the
mood of the times in Greece. Two months before Welch
was murdered, Henry Kissinger urged increased military aid
'to strengthen the position of the present democratic regime'.
With memories fresh about how the military might of Greece
created by the Americans had been used for seven years against
the people of Greece, Kissinger's comment had the subtlety of
a red rag to a bull.

None the less, the Americans pressed the new government
with their plans for an enhanced CIA presence. Karamanlis'
minister believed the only way to stop them was to have the
plans leaked and the extent of the CIA operations in Greece
exposed. Greek editors who discussed possible publication were
reported to have received death threats and so it was deemed
advisable that the story appear first outside Greece. Filias said
that he knew someone who might be able to help and turned
to Packard.

Packard thought of Philip Agee, the former CIA agent and
author of *Inside The Company*, an exposé of the agency's
activities. As gamekeeper turned poacher, Agee had established
a reputation for exposing what he regarded as the illegal activities
of his former colleagues worldwide. As a result of his actions,
he was regarded with deep loathing by those in the agency who
remained faithful to their calling.

Packard contacted Agee in England and arranged a meeting in
Exeter. According to Packard, he passed on documents which
had been forwarded from Karamanlis' office in Athens and,

after a brief conversation, the two agreed to keep in touch. The meeting was observed by British government intelligence agents who were working hand in glove with their US counterparts. The CIA was hungry for any information on Agee and his activities that could be obtained from MI6 and other friendly intelligence organisations around the world. It appears that by approaching Agee, Packard, already the subject of files held by British intelligence and the CIA, set alarm bells ringing in the intelligence community. The CIA, which was told of the Packard–Agee meeting, saw a link between the assassination of Welch and the 'outling' activities of Agee and his ilk.

But there is another possible explanation. In early 1975, Welch had been named as CIA station chief in Lima, Peru, by *Counterspy*, a Washington based anti-CIA magazine run by journalist Winslow Peck. Moreover, it did not take much imagination for 17 NOVEMBER to put two and two together when Welch arrived in Athens under diplomatic cover but took up residence in the house of his predecessor, Stacy Hulse, whose status as station chief had been well known. Peck responded to agency charges that he was responsible for putting 17 NOVEMBER onto Welch by pointing out that Welch had been named as a CIA agent as long ago as 1967 in a book, *Who's Who in the CIA*, a piece of Cold War propaganda produced by the East German intelligence service, the STASI.

In late 1975 when Packard approached Agee, the activities of the former CIA man, Winslow Peck, and Mark Hosenball, a US-born journalist living in London, suddenly overlapped and the CIA moved to try to prevent further disclosures. Hosenball was an investigative reporter working for the magazine *Time Out* and had had dealings with both Agee and Peck. In February 1976, the *Counterspy* editor came to London and stayed with him. The two were discussing CIA activities in Britain which *Counterspy* hoped to reveal in a forthcoming issue of the magazine. But when Peck attempted another visit to Hosenball in June, the then-Labour Home Secretary, Roy Jenkins, refused him entry to the country. Five months later, Jenkins' successor at the Home Office, Merlyn Rees, ordered

Hosenball out of Britain. Two days later, Agee was also given his marching orders.

'Mr Hosenball has, while resident in the UK, in consort with others, sought to obtain and has obtained for publication information harmful to the security of the UK and ... this information has included information prejudicial to the safety of servants of the Crown,' said a Home Office statement.

The explanation for Agee's deportation was that he had 'maintained regular contacts harmful to the security of the United Kingdom with foreign intelligence officers; that he had been and continued to be involved in disseminating information harmful to the security of the United Kingdom, and that he had aided and counselled others in obtaining information for publication which could be harmful to the security of the United Kingdom,' Rees told the House of Commons.

On 23 May 1977, the Irish government, anxious not to irritate London, refused a request by Hosenball that he be allowed to live in Ireland, where he had attended university in the early 1970s. Five days later, he flew to America. Agee moved through a succession of other European countries, dodging repeated US government attempts to harry him.

The British government clung to the implausible insistence that Washington played no part in the two expulsions. Successive governments have remained determined that Hosenball should never again be allowed to enter Britain. In the 1980s, Lord Whitelaw told a journalist friend of the expelled American that, 'so long as I remain in public life, he will not be allowed back here'.

The episode resulted in yet more information being placed in Packard's MI5 and MI6 files and, over the succeeding years, British government agents kept a sporadic eye on him. Almost a decade after the collapse of the colonels, he was still being accorded special attention by immigration officials and Special Branch officers. By this stage in his life, Packard had developed a career in business and the attention irritated him. He asked a former naval colleague with intelligence service connections why he was still apparently on some sort of MI5/MI6 blacklist. 'Once your name is on the list, it stays there,' the colleague replied after asking around. Despite this, Packard was told that he could assume that, since his political involvement had ended with the demise of the junta, there would be no further harrassment from the British services. The diplomatic service took a different attitude, apparently, for as late as 1976, Packard's name was still on a blacklist held by the British embassy in Athens.

If British intelligence interest in Packard waned, the same could not be said for the Greek media. In 1983, a London based correspondent for the Athens newspaper, *Eleftherotypia*, wrote a series of articles about Packard. Yannis Andricopoulos, a sometime reporter and founder of a Greek island holiday centre devoted to holistic studies, claimed that Packard was a dealer in illegal drugs, an accomplice to the murder of a British journalist in Athens, and a British intelligence agent who had infiltrated the Greek resistance and betrayed it, leading to the torture of dozens of its activists.

Not a shred of evidence for these allegations was produced in the three part series of articles, yet still they caused enormous trouble to Packard and his wife, from whom he had earlier separated. When challenged, Andricopoulos and the newspaper refused either to retract the claims or to further investigate Packard's role in Democratic Defence and the CIA in Greece. When offered the latter option by Packard's solicitors, Anrdicopoulos claimed that to write about the agency's activities in Greece would place his life in jeopardy.

Packard sued. During a two-day hearing before a London jury, Andricopoulos was unable to substantiate any of his claims. He offered the bizarre excuse, by way of pleading mercy, that the CIA was behind the articles and that the agency, therefore, bore ultimate responsibility. Packard, on the other hand, produced George Kouvelakis, by now a senior judge and full member of the Greek Council of State, to give testimony in his favour. His evidence was impressive.

'This man', Kouvelakis told the jury, 'did more for the Greek resistance to the dictatorship than any other foreigner I know. He was fantastic. He saved many people. He set up safe houses. He was totally on our side.'

The jury agreed and awarded Packard damages of £450,000.

Andricopoulos claimed to be broke and made only a token payment towards Packard's costs. *Eleftherotypia*, which has one of the widest circulations of any paper in Greece, claimed protection from the government of Andreas Papandreou and has yet to settle a penny of the award. Even after Packard's departure from Greece, what seemed like a dirty tricks campaign was carried on against his wife, Kiki, who eventually lost almost all of her personal wealth and her family business. She and Packard now had separate lives. Kiki is embroiled in trying to sort out her collapsed business affairs while Packard has become involved in joint business ventures between western companies and financiers and the emerging post communist Russia.

Roger Williams, Packard's former partner in Democratic Defence, is a journalist in London. Takis – Nicos Leventakis – returned to Crete and established himself as a successful architect. Their Norwegian comrade in arms, Arne Treholt, joined the Norwegian foreign ministry in 1972. His induction to government service was extraordinary given the fact that Norwegian intelligence had doubts about his loyalty to the country from at least the late 1960s. The tapping of his telephone, which began in 1968, continued, and from 1977 on, he was subjected to 24-hour surveillance, including a stint working in New York from 1977 to 1982 when the FBI was used to keep an eye on him. Treholt's contacts with Soviet 'diplomats' continued even as he rose to a senior foreign ministry position with responsibility for Norway's international maritime obliga- tions – an area of critical importance for a seafaring nation. From 1971 to 1977, Treholt was particularly friendly with Gennady Titov, who worked at the Soviet embassy in Oslo.

For Titov and other Soviet officials, Treholt wrote papers detailing the Norwegian government's position on a variety of international matters. When meeting them, he also brought with him various ministry files. By 1984, the Norwegian authorities believed they had enough evidence to prove he was a Soviet spy. He was arrested at Oslo airport with 66 classified foreign ministry files en route to meet Titov in Vienna, Treholt was tried and, amid considerable public debate as to how he had been able to operate given the long-standing suspicions about him, sentenced to twenty years in jail. He was released in July 1992 on grounds of ill health. His exposure as a spy was big news in Greece where his relationship with Andreas Papandreou did not go unnoticed.

In 1975, Greece tried to purge itself of the memory of the junta by putting its leaders of trial. Panayiotis Pipinelis, in many respects the intellectual force behind the coup, served the junta faithfully but escaped justice. He died in 1970, shortly after failing to pursuade Constantine to return from exile and give the colonels his imprimatur. Papadopoulos, Makarezos and Pattakos were sentenced to death but the sentence was commuted to life in prison. Ioannides was sentenced to life in prison. Efforts to unravel the truth behind the Cyprus fiasco were frustrated when Karamanlis ordered an end to official inquiries and the files closed. He feared that raking over the ashes would only serve to inflame passions to no useful purpose and would expose details of US–Greek relations best left in the dark.

Like George Kouvelakis, the other prominent members of Democratic Defence resumed their normal careers after the restoration of democracy. Kouvelakis continues to serve his country as a senior judge on the Council of State. Many of his former comrades in arms returned to academia. Vassilis Filias resumed life as a sociologist and, in the late 1980s, was appointed president of Olympic Airways by the Greek government. In the immediate aftermath of the collapse of the junta, Filias and many of the others in Democratic Defence were active in politics but most eventually fell foul of Andreas Papandreou.

In October 1974, parts of Democratic Defence amalgamated with Papandreou's Pan-Hellenic Liberation Movement, PAK, to form PASOK the Pan-Hellenic Socialist Alliance – which became the junior opposition party to the Centre Union when Karamanlis formed a new right-of-centre government. Initially Democratic Defence members held a working majority on the central committee but in less than a year, the Alliance was a shambles as the destructive streak in Papandreou's personality emerged once more. Having neutralised a potentially rival political movement by getting it to join him, he set about undermining its members, now his supposed colleagues. The Democratic Defence members of PASOK wanted the Alliance to have a party constitution that established rules and procedures for the organisation and stated its views. Papandreou 'wanted to be Pope', as one former member put it, and began referring to the former members of Democratic Defence as a 'tendency' within PASOK which was bent on undermining him.

The differing views came to a head in mid-1975 when Papandreou loyalists engineered the expulsion from PASOK of 57 people. They included the most prominent members of the defunct Democratic Defence – Vassilis Filias, Gerassimos Notaras, Stellios Nestor and Nicos Constantopoulos among them. But PASOK grew without them and, in 1981, Papandreou was elected prime minister of Greece's first supposedly socialist government since liberation from the Germans. He won a second term of office but in 1989, his government collapsed in a welter of scandal and allegations of corruption. A number of his ministerial colleagues were eventually convicted of fraud and corruption but Papandreou, similarly charged, was acquitted by the thirteen-judge court by a margin of just one vote.

The affair was the most dramatic example of how Greek post-war history had come the full circle. The new government that accused Papandreou was an unprecedented left-right coalition dominated by New Democracy, the party which inherited the mantle of Karamanlis' National Radical Union, and Sinaspismos, a grouping of left-wing politicians ranged against PASOK. New Democracy was led by Constantine Mitsotakis, a former member of George Papandreou's Centre Union. When Papandreou was sacked by King Constantine in 1965, Mitsotakis defected, leaving the ousted prime minister to his fate and earning the undying contempt of the younger Papandreou. The coalition's justice minister was Nicos Constantopoulos, a member of Sinaspismos. One of the parliamentarians who investigated Papandreou and his corrupt colleagues was Stellios Nestor.

The corruption of the Papandreou government made possible the sort of national reconciliation that persistent American interference had denied Greece after the civil war and throughout the

1950s and 1960s. It was fortunate for Greece that reconciliation reached its apotheosis in the same year that the Cold War ended. For the first time in over 40 years, Greece faced the prospect of being able to evolve as an independent nation without the dead hand of superpower rivalry stunting normal political development.

No greater symbol of the break with the past could have been offered than that which took place on a sweltering Athens morning in August 1989, the fortieth anniversary of the ending of the civil war. Taken from the bowels of the Security Police headquarters, a fleet of trucks left the city carrying sixteen and a half million secret files. The files, compiled by right-wing governments since 1944 and assiduously added to by PASOK when in power, contained private and political information on millions of Greeks compiled by the police and the intelligence service KYP. There were files on tens of thousands of prominent people, including many members of parliament and the composer Mikis Theodorakis.

The trucks made their way to a steel mill 21 kilometers northwest of the city. There, a huge crane lifted them high above a blazing furnace. As they were dropped in to be destroyed for ever, there was a great whoosh as flames leapt into the air scattering the ashes of the past across the plant.

Among the onlookers was an elderly veteran of the civil war. 'The misery has now ended,' he said. 'After 40 years of political discrimination, I feel free.'

Bibliography

The following is a select bibliography of books, official records and magazines consulted during the course of research. I have freely used the information in these tracts and gratefully acknowledge the various authors.

Books:

Anon (translated Richard Clogg); *Inside the Colonels' Greece*; Norton and Company, New York 1972.

James Becket; *Barbarism in Greece*; New York 1970.

Ellis Briggs; *Anatomy of Diplomacy*; 1968.

Winston Churchill; *The Second World War, volume VI*; London 1954.

Richard Cottrell; *Blood on their Hands – The Killing of Ann Chapman*; Grafton Books, London 1987.

TA Couloumbis, JA Petropulovs, HJ Psomiades; *Foreign Interference in Greek Politics, an historical perspective*; Pella, New York 1976.

Philip Deane (Philippe Deane Gigantes); *I Should Have Died*; Hamish Hamilton, London 1976.

Milovan Djilas; *Conversations with Stalin*; Rupert Hart-Davis, London 1962.

Denna Frank Fleming; *The Cold War and its Origins, 1917–1960*; New York 1961.

Richard Grunberger; *A Social History of the Third Reich*; Weidenfeld and Nicolson, London 1971.

Seymour Hersh; *Kissinger – The Price of Power*; London 1983.

Christopher Hitchens; *Cyprus*; Quartet, London 1984.

David Holden; *Greece Without Columns*; Faber and Faber, London 1970.

John A Katris; *Eyewitness in Greece*; New Critics Press, St Louis, Missouri, 1971.

Herbert Kubly; *Gods and Heros*; Victor Gollancz, London 1970.

P Lambrias (ed.); *Greek Report*, a monthly publication of uncensored information about Greek affairs and documents; London, 1969 and 1970.

William McNeill; *The Greek Dilemma – War and Aftermath*; 1947.

Brigadier ECW Myers; *Greek Entanglement*; Rupert Hart-Davis, London 1955.

Edgar O'Ballance; *The Greek Civil War*; London 1966.

Andreas Papandreou; *Democracy at Gunpoint*; New York 1971.

Margaret Papandreou; *Nightmare in Athens*; Prentice-Hall, New York 1970.

Elliott Roosevelt; *As I saw It*; 1946.

Yannis Roubatis; *Tangled Webs, The US in Greece 1947–1967*; Pella, New York 1987.

Major-General Stefanos Sarafis; *ELAS Greek Resistance Army*; Merlin Press, London 1980.

Nikolaos A Stavrou; *Allied Politics and Military Interventions: The Political Role of the Military*; Papazissis Publishers, Athens 1970.

Laurence Stern; *The Wrong Horse*; Times Books, New York 1977.

Leland Stowe; *While Time Remains*; 1946.

Taki Theodoracopoulos; *The Greek Upheaval*; Stacey International, London 1976.

Mikis Theodorakis; *Journal of Resistance*; Coward, McCann and Geoghegan (translated from the French), New York 1973.

Michael Tracey; *A Variety of Lives, a biography of Sir Hugh Greene*;

Lawrence A Wittner; *American Intervention in Greece, 1943–1949*; Columbia University Press, New York 1982.

C.M. Woodhouse; *The Rise and Fall of the Greek Colonels*; Granada, London 1985.

C.M. Woodhouse; *Modern Greece: a short history*; Faber and Faber, London 1986.

G Yannopoulos (ed.); *The Greek Observer*, a monthly magazine on Greek affairs; London, 1969 and 1970.

Official publications:

Martinus Nijhoff (publishers); Yearbook of the European Convention on Human Rights – The Greek Case; The Hague 1972.

United States Government; Declassified documents (numerous relating to the White House, State Department, Department of Defence, and NATO ministerial meetings); Washington 1950s, 1960s, 1970s.

United States Government; Foreign Relations of the United States of America; various volumes 1947 on.

United States Government; Greece, Spain and the Southern NATO Strategy, Committee on Foreign Affairs, House of Representatives, hearings before the sub-committee on Europe, 92nd Congress, First session, July, August and September 1971.

United States Government; Political and Strategic Implications of Homeporting in Greece, Committee on Foreign Affairs, House of Representatives, hearings before the sub-committee on Europe and the sub-committee on the Near East, 92nd Congress, Second session, March and April 1972.

Hansard; House of Commons Parliamentary Debates (official report); HMSO, London various volumes, 1944–1975.

Newspapers and magazines:

The Times, The Guardian, The Daily Telegraph, The Observer (London); *The New York Times, The New York Times Magazine, The Washington Post, The Boston Globe, The Nation, New Republic, Newsweek, Covert Action Information Bulletin* (Washington, New York, Boston); various dates 1944–1975.

INDEX